THE DOWNFALL
of Galveston's
MAY WALKER BURLESON

Texas Society Marriage & Carolina Murder Scandal

T. FELDER DORN

THE
History
PRESS

Published by The History Press
Charleston, SC
www.historypress.net

Copyright © 2018 by T. Felder Dorn
All rights reserved

First published 2018

Manufactured in the United States

ISBN 9781467139663

Library of Congress Control Number: 2017960347

To Donna W. Cameron, whose interest in her family history and her unstinting support throughout the past five years made this book possible.

CONTENTS

PREFACE

GLENWOOD CEMETERY

Established in 1871 in a then rural Houston, Texas, Glenwood Cemetery quickly became the burial site of choice for the wealthy, for the social elite and for people prominent in their fields of endeavor. William P. Hobby, governor of Texas (1917–19) and publisher of the *Houston Post*, and his wife, Oveta Culp Hobby, who held the rank of colonel while she was the first commander of the Woman's Army Corps (WAC) in World War II and who became secretary of health, education and welfare under President Eisenhower, are buried there, along with James Anson, the last president of the Republic of Texas; as well as Edward Mandell House, an advisor to President Woodrow Wilson who helped negotiate the acceptance of Wilson's Fourteen Points, and many businessmen of great wealth in fields such as banking and the petroleum industry.[1]

About one-tenth of a mile from the grave site of billionaire Howard Hughes, known for his contributions to the movie industry and aviation, but who became reclusive near the end of his life, is the Walker family plot.[2] At rest there, near the graves of her prominent Galveston parents John Caffery and Clara Wilson Walker, is May Walker Burleson. Mrs. Burleson had a brief period of national fame in 1913 when she served as grand marshal for a parade in the nation's capital on behalf of woman suffrage. Riding a black horse, she led a huge procession, with floats, bands and an estimated eight thousand persons, mostly women, down Pennsylvania Avenue from the Capitol to the White House grounds. She continued to work for woman suffrage, and after the Nineteenth Amendment was approved, she was active in the Democratic Party. These accomplishments later were eclipsed, however, by the sensation that resulted when May Burleson fatally shot her ex-husband's second wife during lunchtime in a hotel cafeteria.

This work covers the roles of both Mrs. Burleson and her husband in their unusual marriage and recounts the bitter divorce proceedings that terminated that union. The narrative then moves to the homicide, to her trial and incarceration and finally to her post-prison years. An "Aftermath" section includes reflections on the lives of both May Walker and Richard Coke Burleson.

This book is the third volume in a trilogy about three women who were convicted of crimes involving homicide in South Carolina. For most of the year 1942, these women, one of whom was Mrs. Burleson, occupied adjacent cells in the Woman's Prison of the South Carolina State Penitentiary. One of the other two women was Beatrice Snipes, who had been convicted in 1933 of killing a rural policeman by pistol fire the prior year. The third member of the trio was Sue Logue, who was electrocuted in January 1943 for being part of a conspiracy to have killed the man who had killed her husband in self-defense during an altercation. Mrs. Snipes's story was told in *Death of a Policeman; Birth of a Baby: A Crime and Its Aftermath*. Mrs. Logue's story was the subject of *The Guns of Meeting Street: A Southern Tragedy*.

ACKNOWLEDGEMENTS

Assembling the documentation for this book was done with the assistance of many individuals, including staff members at libraries, newspapers and government institutions. I wish to acknowledge specifically the contributions of the people noted below and to express my gratitude to them and to everyone else who helped with the research that was required.

Donna W. Cameron, assistant district attorney for Galveston County, Texas, and the grandniece of May Walker Burleson, the main character in this narrative, provided me with access to the papers retained by the Walker family that were relevant to the life of Mrs. Burleson. These papers included a significant amount of Mrs. Burleson's correspondence, which revealed many of her thoughts and shed light on the motivations for her actions. This trove of documentation and Donna's recollections—and those of her sister Carol Burns—of the memories, opinions and actions of other Walker family members were of immense value. The book includes many photographs from the Walker family collection. Donna also read and offered valuable suggestions on a draft of the manuscript.

Richard Turner Miller, Esq., and his mother, Mrs. Jack Burleson Miller, contributed material concerning the reactions of the Burleson family to the events described in the book.

A considerable amount of research regarding the divorce proceedings was done by Lynn Blankenship. She and her husband, Jerry Blankenship, PhD, who also contributed to the research, are members of the San Saba County Texas Historical Commission.

Some important preliminary research was done by Marilyn Smiland of Columbia, South Carolina.

The following individuals provided help in securing specific documentation or photographs: Debbie Bloom, manager, and Margaret Dunlap, librarian, of the Walker Local and Family History Center, Richland Library, Columbia, South Carolina; staff, South Caroliniana Library, Columbia, South Carolina; Dale Colson, director, Interlibrary Services, Newark Public Library, Newark, New Jersey; Kim Wells, county clerk, district court, San Saba, Texas; Lois Bradley, deputy clerk, Justice Center, Galveston, Texas; Andrew D. Crews, archivist/librarian, San Antonio Public Library, San Antonio, Texas; Sean McConnell and Carol Wood, archivists, Rosenberg Library, Galveston, Texas; Wendy Scheir, archivist, Johnson Design Center, the New School, New York.

Dennis Mistretta, assisted by other members of the staff at the Millburn Camera ASAP Photo, Millburn, New Jersey, worked diligently to prepare a disk that contained over thirty electronic files of photographs.

Daniel Greenfield, MD, and Thomas Pitoscia, MD, of Millburn, New Jersey, read sections of the manuscript pertaining to mental health issues and offered recommendations thereon. Dr. Greenfield also provided several references.

Dr. Bonnie Kind of Germantown, Maryland, and Dr. Daniel O'Day of Rye, New York, colleagues of the author when all three were serving at Kean University in Union, New Jersey, read drafts of the entire manuscript and made helpful criticism and suggestions.

Sahil Patel, Department of Design at Kean University, drew the illustration that enables the reader to follow the route of the Woman Suffrage Procession.

Ben Gibson, commissioning editor for The History Press, provided help and guidance throughout the process of getting the manuscript in the form required for submission. Abigail Fleming, production editor, copyedited the document, including its extensive endnotes, with great skill.

My wife, Sara Ruth, served as research assistant and in-house editor, making corrections and significant suggestions at every stage of the work. Her encouragement and that of my children, Ruth, Julia and Thomas, kept my spirits up during the many years of research and writing. Finally, I am deeply grateful for the enthusiastic interest and support of my grandchildren, Kristine, Allison and Adam, during the ups and downs of this project.

PROLOGUE

On September 8, 1900, the hurricane that holds the record for causing the most deaths on American soil struck Galveston, Texas. At least six thousand people died, and much of this coastal city of thirty-seven thousand residents was obliterated.[3]

A twelve-year-old girl named Jennie May Walker lived in an area that was battered and flooded. Jennie May and her family survived, and she later wrote the following account of her experiences during the storm.

I Lived to Tell It

A Child's Experience in the Great Galveston Storm of 1900

"Oh, God! Save us! Save us! Save us!" The prayers of the mothers punctuated by the wails of terrified children inside the house were drowned out by the crescendo of the raging storm outside. These were no ordinary prayers such as a child was accustomed to hearing at home or in Sunday School. Instead, they were spontaneous expressions of refugees fearing for their lives.

I was only a child but I remember the 1900 hurricane as if it were yesterday. My two little brothers and I had been transferred from our house, which was but two feet above the ground, to the Kenison's stone castle across the street, which was three stories high surmounted by a tower and situated on a terrace. It was intended that the rest of my family would follow but they never made it, and I did not know until the storm was over that they were saved, and the Kenison's did not know whether or not their son Alphonse was still alive.

When my father took me across the street, it was about 5 p.m. It was pitch dark and the water was over six feet deep. The problem of how to get me across the street, without losing me on the way, was solved by placing me on an ironing board. Father carried one end and Alphonse Kenison, a young man of 20, who was helping father evacuate our family, took the other end. I clung to that board for dear life as we were swept two blocks away before the men could make any progress in crossing the street. By flashes of lightning I saw roofs of houses, with people clinging to them, trees, and timbers go hurtling by before the terrific force of the wind.

"How in the Hell are we going to get this child off the fence," Alphonse shouted to father. For in a flash of lightning I had glimpsed the top of the iron fence around the Kenison place, sticking up out of the water. We were dashed against the fence and I slid off the ironing board, grabbing an iron rod of the fence in each hand.

"I have got hold of something now and I'm never, never going to let go," I cried at the top of my voice. Just then I felt blows on both wrists and kicks on the shins that loosened my grip. No time now for being soft with children. Father and Alphonse knew they had to get me in the house with the utmost speed, and go back for the others, as the storm was increasing in violence, and the water was rapidly rising higher and higher.

The next thing I knew, father was banging on the great oak doors of the Kenison house with a telephone pole he had seized from the whirling water. Suddenly the door flew open and in I went, propelled by the blinding rain and wind. Alphonse and father had vanished in the storm. Blood was flowing from my wounds, caused by the terrible lashing of the wind driven rain. I was wrapped in a blanket and laid on a sofa. . . .

To avoid panic, should water come into the house, Mr. Kenison called to all the people to assemble on the great stairway, while he talked with them as quietly as the elements permitted. Mrs. Kenison was wonderful too. She stayed in the kitchen, calming the servants and made gallons of hot coffee and served it with other food to the refugees. Some of the men then went about with Mr. Kenison trying to find enough boards, nails, and hammers to cover the windows and keep out some of the wind and rain.

As the pale dawn began to filter in, the storm had somewhat abated. Mr. Kenison took Lucy Kenison, my playmate, and me up to the tower to get some sleep. The place was a shambles. All the furniture was in *splinters, walls and floors were running with water and not a window frame remained. Mr. Kenison pulled a dry mattress from a closet, put it on the wet floor, and the three of us laid down and slept.*

When I woke up, the sun was shining, the Gulf had receded and was blue and sparkling. Was this a dream or a nightmare? Had there really been a terrible storm?

I began to make my way across the street, which was blocked by the roofless top story of a house. I managed to burrow through the wreckage surrounding the roofless dwelling...

When I reached home, I saw the first floor covered with a deep layer of slimy mud, and a huge black scorpion came forward to greet me. I saw that

Storm of 1900: Devastation in Residential Galveston, I. *Galveston and Texas History Collection, Rosenberg Library, Galveston, Texas.*

Storm of 1900: Devastation in Residential Galveston, II. *Galveston and Texas History Collection, Rosenberg Library, Galveston, Texas.*

everything except the heavy dining room table had been swept away. The scorpion eyed me evilly and sent me flying upstairs into the arms of my father and mother.

All my father's famous library was gone with the wind and waves. Paintings by Degas, Van Gogh, Toulouse Lautrec, Monet, Renoir, and others that father had collected when he was a bachelor in Paris now belonged to the denizens of the deep sea. I loved those paintings, and ran down stairs again to see the vacant places where they had been hanging. In spite of my fear of the scorpion, I sat down in the mud and sobbed....

Mother had used great presence of mind when she saw that the storm was going to be destructive, and we had filled the bathtub and all available

Preparation for funeral pyre after 1900 storm in Galveston. *From Clarence Ousley, Galveston in Nineteen Hundred.*

vessels upstairs with fresh water from the high cistern before it was blown away....Mother handed out food and fresh water to the survivors who came and asked for it until we had no more.

Father did not lose a minute. He found an axe in the mud, then rounded up a gang to help dig out bodies from the wall of wreckage, for there was 6000 casualties.

The dead were put on barges and towed out to sea, but they floated back. It was then necessary to pile them up like cordwood and burn them. A pall of smoke hung over Galveston Island for weeks, and I shall never forget the awful stench of burning bodies and decaying flesh.[4]

I still have the little dress which I had on that terrible night of September 8, 1900, when I crossed the street on an ironing board in over six feet of raging water. It is just shreds of material hanging from a split bodice.

Washington crossed the Delaware under unfavorable conditions, but I have been through a horrifying experience in crossing the street in front of our house in Galveston, Texas.[5]

EARLY MARRIED LIFE

Service and Society

Captain and Mrs. Richard Coke Burleson

In Galveston, Texas, on Saturday, September 5, 1908, the engagement of Jennie May Walker and Richard Coke Burleson, captain, Ordnance Department, U.S. Army, was announced at a luncheon held in the home of the parents of Miss Walker.[6] John Caffery Walker, May's father, was a distinguished jurist in Galveston, and Richard came from a well-established Texas family in San Saba, where his father, Leigh Burleson, was a prominent attorney.

The prospective groom, age twenty-seven, was a graduate of the U.S. Military Academy at West Point, class of 1906, who had been posted on July 1, 1908, to the Watervliet Arsenal in Watervliet, New York.[7] The twenty-year-old Miss Walker was a stunning beauty who would complete that fall a course of study at an art school in New York. The two had met at a dance at West Point soon after Richard was graduated from the U.S. Military Academy. Their courtship had lasted eighteen months, during which the young lieutenant had taken Miss Walker and her mother to dances and the theater in New York.[8]

Four days after the engagement announcement, May Walker sailed to New York and returned in late October. Plans for the wedding then began in earnest, and several prenuptial parties were planned for the weeks just prior to the announced date of December 23.[9]

Left: Clara Wilson Walker, mother of Jennie May Walker. *Walker Family Collection.*

Right: Judge John Caffery Walker, father of Jennie May Walker. *Walker Family Collection.*

Unexpectedly, and quite suddenly, however, Burleson was ordered to Cuba, presumably to help with the evacuation of U.S. forces from there. Cuba had been occupied by the United States since 1906. The decision to withdraw the U.S. "Army of Cuban Pacification" was made after the election in November 1908 of José Miguel Gómez as president of Cuba. President Theodore Roosevelt felt that Gómez's election would result in a stable government on the island. Arrival of these orders for Captain Burleson mandated a change in schedule. Instead of a church wedding on the date planned, a simple ceremony attended only by relatives was held at the Walker home on December 9, and the pre-wedding parties were cancelled.[10] After the 3:30 p.m. rites were performed, the newlyweds departed almost immediately for the railroad depot, with the bride wearing a "going-away frock that was a stunning coat suit of taub gray with which was worn a Parisian hat of soft crush felt in gray with blue rosette." The couple left Galveston on the 6:00 p.m. train for New Orleans, from which city they sailed for Havana on December 15.[11]

The occupation of Cuba by military forces of the United States ended in February 1909, so that Captain Burleson's assignment to Cuba was necessarily brief.[12] By March 17, 1909, the Burlesons were located at the Watervliet Arsenal in Watervliet, New York, to which Richard Burleson

The Burleson family of San Saba: (*back row*) Mary Armour Longley Burleson, Worth Burleson and Richard C. Burleson; (*second row*) R.W. Burleson, Mary Leigh Burleson Price, Mrs. Leigh Burleson and Leigh Burleson; (*front row*) Armour Leigh Burleson, Wade Burleson and Bob Price. *Family album of Mrs. Jack Burleson Miller.*

had been posted before his marriage.[13] Their stay in Watervliet ended on April 9, 1909, and immediately, Captain Burleson was ordered to the Philippines, where he and his wife were resident at the U.S. Army post in Manila. May's charm and social skills enabled her to assume easily a role in the entertainment and other activities of a military base. Following a polo tournament, Captain and Mrs. Burleson hosted a dinner for a group of cavalry officers and their wives. Dinner was prepared by the Burlesons' Chinese cook, and the guests "declared that they would like to find his equal." The Burlesons, in fact, had four servants and entertained frequently. May Burleson wrote her friends in Texas about the horseback rides in which the officers and wives all participated and reported that much social activity was expected in connection with a coming visit to Manila by the U.S. Secretary of War.[14]

Although she enjoyed the active and varied social life on the army base, Mrs. Burleson began there her pattern of involvement in interests beyond home and society. During her time in Manila, that interest was art. At a

21

young age, Jennie May Walker ("soon after she put on frocks," according to a columnist who interviewed her) had gone to New York City to study under the painter William Merritt Chase.[15] When she was graduated from the Chase Normal School, she had earned a teacher's certificate, which opened an employment opportunity in Manila. She spoke about this with a journalist a few years later:

It was after I married and my husband had been stationed in the Philippines that this little certificate of graduation from Mr. Chase's normal school proved a very desirable thing to have.[16] After we were established in Manila, I found owing to the efficiency of Filipino and Chinese servants, my housekeeping duties would be next to nothing. Now we all know that in order to keep her health and youth, every woman must have an occupation of some sort. In casting about for a way in which to fill my time, I thought about the teacher's certificate in the bottom of my trunk. It secured for me the appointment of supervisor of art in the public schools of Manila, and I entered upon two years of fascinating work. I directed the teaching of five hundred interested and enthusiastic teachers, under whom there were thousands of children.[17]

Mrs. Burleson also sent "souvenir postals of Filipino belles" to her friends in Galveston. She thought that these Filipino women were very pretty and remarked that they were the native "society girls." She added, though, that the natives may be "little brown brothers of Mr. William Taft, but they ain't any of mine."[18]

In April 1911, near the end of their stay in Manila, the Burlesons took a quick tour of the Far East, during which May sent picture postcards to family and friends. Her father was favored with a picture of a Daibutsu in Kamakura, Japan. Her mother received an enthusiastic postal about the shops in Canton. Other stops were at Japanese temples, including ones in Kyoto and Nagasaki.[19]

Captain Burleson was relieved from detail to the Ordnance Department on June 19, 1911, and he and his wife soon were back in the United States.

Above: Lieutenant Colonel Richard Coke Burleson, early 1930s. *Walker Family Collection.*

Opposite: Jennie May Walker Burleson about the time of her marriage to Richard Coke Burleson. *Walker Family Collection.*

Class at Chase Normal School, in 1903, with William Merritt Chase as instructor. Jennie May Walker attended this school and was taught by Mr. Chase. She was awarded an art teacher's certificate in 1908. *From the Archives of the New School in New York.*

The Walker family of Galveston, about 1920–21: *(from left to right)* Clara Wilson Walker, May Walker Burleson, Richard S. Walker, Judge John Caffery Walker, Major John C. Walker Jr. *Walker Family Collection.*

Hotel Galvez on Galveston's Waterfront. An event honoring the officers of two U.S. battleships anchored in Galveston Harbor was held at the Galvez in 1912. *Galveston and Texas History Collection, Rosenberg Library, Galveston, Texas.*

He was based at Fort Sam Houston in Texas, but Mrs. Burleson did not join him immediately, instead spending several months with her parents in Galveston. Richard joined her there for the short leave of absence that he was granted in September.[20]

For May, a not-to-be-missed occasion occurred in early January 1912: a large and elaborate social event hosted by two prominent families of Galveston. Among the guests were thirty-five officers from two U.S. battleships, the *Florida* and the *Utah*, that were in port at Galveston. The highlight of this affair at the Galvez Hotel was a ball featuring peasant dances from many countries. Many of the female guests wore peasant costumes and were noted in the *Galveston Daily News*, including "Mrs. Richard Coke Burleson, wife of Captain Burleson, Fort Sam Houston, San Antonio."[21]

When May Burleson finally moved to Fort Sam Houston to be with her husband, her mother came for a three-month visit with her daughter and son-in-law. In addition to his duties at the fort, Richard was enrolled in a civil engineering program offered by Texas A&M. May began to participate in the social and other activities of the army base. Captain Burleson's assignment at Fort Sam Houston ended in August 1912. His next assignment was a four-month stint as an instructor at West Point. After that, Richard Burleson, who had been returned to the rank of first lieutenant in the field artillery, was posted to Fort Myer, Virginia, on December 16.[22]

SUFFRAGIST

The 1913 Woman Suffrage Procession

Mrs. Burleson promptly joined her husband at Fort Myer, which was near Arlington Cemetery, immediately across the Potomac from Washington, D.C. The nation's capital was a venue to May's liking, where her beauty, charm and social skills would enable her to achieve prominence in society. It was also a venue, moreover, that provided opportunities for service and political activities. She plunged first into the struggle for woman suffrage and soon was chosen for an important part in a major event being planned to promote that cause.

In mid-December 1912, about the same time Mrs. Burleson arrived on the Washington scene, an ardent crusader for woman suffrage named Alice Paul arrived in the nation's capital. Her task, on behalf of the National American Woman's Suffrage Association, was to organize a parade in Washington that would generate momentum for the cause of voting rights for women and support for a constitutional amendment that would grant suffrage to women all across the United States.

Paul's vision was sweeping. She preferred the term *procession* rather than parade, and the procession was to include women marchers from all over the United States and other countries, as well as bands and floats, and would feature prominent supporters, male and female, of the cause. Also included would be a pageant or allegory that would symbolize what America was striving for—a quest that would be advanced by woman suffrage. Alice wanted the procession to occur on March 3, the day before Woodrow Wilson was inaugurated as president, and she felt that the route had to be down Pennsylvania Avenue, starting at the Capitol. Other well-known suffragists such as Dr. Anna Shaw, Rosalie Jones and Inez Milholland would participate and help, but the bulk of the huge organizational tasks of assembling and determining the order of march for the thousands of procession members fell to Alice Paul and her assistant, Lucy Burns.[23]

In spite of the urgency of the organizational tasks, first priority had to be given to securing a permit to hold the procession. Power to grant that permission rested with Richard H. Sylvester, Washington's superintendent of police, and the last thing he wanted was a large parade the day before the inauguration. He cited the proximity of Pennsylvania Avenue to bars on adjacent streets and the large number of men who would be in the city for the ceremonies the next day—men emboldened by alcohol who might very well enjoy making trouble for a woman suffrage parade. He wanted both the date and the route changed. Alice Paul remained firm in her position that Pennsylvania Avenue was where the men marched; hence, the women had to march there also. Also, holding the march just before the swearing in of a president chosen in an election in which women did not have full suffrage would send a powerful message. Superintendent Sylvester and his boss, Commissioner John A. Johnson, remained adamant, however, in spite of a barrage of calls and visits that they received in support of Paul's request. Then, in late December, Sylvester granted approval for the March 3 date, but not for the Pennsylvania Avenue route. After a session with Commissioner Johnson, it appeared to Alice Paul's coworkers that the time had come to concede on that issue, but Alice continued to hold out, taking her case to the newspapers. From January 3 through January 9, articles appeared in the *Washington Post* almost every day, each of which made note of the permit controversy.[24] Even President William Howard Taft weighed in to support the suffragettes.[25] Finally, on January 9, 1913, Sylvester granted approval for the Pennsylvania Avenue route. March 3 was under two months away, but it was clear from page one of the *Washington Times* on January 10 that plans for the procession were in full swing. A large picture of Mrs. Burleson appeared there under the heading:

"Army Officer's Wife to Lead Suffragists' Pageant"

The article that accompanied the picture had a quartet of headlines, the first of which proclaimed: BIG PAGEANT BEING PLANNED BY SUFFRAGISTS, a second headline noted that an army woman had been named as grand marshal, the third announced that "Hikers" were coming from New York and the last stated that three societies would have parts in the march.[26]

The story opened by revealing that a permit had been granted for a march down Pennsylvania Avenue and that suffragettes were now "settled down" to work on "the preliminary tasks incidental to the largest and most spectacular parade known to the votes-for-women cause."

The second paragraph was devoted to Mrs. Burleson:

> *Mrs. Richard Burleson, the beautiful wife of a Fort Myer army lieutenant, will be the grand marshal of the suffragette parade. Mrs. Burleson, familiar with the details of the military end of a procession, was selected for this reason, and in the pageant she will instill the discipline which her life at a military post has taught her.*[27]

Army Officer's Wife to Lead Suffragists' Pageant

Picture of Mrs. Richard Burleson that accompanied stories about the forthcoming Woman Suffrage Parade in Washington, D.C. *The* Washington Times, *January 10, 1913.*

Mrs. Burleson's appointment as grand marshal was widely reported, and newspaper articles described her as "the athletic young army officer's wife who will be the grand marshal of the suffrage parade in Washington."[28]

May Burleson did her part to help publicize the coming parade and the cause it symbolized. She joined other suffragists in passing out literature on the streets of Washington in the weeks before the procession, and once, as a publicity stunt, at the request of Alice Paul, rode her horse in "full riding regalia" down F Street in Washington, the street on which Miss Paul's headquarters were located.[29]

By the middle of January, therefore, Mrs. Richard Coke Burleson had been selected to lead the huge Procession for Woman Suffrage, which was firmly scheduled for March 3, 1913, in Washington, D.C. Mrs. Burleson, as grand marshal, would ride a black horse and be accompanied by attendants. She was to be followed by the herald, Inez Milholland, riding a white horse and accompanied by attendants. Milholland, an attorney, was a prominent suffragist whose beauty, as well as her advocacy of women's rights, received notice in the press.[30]

After this lead contingent, the procession was divided into seven sections. The first section included women representing other countries, grouped according to the status of woman suffrage in the countries concerned. The next section focused on the status of woman suffrage in the United States at intervals during the period 1840–1913. Next came three sections featuring women in various roles and occupations with the women marchers in uniforms, the color of which reflected a particular profession or occupation. Government workers, teachers, businesswomen, lawyers, librarians and physicians were among those represented. A fifth section also included representatives of various fields of endeavor, but these women were not to wear uniforms. Section six was to be made up of delegations from political parties, delegations from equal suffrage states and representatives

Mrs. Richard Burleson, grand marshal of the Woman Suffrage Procession, seated on her charger. New York American, *March 4, 1913.*

of the Men's League for Women Suffrage. A final section was composed of representatives from the various states in the Union, beginning with those states in which a woman suffrage amendment already had passed both houses of the legislature. Marching in this last part of the parade were the "Pilgrims" under the command of "General" Rosalie Jones and "Colonel" Ida Kraft, who had hiked from New York to Washington, distributing suffrage literature and speaking to groups encountered along the way.[31] The pilgrims were greeted by crowds of spectators upon their arrival in Washington on February 28, and on March 3, many spectators had a particular interest in General Jones and her band of hikers.[32]

A program for the procession, eighteen pages in length, was assembled so that spectators and others who were interested could purchase copies.[33]

The procession was to form near the Capitol, with sections on First Street, South Capitol Street and New Jersey, Maryland and Delaware Avenues. Mrs. Burleson and her attendants were to assemble by the Garfield Monument and enter Pennsylvania Avenue at the Peace Monument to begin the parade. The parade then was to move along Pennsylvania Avenue until it reached Fifteenth Street, at which point it was to bear right to go by the south front of the U.S. Treasury Building, where an allegory was scheduled for presentation on the steps. From there, the procession was to proceed along the street south of the treasury and then to Continental Hall by the White House grounds. The designated disbanding area for the parade was on B Street and the White House grounds just above.[34] The procession route is shown on the map provided.

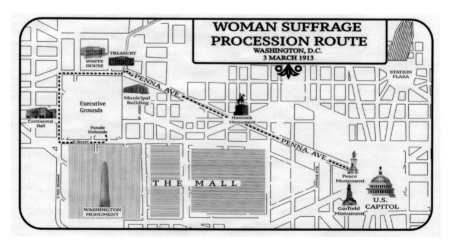

Line drawing of Woman Suffrage Procession. *Drawing by Sahil Patel, Department of Design, Kean University.*

Mrs. Richard Burleson on horseback, leading the Woman Suffrage Parade in Washington, D.C., on March 3, 1913. *Public domain.*

In the pageant or allegory to be presented on the steps of the Treasury Building, German actress and opera singer Hedwig Reicher was cast as Columbia, who was to summon to her side five other women, each of whom represented one of the following: Justice, Charity, Liberty, Peace and Hope, namely the five ideals toward which women and men were striving under Columbia's wing. The progress toward equality, a prerequisite for achieving those ideals, was signified by the procession. The allegory was to commence as the procession began, and the parade would pass by its final tableau on the treasury steps.[35]

Estimates of the number of people who marched in the March 3 procession varied from 5,000 to 8,000. Newspaper estimates of the crowd of spectators generally were in the 225,000 to 250,000 range.

Mrs. Burleson began moving the procession forward about twenty minutes later than the scheduled 3:00 p.m. start time. Trouble began soon, when after the first block or so, the crowd surged into the street and soon enveloped her and her heralds and immediately thereafter began to surround Milholland and her aides. Progress was slow, with frequent halts for many blocks, until a contingent of cavalry from Fort Myer moved the crowd out of the street, which enabled Mrs. Burleson to lead the procession reasonably unimpeded for the last few blocks. It took an hour, however, to travel ten blocks before the cavalry was called.

It was clear from newspaper accounts and photographs of the procession and the crowds of spectators that the parade route was obstructed not just at the beginning of the procession but in many places by the presence of onlookers in the street, in front of and alongside the marchers.[36] The leaders of the woman suffrage movement who were in the procession were outraged at the lack of arrangements for crowd control and the failure to provide clear streets for the marchers. These women voiced their anger at a meeting in Continental Hall after the parade ended. One result of that meeting was a petition to Congress that there be a congressional inquiry to determine the causes for the breakdown in security arrangements for the procession.[37]

The petition was honored, and on March 6–17, a special subcommittee of the U.S. Senate Committee on the District of Columbia held hearings to investigate the conduct of the "District Police and Police Department of the District of Columbia in Connection with the Woman's Suffrage Parade on March 3, 1913." Ninety-four witnesses were examined by the subcommittee, and a number of sworn statements also were read into the record of the hearings.[38] The various witnesses testified regarding instances of harassment (unkind, sometimes vulgar, remarks made to the women and attempts to take down banners or impede the floats) and rude or indifferent behavior by individual policemen. Some witnesses praised the performance of individual police officers, but a clear message from the testimony was that security arrangements had been inadequate.

The testimony by Mrs. Burleson in particular made clear that the attitude of some men in the crowd, the conduct of some policemen and the inadequacy of the security provided by the District police all contributed to impeding the progress of the lead section of the parade on Pennsylvania Avenue from Third or Fourth Street until the parade met the cavalry at Fifteenth Street. Excerpts from her testimony are provided here.[39]

The first excerpt is from the early part of Mrs. Burleson's testimony. She was being questioned by Senator Wesley L. Jones of Washington State, who chaired the subcommittee. The excerpt begins a discussion regarding the distance that Pennsylvania Avenue remained clear after the procession began at the Peace Monument. At the start of the parade, it was led by sixteen mounted policemen, and several police automobiles also went ahead of the procession.

Mrs. Burleson: *Then we started, and for about a block and a half the way was fairly clear.*

The Chairman: *For about a block from the peace monument.*

Mrs. Burleson: *For about a block from the Peace Monument only; then I noticed that they began to come out into the street and stand around, and commenced a hooting, and I thought, "How unusual." I thought of Maj. Sylvester's promise to have the streets clear.*

The Chairman: *Please state not so much what you thought as what actually happened.*

Mrs. Burleson: *They came out gradually, then closed around us, closed around me. We proceeded haltingly for about a block to, I should say, about Fifth or Sixth streets; but suddenly we found ourselves up against this horrible howling mob, this jeering mob, exactly as it is here* [indicating on photograph]. *I, with these two women in front of me, suddenly found myself surrounded by the mob. I looked for the police. The police were not there.*

The Chairman: *Had you seen any police along there?*

Mrs. Burleson: *Sixteen policemen had gone ahead of us while the Avenue was clear. The automobiles had preceded them but when I found myself with these two women bearing the flags face to face with this howling mob, there did not seem to be a policeman anywhere near. They seemed to have evaporated, to have disappeared, and I wondered where the police were, and I looked for them. They seemed to be mixed up in the crowd and the automobiles also.* (496)

As the procession moved forward, the interference of the unruly crowd spread to the sections of the parade behind Mrs. Burleson. She witnessed this, as indicated in the next excerpt:

The Chairman: *Who was behind you?*

Mrs. Burleson: *The six mounted women—my aides.*

The Chairman: *They were behind you, were they?*

Mrs. Burleson: *They were behind me; yes.*

The Chairman: *Did the crowd get in between you and them?*

Mrs. Burleson: *It did not. I managed to keep them together.*

The Chairman: *Did the crowd get in between them and other parts of the parade?*

Mrs. Burleson: *Indeed it did. It got in between them and Miss Milholland and completely surrounded her, and she was, I thought, in* *danger. I looked back along the line of march when I was halted—and I was halted for 10 or 15 minutes at a time by my wrist watch—and thought that Miss Milholland was in danger twice. There was not a policeman near her.*

The Chairman: *You did not really know very much about her situation, did you? You were concerned about your own part of the parade, were you not?*

Mrs. Burleson: *Yes, I did, because I watched her situation. There was no one to protect her, and I was afraid that she would be mobbed and pulled from her horse.* (499–500)

At one point during her testimony, Mrs. Burleson gave her assessment of the composition of the crowd:

Mrs. Burleson: *I should like to state the crowd was not composed of women and children, because I was the first one to see the crowd—the very first one in it—and it was composed of young men, rowdies, hooting hoodlums. There were very few women and children. I did not see any children, and I looked for them.* (505)

According to Mrs. Burleson, once the spectators had moved into Pennsylvania Avenue, the police escort that had been leading the parade "disappeared into the crowd," and she was left alone to fend for herself. Several of the leading women in the parade, who were traveling in automobiles, however, came to her aid. There were three automobiles, with Mrs. Patricia M. Street in one, Mrs. David S. Tinnen in another and Miss Alice Paul and Miss Lucy Burns in the third. These women, with some help from a few of the policemen whom they could locate and get to assist them, forced a path in the crowd that enabled the procession to edge forward. This was the story of the parade along Pennsylvania Avenue until Fifteenth Street:

The Chairman: *You went ahead a little bit at a time, did you?*
Mrs. Burleson: *Yes.*
The Chairman: *And still the crowd kept in behind these women who were behind you, and they proceeded about that way all the way along the Avenue, did they?*
Mrs. Burleson: *Yes; halting. They would crowd up. The crowd would make remarks to my aides. We would have to go just a few steps at a time,*

and the only way we could go was when Mrs. Street and Mrs. Tinnin had cleared the way.

The Chairman: *Were there any foot policemen along there?*

Mrs. Burleson: *I did not see one. I looked; I watched, and I did not see one. I saw a few men with policemen's badges. Maj. Sylvester had assured me he would have a great many men sworn in as special policemen, so I looked for them. I saw them with their badges, standing perfectly idle watching the crowd.*

The Chairman: *You say you saw no uniformed policemen?*

Mrs. Burleson: *No uniformed policemen.*

The Chairman: *But you did see some civilian policemen?*

Mrs. Burleson: *Yes: I saw some civilian policemen.*

The Chairman: *But you saw no uniformed policemen on foot between what points?*

Mrs. Burleson: *Between the whole parade. It seemed to me there were no policemen, except the original 16 we started out with.*

The Chairman: *You did, however, see several special policemen?*

Mrs. Burleson: *I saw several special policemen with badges.*

The Chairman: *Tell us what they were doing.*

Mrs. Burleson: *They were doing nothing. They were standing watching the parade in many instances.*

The Chairman: *They appeared to be just a part of the crowd?*

Mrs. Burleson: *They seemed to be just a part of the crowd, as the 16 mounted policemen who started out with us appeared to be when they first cut us off and allowed the crowd to surge in between me and them.* (500–501)

Evaluation of Procession and Mrs. Burleson's Role

When Mrs. Burleson and her attendants finally reached Fifteenth Street, a contingent of cavalry arrived from Fort Myer that cleared the crowd from the streets for her and the rest of the parade. The pageant on the U.S. Treasury steps, which had begun about three o'clock, was viewed by thousands and was a stunning success.[40] The expected coincidence in time of the allegory's final tableau with the arrival of the parade, however, did not occur. Because of the delay caused by the uncontrolled crowds along its route, the parade arrived well over an hour late, and the final tableau cast, some members of which had worn thin dresses and were barefooted, had gone into the Treasury Building to seek warmth. They did return when the parade finally came.[41]

The 1913 Woman Suffrage Procession in Washington was a brilliantly conceived, carefully planned and well-organized event that called attention all across the United States to the cause of voting rights for women. The abysmal failure by the Washington police to provide adequate crowd control did lessen the enjoyment of the procession for those spectators who had come simply to see the parade and certainly made the event less enjoyable—terribly distressing for many—for the participants. In spite of that difficulty, a large number of those witnessing the event saw and were moved by the various sections of the parade: Inez Milholland, Rosalie Jones and her hikers; the great masses of women from different places in the United States and abroad; and the allegory at the U.S. Treasury. Perhaps of even more importance, the lack of crowd control and the associated incidents intensified the impact of the parade and forced the public to confront the suffrage issue. There is no doubt that the parade energized those supporting the movement for providing voting rights for women by constitutional amendment.

Mrs. Richard Coke Burleson was given the responsibility of leading down Pennsylvania Avenue this huge procession that would be viewed by hundreds of thousands of spectators. Her real task turned out to be keeping calm and focused in the midst of unexpected chaos and harassment. A failure in her resolve to move forward could have had a disastrous effect on the parade. Mrs. Burleson, however, although frightened at times by lack of a police presence and being at the mercy of a crowd, held her ground when halted and moved resolutely forward whenever she could. Her determination, courage and horsemanship made her an excellent choice for grand marshal of a procession that was hampered by lack of crowd control.

Continuing Suffrage Activity

Although the procession in Washington was the point of highest visibility for Mrs. Burleson in her involvement in the movement for women's rights, she remained active in the suffrage cause. On March 25, 1913, she sent a telegram to the Equal Suffrage Association of Galveston, asking the association to endorse a resolution of the National American Woman

Suffrage Association (NAWSA) calling for a constitutional amendment that would grant women throughout the United States the right to vote. The Galveston Association did so, and Mrs. Burleson presented the resolution to Dr. Anna Shaw, president of the NAWSA.[42]

In January 1914, she took a leave of several months from significant participation in both suffrage activities and society functions. She enrolled as a special student in George Washington University to study sociology and economics. She noted that the reason for "surprising" her friends in this way was that these "subjects bear closely on the management of the modern home" and that the successful housekeeper will have to have a knowledge of them."[43] Given her lifestyle and the direction her interests were taking, however, one has to wonder if she might have been seeking background knowledge that might be helpful in her activist undertakings. Her picture appeared in the *Washington Post* in January 1914, with a caption that reported both her enrollment at George Washington University and the fact that her popularity there led to her selection for membership in the Pi Beta Phi sorority.[44]

By August 1914, she was in New York City for a stay of three months to assist the Woman's Suffrage Union with its campaign for woman suffrage in the state of New York. Her specific task was to circulate petitions among professional men, petitions that were to be presented to both the Democratic and the Republican state conventions. A brief article in the *Washington Post* with the headline Quits Society for Suffrage described Mrs. Burleson as a "most vivacious and energetic young woman [who] is enthusiastic of the prospects for suffrage in New York." In particular, Mrs. Burleson was confident that the two parties, each in convention, would adopt resolutions of support for a woman suffrage amendment to the U.S. Constitution.[45] Her picture appeared in the *Post* two days later with her quip about why she was undertaking the task: "I was driven to it by summer dancing."[46]

Mrs. Burleson's mode of travel to New York was unusual. She rode the three hundred miles from Fort Myer, Virginia, to Manhattan on horseback, traveling with the Second Battalion of the Third United States Field Artillery. The trip took twelve days, moving out at 5:00 a.m. each day and riding until noon before setting up camp. She described the trip as "wonderfully refreshing" and declared that she "had a perfectly corking time" on the trek.[47]

In November 1915, Mrs. Burleson was part of a deputation of women who met with William A. Jones, member of Congress from the First District in Virginia, for the purpose of urging him to support the proposed

Mrs. Richard Burleson leading horse before mounting. *Walker Family Collection.*

constitutional amendment extending the right to vote to women. Mrs. Burleson was one of the three speakers who presented the case on behalf of the delegation. Her remarks were from the perspective of an army wife whose husband was stationed in Virginia.[48]

Several years later, after the Nineteenth Amendment was incorporated into the U.S. Constitution in August 1920, she began to devote time and energy to promoting the participation of women in the political process, not only through voting, but also through women's organizations that supported particular programs or candidates.

HOME LIFE AND SOCIAL ACTIVITY, 1914–17

In the years 1914–17, besides being an active suffragist, May Burleson assumed two other roles. One was simply that of daughter. During this period, for an average of three months each year, Mrs. Burleson either lived with her parents, or her mother, Clara Walker, visited with her daughter and her son-in-law. In 1915, May Burleson accompanied her mother to Rochester, Minnesota, for treatment of a medical condition and then remained in Galveston with her mother for more than a month after their return. Near the end of her stay, Mrs. Burleson hosted a luncheon at home to introduce her mother to army wives who lived in Galveston and its environs.[49] After May rejoined Colonel Burleson in Virginia, Clara Walker arrived in Fort Myer in mid-December 1915 for a visit that lasted through March 1916.[50]

While in residence at Fort Myer, May Burleson was active both as a hostess and as a guest in demand on the Washington social scene. Her picture appeared numerous times in the *Washington Post* and in columns about Washington society in many other cities. She was one of "three beauties" (of Washington society) featured in a picture in the *Washington Post* in November 1913.[51]

Lieutenant and Mrs. Burleson's place in Washington society was enhanced by the fact that Richard's uncle Albert S. Burleson was postmaster general of the United States. On New Year's Day 1916, Mrs. Albert Burleson held an "at home" at which May Burleson joined her on the receiving line.[52] In March 1916, no doubt through arrangements by Mrs. Albert Burleson, Clara Walker received an invitation to a reception at the White House. Lieutenant and Mrs. Burleson were in the postmaster general's box at the Army-Navy football game in 1915, held at the Polo Grounds in New York.[53] On December 4, 1915, President Wilson and his fiancée, Edith Galt, viewed a drill at Fort Myer. May Burleson assisted with the arrangements for the reception that followed.[54] During the 1916 social season, which opened in January, there were bridge parties, elaborate balls, tea dances and a plethora

Right: Mrs. Richard Burleson. This photograph appeared with those of two other women in the *Washington Post* Society section of November 2, 1913. *Walker Family Collection.*

Below: Invitation to Mrs. Burleson's mother to a reception at the White House on March 3, 1916. *Walker Family Collection.*

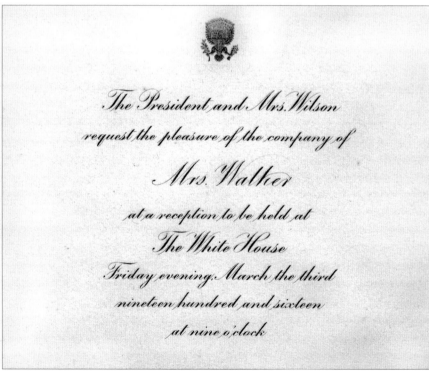

The President and Mrs. Wilson
request the pleasure of the company of

Mrs. Walker

at a reception to be held at
The White House
Friday evening March the third
nineteen hundred and sixteen
at nine o'clock

of luncheons. Clara Walker came with her daughter to several of these functions, including a tea dance at which she was asked by the hostess to pour the tea.

In April 1916, after almost four years there, Lieutenant Burleson's assignment at Fort Myer ended.[55] During the next twenty-three months, he was given a dozen assignments, but most of his time was spent in postings near San Antonio, Texas, working with field artillery units.[56] By November 1916, the Burlesons had appeared in the society column of the *San Antonio Light* and soon thereafter were noted in Galveston and San Saba newspapers as well.[57]

In late October 1917, May Burleson was the "head nurse" at a Red Cross charity ball in San Antonio. Her duties were to direct other "nurses" in Red Cross uniforms in the collection of ten cents a dance from all the gentlemen dancers at the ball.[58] Two days after Christmas in 1917, Richard and May attended the Burleson family reunion in San Saba.[59] It was the last big social event that they attended together until after the war.

Richard Coke Burleson, Artillery Commander, 1916–20

From 1910 through 1920, Mexico was in almost constant turmoil, with presidents being installed or removed by force of arms. The United States, which had a long border with Mexico and American citizens working for U.S. companies and industries based in the country, at times became diplomatically involved in the events of this revolutionary period. In late 1915, the United States gave official recognition to the government of Venustiano Carranza, who had proclaimed himself president. This action angered Pancho Villa, a revolutionary leader and former ally of Carranza's who was now seeking to depose him. Villa began retaliation against the United States by killing a number of American citizens working in Mexico, and then, on March 9, 1916, he led a raid on Columbus, New Mexico. The town was burned; four American civilians and three U.S. soldiers were killed; and guns and ammunition, as well as other property, were seized. President Woodrow Wilson immediately sent General John J. Pershing with a force of 4,800 men into Mexico with the objective of capturing or killing Pancho Villa and putting a stop to attacks on U.S. border towns by Villa's forces.[60] In June 1916, President Wilson also called up 110,000

National Guardsmen to be deployed along the Mexican border in order to repulse any attempts at raids on American soil. This National Guard force was supplemented by units of the regular army.[61] Richard Burleson was an officer in one of those units.

After his tour at Fort Myer ended in April 1916, Lieutenant Burleson was detailed for a month as an instructor-inspector with the New York National Guard; then he was sent to join his regiment at Leon Springs, Texas. Between June 27 and October 12, his station was Camp Eagle Pass, Texas, from which he and his artillery battery moved to a position to guard against border intrusions by armed raiders from Mexico. The *San Saba News* was clearly proud that a native son, "a scion of the illustrious family of his name in Texas history, West Point graduate, and brilliant young artillery expert," was serving with "one of the crack light batteries of the Third artillery on the Mexican border."[62] On July 1, soon after his arrival on the border, Richard Burleson was promoted to the (permanent) rank of captain.[63]

The action seen by the large force of guardsmen and regular troops during this border deployment was limited, but Captain Burleson and other officers used this time for training and preparation for future wars, one of which was soon to start. By February 7, 1917, the Pershing expedition had ended, and National Guard forces were in the process of being withdrawn.[64] Captain Burleson spent October 1916 to early March 1917 commanding a provisional unit of National Guard Field Artillery at Camp Wilson in San Antonio, Texas.

President Wilson had struggled to keep the United States out of the European conflict, but on January 31, 1917, the German Ambassador notified the United States that Germany intended to resume unrestricted submarine warfare, which meant that U.S. ships entering the European war zone could be sunk by German U-boats.[65] It was also discovered that Germany had secretly proposed to Mexico that, should the U.S. declare war on Germany, Mexico should declare war on the United States. The proposal noted that by doing so, Mexico, with German support, could regain the territory comprising the states of Arizona, New Mexico and Texas.[66]

On April 2, 1917, President Wilson asked Congress for a declaration of war, and four days later, after Congress had acted, the president issued Proclamation 1364, which stated that a state of war existed between the United States and the Imperial Government of Germany.[67]

Richard Burleson's military duties immediately focused on getting the U.S. Field Artillery, himself included, ready for war, and he began by serving as a field artillery instructor at army bases in Arkansas and Texas. In August

1917, he was promoted to the (temporary) rank of major, and in January 1918, he was made lieutenant colonel (also temporary).[68]

By late March 1918, Burleson was in France. He started his tour overseas as an observer with an artillery brigade and then spent five months as an instructor in artillery training schools. On September 9, 1918, however, he was assigned command of the 107th Field Artillery Regiment, and on September 11, he was promoted to colonel.[69] The 107th Artillery was part of the 53rd Field Artillery Brigade within the 28th Division, a division composed of activated units of the Pennsylvania National Guard.[70] There were two battalions within the regiment, each of which included three batteries. Each battery consisted of 180 to 190 enlisted men and several officers. On October 5, 1917, the regiment was listed as having 1,283 enlisted men and 44 officers.[71] The batteries were equipped with French 75mm howitzers.

The 107th Field Artillery was called up for duty in July 1917, sailed from Brooklyn on May 18, 1918, and arrived in France on June 3. After two months of training at Camp Meucon that focused on the use of the 75mm artillery pieces, the regiment left camp on August 9 and was in action by August 14. The regiment had remained on the front lines for nearly a month and was completing two days of rest when its new commander arrived. Burleson's assumption of command reflected implementation of a U.S. military policy that stipulated placing regular army officers in command of field forces. Lieutenant Colonel Albert Crookston, a Pennsylvania guardsman who had been in charge of the 107th since its arrival in France, became the second in command. There is no evidence of friction when Burleson arrived, but the transition must have been difficult; this was a Pennsylvania unit, and most of its members had been together through the period of being called up, preparation in the United States and training in France—and Crookston just had led the regiment successfully in combat.[72]

Under Colonel Burleson, the 107th participated in two major Allied offensives—the Meuse-Argonne Offensive in September and October and the Lys-Escaut Offensive on the Lys front in late October/early November—actions, as it turned out, that were the culminating Allied offensives of the war.[73] The artillery of the 107th provided cover fire to support an infantry attack in the Argonne Forest from September 24 until the night of October 9 and contributed to the success of the offensive.[74] On October 3, a German shell landed on a dugout, killing two officers and five enlisted men in Battery C of the regiment.[75] Colonel Burleson found it necessary to relieve Captain Whittaker of Battery C—who was temporarily in charge of the 1st Battalion—of his command for failure to get his battalion forward as ordered. This action did not endear the colonel to the men of Battery C.[76]

After its participation in the Argonne, the 107th was given a rest before moving to the Lys front. Richard Burleson sent a terse Western Union cablegram, dated October 18, 1918, to his wife. It remained in May Burleson's possession until her death:

OUT OF LINE FOR REST. LOVE AND DEVOTION, RICHARD.

The action by the Lys River lasted from October 31 through November 4, and again, the 107th was part of an attack that went well. In the regimental history, though, Belgium was referred to as a "mudbath," and the delousers and rest billets that came after were a welcome relief from fighting in Belgium. A difficult scene to watch occurred whenever a horse was wounded or injured such that it had to be shot. The animal would be killed in an open field, and its bones quickly would be "picked clean" by starving Belgians in the area.[77]

Colonel Burleson was awarded a Belgian Croix de Guerre for meritorious and distinguished service during the Lys Offensive.[78] He was also awarded the Order of Prince Danilo I (3rd Class) by the government of Montenegro.[79]

When the war ended, Colonel Burleson remained overseas until March 1920, retaining for a time the command of the 107th Field Artillery and then being given various staff assignments at General Headquarters of the American Expeditionary Force (AEF).[80]

May Burleson was with her parents in Galveston for an "extended visit" in February 1919 when she hosted a charity bridge luncheon for the Merry Wives to benefit the Armenian Relief Fund.[81] In May, she left Galveston for New York and soon joined her husband in Europe.[82] Richard was able to take the time to travel with his wife across France and Germany, and their trip is documented by postcards that May sent to her mother.[83] She wrote home in November to report that she and Colonel Burleson had just completed their tour and were in Paris "awaiting further orders."[84]

SEPARATE WAYS

Colonel Burleson's assignment at General Headquarters of the AEF ended in January 1920, and he departed Paris, France, to begin the return

Mrs. Richard Burleson in 1920. *Walker Family Collection.*

trip to the United States. His wife, however, remained in Europe. Mrs. Burleson, in fact, undertook a trip across Western Europe that began in Paris and included stops in Saint-Nazaire and Biarritz, France; then Madrid, Barcelona and Toledo, Spain; and finally Milan, Turin, the Villa Medici in Fiesole, Rome and Naples, Italy. Her visit to Rome lasted ten days. She returned to France and visited Antwerp, Belgium, before sailing back to the United States. May Burleson obviously loved travel, and her enthusiasm shone through in postcards that she sent at each stop. From Naples, she wrote her mother: "They say 'see Naples and die.' It is very lovely and beautiful, truly! But I am not ready for the bone yard." She sent many cards to her husband; on one written from San Sebastian, Spain, she wrote: "'The bridge of Spain will groan with pain.'[85] It is wonderful here. How I wish you were with me." She sent her father a picture postcard showing the ruins of the Temple of Apollo at Pompeii, with this message: "This recalls the days I studied Latin with you." The card was signed "Jenny." One of her friends received a card with a "wonderful painting" (a portrait) from the Prado on the obverse. On a card to her mother, she referred to Toledo as the "artists' paradise" and expressed the wish that she could stay there and paint—but noted that it was too cold in the morning and at night. May Burleson's European tour lasted seven months, from February through August. She arrived home in mid-September 1920.[86]

Colonel Richard Burleson had arrived in New York on March 8, 1920. The *San Saba News* put on page one the news that his parents had received a wire from their son just after he landed. The paper also noted that Colonel Burleson was one of the last members of the AEF to come home.[87] After field artillery assignments at Camp Travis in Texas and Fort Sill, Oklahoma, he was granted a leave of absence in September 1922 and returned to duty in June 1923 at Fort Leavenworth, Kansas, where he attended the Command and General Staff School. He was a student officer and was graduated with honor. Successful graduates were put on a list of officers suitable for brigade command in case of mobilization for war.[88]

Richard Burleson returned to his peacetime rank of captain shortly after his return to the United States, but on July 1, 1920, he was promoted to the permanent rank of major of field artillery.[89] While her husband was stationed in Kansas, Mrs. Burleson spent much of her time at her parents' home in Galveston, where she was active in civic and charitable events.[90]

AN ARTICLE ON AIR POWER

After completion of his course in Kansas, Major Burleson was posted to duty in Washington, D.C., with the Historical Section of the Army War College. During this period, Major Burleson published an article in the *Field Artillery Journal* titled "THE AEROPLANE: A Means of Transport with Special Reference to Its Adaption to the Conduct of War." His thesis was stated unequivocally in the opening paragraph:

> *The aeroplane must be considered only as a means of transport. To treat the subject on any other assumption is false and therefore leads to faulty deductions. This statement probably will shock the reader. However, before this paper is thrown down in disgust, I would invite the reader to call forth from the dormant recesses of his brain, the many claimants for the throne in the scheme of war, which have been presented in the last two score of years.*[91]

He went on to cite the Pneumatic Drill (which fired darts), the torpedo boat and the submarine as being among the many innovations that had been hailed as instruments certain to revolutionize warfare—but either "fizzled" or were simply incorporated among the weapons employed. The submarine, for example, had its place in modern warfare, but it had not made battleships obsolete, as some had proclaimed that it would.[92]

Burleson saw the aeroplane as having an important role in observation, as eyes for the artillery units on the ground, but added that the driver (pilot) should be under artillery command. He did feel that planes could also serve a broader intelligence role for high command, and cited examples, some applying to the German side, some to the Allied side, in which, had good observation information been available on the disposition of enemy forces, a great victory could have been won.

Burleson clearly was ambivalent about the importance of the bomber, which in his view, was a type of delivery system for explosives—a form of artillery. He saw a role for bomber aircraft but felt that the development of pursuit planes would be faster than that of the bomber and therefore would limit the effectiveness of the latter. His article concluded with this sentence:

> *Thus we see that the Aeroplane in all its adaptations to the armed forces of the nation is only a means of transport and that its future development, which undoubtedly will be great, must be pushed with that end in view.*[93]

At one point in his article, Burleson noted that no one had suggested a separate branch of the service for horse riders. This comment, and the skepticism about the aeroplane that pervades the piece, suggests that he was at least partially motivated by a desire to refute the line of thought espoused by Billy Mitchell, prominent air power advocate, predicting a revolution in warfare to be brought about by the airplane. Major Burleson's point of view may have gained him favor with military commanders who agreed, but events in the not-too-distant future would reveal that his views on air power had missed the target.

STRONG RECOMMENDATIONS AND IMPORTANT ASSIGNMENTS

Major Burleson's assignment to the War College in Washington was extended to permit him to complete a course of study at the college, during which he served as a student officer. In the fall of 1926, he visited his parents in San Saba, Texas, where the *San Saba News* reported that he was working on "a complete and authoritative history of the World War."[94] While at the War College, he was nominated for the presidency of Texas A&M. Among the letters sent to the board of directors of that institution in support of Burleson's nomination were ones from Major General Hanson E. Ely, president of the Army War College, and Major General Charles P. Summerall, commanding general of the Second Army Corps.[95] General Summerall pointed out that he had known Richard Burleson as a cadet at West Point and as a field artillery officer under his command in Europe during the war. The key paragraph in Summerall's letter, dated June 15, 1925, stated:

> *Major Burleson has one of the finest minds I have ever known in any walk of life. He has an exceptionally strong personality with great force of character, and he possesses dominant leadership. His judgment and common sense are marked qualities, and he has ability to secure results without antagonism or conflict. His service in the line of the Army and in administrative section and his education eminently qualify him for the head of a great institution, I heartily recommend him for appointment, and I believe that he will administer the affairs of the college in a manner that will redound to his credit, and will bring success to the State.*[96]

Charles P. Summerall became chief of staff of the army in November 1926 and was promoted to four-star general in 1929. He retired in 1930 and, in 1931, was made president of The Citadel, the Military College of South Carolina, and served in that capacity until 1953.[97]

In spite of glowing recommendations from his superior officers, Major Burleson was not chosen as president of Texas A&M. In December 1926, he departed for his next assignment, which was to Paris, France, where he was attached to the U.S. Embassy as a representative of the Historical Section of the Army War College. While serving in that capacity, he visited World War I battlefields in France for the purpose of writing histories of the battles that occurred. He was relieved from that duty in April 1928.[98]

The next posting for Major Burleson was to San Antonio, Texas, where he spent nearly five years in various capacities at Fort Sam Houston. His promotion to lieutenant colonel became effective on November 16, 1929.[99]

In March 1933, he was transferred to Boston, where he served as a senior instructor of field artillery for the Officers Reserve Corps until August 1936. On August 1, 1935, he was promoted to the rank of colonel of field artillery.[100]

Society, Civic Service and Archaeology

The decade that began in 1925 was a remarkable one for Mrs. Richard Coke Burleson. When her husband was transferred from Kansas to Washington, D.C., May Burleson appeared to return with ease to a prominent role in Washington society. She also assumed a leadership role in women's clubs and began involvement at both the state and the national levels in the Democratic Party. In July 1924, she attended the Democratic National Convention held at Madison Square Garden in New York City and while there was photographed during a break in the balloting that eventually resulted in the nomination of John W. Davis.[101] The picture was posed, with Mrs. Burleson standing between William Jennings Bryan and Senator Thomas Walsh, from Montana, permanent chairman of the Democratic National Convention.[102]

Mrs. Burleson was elected to the board of governors of the Women's National Democratic Club (WNDC), and her work in that organization, together with her place in society, were recognized on March 8, 1925, when the *Washington Post* featured a full portrait of her along with a story about women's clubs and their planned activities in the nation's capital during the coming inauguration of Calvin Coolidge.[103] When the Washington office of the WNDC reopened in November 1925 after being closed for the summer season, Mrs. Burleson, who had been named assistant secretary, assisted the president, Mrs. Borden Harriman, with arrangements for political programs and social activities.[104]

There was a hiatus from late 1926 through the first part of 1928 in Mrs. Burleson's social life and political activities, due partly to her interest in archaeology (which will be described later) and partly to her husband's assignment as military attaché to the American Embassy in Paris. In June 1928, Major Burleson was assigned to the Twelfth Field Artillery at Fort Sam Houston, Texas.[105]

Mrs. Burleson and Mrs. Cordell Hull worked together to set up a hospitality stand on behalf of the Women's National Democratic Club at the 1928 Democratic Convention held in San Antonio, Texas, beginning in late June. A news story listed Mrs. Burleson as the wife of the military attaché in Paris and Mrs. Hull as the wife of the Tennessee candidate for the presidential nomination.[106] The nominee of this convention was Governor Alfred E. Smith of New York, who lost the presidential election to Herbert Hoover.

The fall 1930 social season began for Mrs. Burleson when she was inducted into the Army Civilian Club of San Antonio at its first fall luncheon on October 13.[107] Soon after that, Mrs. Burleson was one of two honorees at a Friday afternoon tea that was attended by seventy-five guests, and this was followed by bridge party invitations for Mrs. Burleson.[108] Before long, the Burlesons were appearing in the society columns of the San Antonio papers as having hosted meals and other functions in their quarters. Major and Mrs. Richard C. Burleson of Fort Sam Houston, Texas, were listed in the *Social Register of Washington* for 1931.[109]

The early 1930s, in fact, were peak times in the social lives of the Burlesons. In September 1932, Mrs. Burleson began Wednesday evening open houses.[110] May Burleson was an excellent conversationalist, and these functions gave her a chance to demonstrate her skills with the officers and wives on the base.

Easter Sunday afternoon in March 1932, Colonel and Mrs. Burleson held an Easter egg hunt for the children of the Twelfth Artillery. The hunt was in their quarters at Fort Sam Houston. The following year, although Colonel Burleson had already reported for duty in Boston, Mrs. Burleson held the event, after which tea was served for the officers and wives of the Twelfth and Thirteenth Artillery Regiments who had brought their children. Mrs. Burleson had vacated quarters at the fort, and she held the egg hunt at a house off base in which she was living until moving from San Antonio. A description of the hunt in the *San Antonio Light* included the following paragraph:

> *There were 50 children present. Master Maury Maverick won the prize for finding the most eggs, and Master Tom Edwards won a prize for the game of "eggs in a basket." Miss Helen Coburn drew the lucky number which gave her a live bunny in a market basket painted blue and decorated with carrots tied with ribbons.*[111]

The early 1930s, especially 1932, were also years for May Burleson of intense involvement in public service and in political activities that were facilitated by her social contacts and increasing prominence in society. Her social connections were a definite asset in advancing her other interests, including civic responsibilities and political goals. In late January 1932, Mrs. Richard Burleson and her friend Dr. Mary King Robbie were instrumental in the formation of the Alamo City Woman's Democratic Club (ACWDC), open to the women of Bexar County, Texas. The club was affiliated with the Woman's National Democratic Club, on whose board of governors Mrs. Burleson had served in the 1920s. The club's membership goal was 2,500, and 500 invitations were put in the mail as the first step in the membership drive.

An article in the *San Antonio Light* on February 11, 1932, featured a photograph of Mrs. Burleson and Dr. Robbie along with the chairman of the Bexar County Executive Committee under the heading, "S.A. Disciples of Jefferson." The article stated that the women forming the new club had "girded themselves in the armor of Jeffersonian doctrines." A prime and immediate purpose of the organization, according to Mrs. Burleson, was "to bring about the nomination of a candidate for the presidency that every Texan will loyally support." Club policy also stipulated that the ACWDC would take no part in city politics except to support all Democratic nominees. A partisan aim would be "to prevent the republicans from getting a stranglehold" in Texas.[112]

Soon after the initial meeting, Mrs. Burleson announced that the ACWDC would meet weekly in the club headquarters at the Plaza Hotel to discuss "leading problems of the day." On April 13, a pageant was presented as part of a Jefferson Day reception at the Plaza. The pageant was accompanied by "appropriate music" and portrayed "interesting events" in Jefferson's life. Scenes included a reading of the Declaration of Independence by an army major who played the role of Jefferson and a scene in which a young child who was a descendant of one of the signers of the Declaration of Independence portrayed a "little page." Among the cast was Lieutenant Colonel Richard Coke Burleson.[113] Mrs. Burleson began giving teas at the Burleson quarters in Fort Sam Houston in honor of club members.

Mrs. Burleson and Dr. Robbie were both alternate delegates from Texas to the 1932 Democratic National Convention in Chicago. Colonel Burleson attended the convention with his wife, and the Burlesons and Dr. Robbie were guests at a dinner given by Governor Albert Ritchie of Maryland, who was one of the nominees for president. After the balloting, Mrs. Burleson was especially happy that the nominee for vice president was Congressman John Nance Garner of Texas, who was serving as Speaker of the House of Representatives. When Garner and his wife made Galveston a stop on their post-convention tour, Mrs. Burleson presented Mrs. Garner with a bouquet of flowers on behalf of the Alamo City Women's Democratic Club.[114] Unlike the 1924 and 1928 conventions, after which the Democratic nominee had been defeated in November, the 1932 convention gave Mrs. Burleson the opportunity to witness the nomination of the winning ticket.

Mrs. Burleson also served as corresponding secretary and chairman of education work for the Texas School of Politics, a nonpartisan club that sponsored educational programs on politics and government. In August 1932, she spoke on "Politics and Organization" at a club luncheon and the next month was in charge of arranging the program.[115]

The Alamo City Women's Democratic Club and its board of governors honored Mrs. Burleson for her service as president at a luncheon in August 1932.[116] The ceremonies included the reading of communications sent by the Democratic Party and others praising Mrs. Burleson and remarks by Mrs. J.K. Beretta, toastmaster, who reviewed the honoree's service with the Women's Political Union in Washington, D.C., her work for Democratic presidential candidates in several elections and her efforts on behalf of woman suffrage (including being grand marshal of the 1913 parade). Another admirer spoke of Mrs. Burleson's work in organizing the Alamo City Women's Democratic Club. Mrs. Burleson made brief remarks, urging the members to support "a return to states' rights and the sound principles of Washington and Jefferson" and a "united effort for harmony and determination" on behalf of Democratic candidates.[117]

Earth's résumé *entire floats on thy keel, O ship!*
—is steadied in thy spars[118]

The impressive ceremony concluded with a reading of Walt Whitman's "As a Strong Bird on Pinions Free," which had been read at the commencement ceremony at Dartmouth in 1872. This paean to America reflected the ideals for which the members of the club should strive.

Mrs. Burleson remained president until April 1933, when it became clear that she would leave San Antonio. One of her last official acts was to call a meeting of the ACWDC in late April for the club members to join a pilgrimage to the Alamo, where a wreath was laid in honor of Texas heroes.[119]

Finally, the early 1930s were productive years for May Burleson's work in archaeology. For eight years, beginning in 1926, Mrs. Burleson pursued the study of that field and participated in some important expeditions. Although she visited several sites, her focus was on the ruins at Monte Alban in Oaxaca, Mexico. She spent the last four months of 1926 alongside archaeologists, observing their finds at sites in or near Oaxaca. In spite of a busy schedule of civic service and social engagements, she maintained her interest in archaeology with revisits to Oaxaca and home study for several years. A rally in San Antonio for John Nance Garner in February 1932 did cause a brief hiatus in her archaeological work, as indicated by an article in the *San Antonio Light* concerning Washington's birthday, February 22. That day, there was a celebration luncheon at the Gunter Hotel cosponsored by the Army-Civilian Club (of which Mrs. Burleson was a member) and the Pan American Round Table. The festivities overlapped with the Garner rally, and Mrs. Burleson and some others at the luncheon had decisions to make. Referring specifically to her, the *Light* piece noted:

> *She finally had to leave for the rally, so interested is she in that movement to put a real sure-enough Texan in the White House. Mrs. Burleson is so enthusiastic over the coming campaign that she is stopping for the time being her activities along archaeological lines, in Mexico and other parts of the world.*[120]

Then, beginning in late 1932 until late 1934, Mrs. Burleson spent about one-fourth of her time in Mexico with excavation teams. For a good portion of the five months prior to April 1933, Mrs. Burleson was with an archaeological expedition at Oaxaca that was under the direction of Alfonso Caso, an outstanding young archaeologist from Mexico who had recently discovered a tomb, labeled Tomb 7, at Monte Alban and excavated from it an array of artifacts unlike anything previously found in the New World. These artifacts included golden ornaments, gold and silver rings, precious jewels, urns, a skull embedded with jewels and other precious relics. The artifacts were from the Mixtec civilization. The discovery of this site, which also included mummified remains, was quickly hailed as the most significant archaeological find since King Tut's tomb.[121] The artifacts were placed in the National Museum of Mexico, of which Dr. Caso was appointed director in April 1933.[122] Caso became recognized as a leading, perhaps *the* leading archaeologist on Mesoamerica. Alfonso Caso passed through San Antonio on a train in June 1933, carrying with him the jewels and a selection of other artifacts from Tomb 7. His destination was the 1933 Chicago World's Fair, where he and a fellow archaeologist were to supervise the display of the Tomb 7 treasures in an exhibit at the fair. Professor Caso continued to lead excavations in the Oaxaca area for some sixteen years after the discovery of Tomb 7. Mrs. Burleson was involved in some of those excavations, the last being in the year 1934.

After her return from the Mexico expeditions of the winter of 1932–33, Mrs. Burleson gave talks in San Antonio about her archaeological experiences, including one before the Alamo City Women's Democratic Club and another before the Army-Civilian Club. In the latter talk, she used illustrations from the Tomb 7 excavations that had appeared in the *New York Times Magazine*.[123] In May, she spent a good part of the month in Mexico, including a ten-day visit with friends in Tlahualilo, Durango, after which she returned to Galveston to visit her mother. She then joined her husband in Cambridge, Massachusetts. Lieutenant Colonel Burleson was serving in an instructional capacity with the organized reserves in Boston. To broaden her background in archaeology, May took a summer course on the subject at Harvard University. By January 1934, she was back with another expedition in Mexico. The *San Antonio Light* reprinted a piece concerning her work in the Yucatan that first appeared in the *Diario de Sureste* of Merida, Yucatan, Mexico:

> *Mrs. Burleson, who is a cousin of Jeffrey Caffery, United States Ambassador to Cuba, has returned from a trip to distant Maya ruins, and is about to start to Chompton and Monte Cristo where she will study the little-known ruins in that vicinity. She will be accompanied by a guide who speaks both English and Maya. She will travel over the ancient Maya road that Dr. Solias Flores recently located and that we reported in this column.*

The *Light* article went on to report that Mrs. Burleson had been at Chichen-Itza for the past month as the guest of the Carnegie Institute of Washington. While there, she had studied the ruins of the city, the sacred well and the excavations and constructions that had been done by the Carnegie Institute and the Mexican government. Mrs. Burleson, it was stated, would leave Yucatan for Mexico City about the middle of February in order to revisit the archaeological zones of the state of Puebla and Oaxaca before returning to Texas to visit Galveston and San Antonio. The piece concluded with the note, "Col. and Mrs. Burleson who are stationed in Boston at present, were at Fort Sam Houston for a number of years."[124]

Mrs. Burleson began to establish herself as a lecturer on those phases of Mexican history that were being illuminated by the archaeological work in which she was participating. She actively sought speaking engagements by writing administrators at schools and other organizations concerning the talks that she was prepared to give. In a letter to a school administrator in Pittsfield, Massachusetts, she described two lectures that she was prepared to offer for girls between the ages of fourteen and twenty. The fee for one talk was twenty dollars, and the other was thirty-five dollars, plus expenses in both cases. She noted that "her knowledge of Mexican archaeological zones was first hand" and mentioned her association with Alfonso Caso.[125]

Her lecture at the Hale House, Woodson Institute, in Dover, New Hampshire, on October 8, 1934, was praised highly in an article in the local paper. The article stated that when introduced, "Mrs. Burleson made her entrance, wearing an authentic Mexican costume, and carrying on her head, in typically Mexican fashion, a basket full of fruits and vegetables."[126] The newspaper piece also noted the "beautifully prepared slides" that served as illustrations and went on to describe the lecturer's treatment of human sacrifice and then her discussion of the rise and fall of the Toltec, Aztec and Mayan civilizations. The article concluded:

> *Mrs. Burleson's talk was most comprehensive, and her word pictures most alluring and as she concluded her talk it made the members of the audience wish that they might visit our neighbors in the south and see for themselves the many wonders that are Mexico's.*[127]

The culminating event of Mrs. Burleson's work in archaeology also occurred in October 1934, soon after her talk in Dover, when she presented a paper at the Boston Library titled "Yucatan and the Isthmus

Laughing Boy, an artifact excavated by Mrs. Burleson during one of her archaeological expeditions to Mexico. *Walker Family Collection.*

of Tehuantepec." The article in the *Galveston Daily News* that reported on the talk asserted that Mrs. Burleson was considered an authority on the subject.[128]

Mrs. Burleson retained some of the artifacts that she excavated, including the Laughing Boy piece pictured here. The Mixtec, Zapotec and Teotihuacan cultures of Mesoamerica were represented in her collection of about fifty artifacts. These pieces no doubt were used in preparation for her talks and as examples when she spoke to groups.[129]

Several weeks after her talk at the Boston Library, Mrs. Burleson spent four weeks in Washington, D.C., returning to Boston to join Colonel Burleson just before Christmas. Her Washington itinerary included a White House musicale at the invitation of President and Mrs. Franklin D. Roosevelt, a reception at the Italian Embassy in honor of the Archaeology Society of Washington (of which she was a member) and a reception for the delegates at a conference on crime at the invitation of Attorney General and Mrs. Homer Cummings, who hosted the reception.[130]

2
MARITAL PROBLEMS AND PROFESSIONAL DIFFICULTIES

TROUBLED WATERS BENEATH A CALM SURFACE

As the year 1935 dawned, the one factor that suggested that there might be marital problems brewing for the Burlesons was the amount of time that they spent apart. At the heart of these separations was the strong bond between May Burleson and her mother, Clara Walker. For stretches of time, usually months, each year, May Burleson would leave her husband to be with her mother, sometimes to take trips, but often just to live at home. This pattern began immediately after the Burlesons returned from Manila and was compounded by the fact that Mrs. Walker also came to live with the Burlesons for long periods during most years.

The usual routine of upheaval in place of residence associated with army life facilitated visits by May Burleson with her mother. Orders would be issued for Richard's reassignment, and May would spend time with her mother while he began his new assignment and made the necessary housing arrangements—and May did not join Richard promptly after those arrangements were completed.

May Burleson's outside interests also resulted in separations, beginning with a project in New York City early in her married life to work on building support for a constitutional amendment for woman suffrage. Later, her interest in archaeology led to lengthy periods away from her husband.

The public face of the Burleson marriage through the year 1934, however, did not reflect a strained or crumbling relationship. Richard Burleson was a career army officer who had been given a variety of responsible assignments. Mrs. Burleson's involvement in activities ranging from woman suffrage to expeditions in the Yucatan apparently had been with her husband's blessing, and she had been socially active, often a social leader, in some of the various places where Richard had been stationed—from Manila to Washington to San Antonio. His wife's social skills seemed, in fact, to be an asset to Colonel Burleson's career. Her beauty and prominence in activities such as the suffrage movement, politics and women's organizations no doubt added a ripple of excitement when she hosted or attended social functions with her husband. For her part, May Burleson seemed to be pleased and proud to have as part of her identity being the wife of an army officer who had commanded a regiment in combat during the war and who was being promoted to increasingly high rank.

This untroubled public face of their marriage shattered in November 1935 in a San Saba, Texas courtroom when Colonel Burleson brought a divorce suit against his wife, and she vigorously contested the suit. The divorce proceedings came after about a year of intense discord between them. Their marital troubles, however, had begun long before. The first root of the troubles was the amount of time May chose to spend apart from her husband; the second, no doubt derivative, root was Richard's involvement with other women.

When Major Burleson's assignment at the War College in Washington, D.C., ended in 1926, he was assigned as a representative of the War College, stationed in Paris, France.[131] While there, he received authorization to study the battlefields in France.[132] He set sail from New York in December 1926. He soon met another passenger, Nellie Kemp von Ee. Von Ee and Major Burleson were attracted to each other and spent time together both on ship and later in Paris—their relationship became intimate.

He arrived in Paris in January 1927 and soon thereafter began living with a French family. Major Burleson made this arrangement to force himself to have daily practice in speaking French, in that his command of spoken French needed to be strengthened. In the meantime, his wife traveled to Europe with her mother. Mother and daughter remained for a time in Copenhagen and then came to visit briefly with Major Burleson in Paris before locating in a small town in southern France, where they lived with a French family. May Burleson began improving her skills in speaking French. The sudden death of May's brother Major John Walker, a West Point graduate, in May 1927, however, made it necessary for her mother to return home immediately, and May accompanied her. Sometime after this sad event, when her mother was resettled in Galveston, Mrs. Burleson returned to Paris to see her husband.

When May Burleson came to Paris, she discovered the affair between Major Burleson and Nellie von Ee. In a March 1928 report to the War Department in Washington, D.C., Brigadier General William W. Harts, U.S. Military Attaché in Paris, gave an account of what then unfolded:

> *Sometime after the departure of her mother Mrs. Burleson returned to Paris but still lived apart from her husband, but apparently still on good terms with him. Several months ago she came to my house one evening with a very badly blackened eye, which she stated had been caused by a blow in a quarrel with her husband, the details of which I did not know. From her statements it appears that she had learned that Major Burleson on his way to Paris had met some other woman on the steamer...and had fallen in [love] with her. Sometime later while Major Burleson was sick in the hospital Mrs. Burleson had visited his office and had searched his desk, as she was suspicious of certain presents Major Burleson had received. There she found a number of notes disclosing conditions of intimacy with the other woman, which she said caused her great anguish....*
>
> *From these letters she discovered also that Major Burleson had received presents of clothing, a wrist watch, and other articles from the other woman, which she insisted on his returning. These Major Burleson sent back, through the intermediary of the Embassy pouch, to this other woman who had returned to the United States by that time. In some way the officers of the State Department were warned and this package was opened in Washington and returned later to the Embassy for an explanation. To the Counselor of the Embassy Major Burleson admitted using the pouch for this purpose contrary to regulations, and admitted further that he had misinformed the Embassy mail room personnel as to the official character of its contents.*[133]

Although May Burleson's first reaction was that her husband's actions should result in his being "court-martialed and dismissed from the army," she came to see General Harts many times over a period of months, each time asking his advice as to how she should proceed in her relations with her husband. Harts felt that "there was considerable grounds for complaint on both sides of the family," especially given the impact that the relationship between Mrs. Burleson and her mother must have had on the marriage. He therefore urged Mrs. Burleson to return to her husband in order to avoid divorce and the "future unhappiness" that would result. Harts indicated in his report that Mrs. Burleson promised on several occasions to follow his advice.[134] General Harts reported that Mrs. Burleson also had told her troubles to others, including

> *the Counselor of the Embassy, to Major Cotchet, a former member of the Embassy, to General Chester Harding, Retired, who is living in Paris, and doubtless to many others. She even proclaims her family difficulties to total strangers. This latter is particularly unfortunate in view of the prominence which any American officer on duty in Paris naturally assumes in French eyes. Hence her difficulties are far from secret and have been commented on rather widely.*[135]

Harts was very much concerned about the gossip surrounding the Burlesons' marital difficulties and finally gave Mrs. Burleson the choice of either returning to her husband and "adopting a normal manner of life" or returning to her mother in the United States. Once again, she promised to return to her husband, but General Harts reported that instead

> *She informed me just before going home on the 22nd of February [1928] that she had not done so, and on the contrary had left for Rome, where she went to visit some friends. She confessed to having disobeyed me and to having broken her promises to me.*[136]

Harts's concluding comment about Mrs. Burleson in his report to the War Department was as follows:

> *My experience with Mrs. Burleson on several occasions convinces me that she is highly nervous, none too faithful to facts, impractical at times, and somewhat unbalanced. At one time she referred to the plan she had in mind of marrying again so that she would not waste the rest of her life. Whatever she says should, I think, be received with a margin due to these ideas.*[137]

General Harts's report to the War Department was made in compliance with instructions received from the adjutant general by cablegram. The cablegram stated that Mrs. Burleson had made "serious allegations against Major Burleson." In the same communication, the adjutant general requested a statement regarding the major's conduct and a recommendation as to whether or not Major Burleson should be relieved of duty in Paris and reassigned.

Harts did not attempt to excuse Major Burleson's conduct, especially the misuse of the embassy pouch, but he did recommend that any action on Burleson's assignment be taken only after due deliberation, during which the major would be given the opportunity to respond to any allegations made by his wife. The War Department, however, acted swiftly. The Harts report was dated March 2, 1928, but apparently the decision to reassign Major Burleson had been made before General Harts's report arrived. Richard Burleson was relieved of his Paris assignment effective April 7.[138]

A recollection by Mrs. Burleson seven years later (November 1935) is consistent in broad outline with the Harts report but, of course, gives her perspective on the Paris affair. The only significant difference is that, according to her recollection, she had been alerted by a letter from her husband in June 1927 (while she was in Galveston for her brother's funeral) that he wished to divorce her. The extract below from a 1935 letter written to the chief of staff of the U.S. Army also presents her concern about Richard's seemingly inveterate involvement with other women:

> *In 1927, Col. Burleson lived with one Mrs. Nellie Kemp von Ee in France and with me at the same time and wrote love letters to her and to me at the same time. He wrote to Mrs. Kemp von Ee that he would "force a break with me" and force me to divorce him "if he had to force his rights in my father's estate as fortunately both of us are Texans" and "he would commit murder to get her" and that "the facts that he wanted to marry her and divorce me to do so were enough grounds for him to divorce me." In June 1927 he wrote me a letter and told me he wanted me to divorce him so he could marry another woman. I went to Paris and effected a reconciliation after receiving this letter, and upon his promise to break off his affair with the woman [Mrs. Kemp von Ee] resumed our life together. After our reconciliation he wrote to Mrs. Kemp von Ee that he had told me that he would break it off with her but would yet find a way to divorce me and marry her.[139]*

Mrs. Burleson then advised the chief of staff that she had left her husband "for one year and some months to get a proper perspective on the situation." One of the options on her mind in October 1929 is revealed in an inquiry to the adjutant general:

Will you kindly forward information regarding the following query to me at your earliest convenience. It is important that I am correctly advised.

In case a suit for legal separation is filed in the State of Virginia, by the wife of an officer in the U.S. Army, against said officer, and the suit is won by the wife and alimony awarded her by the Court in the State of Virginia, the wife being a resident of that state, and the officer refuses to pay said alimony, he not being a resident of the State of Virginia and the state having no jurisdiction over him, will the War Department enforce payment of said alimony to the wife as long as the officer remains in the service of the U.S.?[140]

Mrs. Burleson received a reply to the effect that it was "contrary to the policy of the War Department to act on abstract matters" and was advised that she must submit "concrete data" in order for her request to receive consideration.[141] (In effect, this meant that the circumstances set forth in her letter would need to be a reality before the War Department would render a decision.)

In her November 1935 letter, Mrs. Burleson advised the U.S. Army Chief of Staff that during their months of separation in 1928–29 her husband had written her

ardent love letters repenting of his "dastardly action against me; burning was too good for him," etc. He implored me to return and stated that "were a thousand years to pass I would still be the dearest thing on earth to him and never would he cease to love me and care for me." On the strength of this, I returned to him at Ft. Sam Houston, Texas, in 1930. I had heard that Mrs. Jane Polk Ball, now Mrs. B.M. Bathurst of San Antonio was trying to force a divorce in order to marry my husband, I wrote to her mother and asked her to restrain her daughter from the pursuit of my husband, but even so, from that day to this, I have been embarrassed and humiliated by the ever present and constant gossip associating the name of my husband with that of Mrs. Jane Polk Ball, now Bathurst....

After my return to Colonel Burleson in 1930 he told me he was planning to divorce me, not to marry Mrs. Ball, as she thought, but to marry one Mrs. William Roberts of the Green Spring Valley, Maryland. After my return, I found over one hundred love letters from Mrs. Roberts to Colonel Burleson acknowledging the fact she expected to marry him. I took no action in this matter except to return handsome gifts Mrs. Roberts had sent to Colonel Burleson and to request Colonel Burleson to break off the affair with Mrs. Roberts. I still have the clothes that Mrs. Kemp von Ee bought for Colonel Burleson and that he wore while living with me.[142]

In spite of what clearly was a rocky beginning to their reconciliation, Richard and May began in 1930 a period of over four years without threat of marital rupture:

We took up our life at Ft. Sam Houston and were happy and harmonious. Colonel Burleson wrote beautiful love letters to me when I was in Mexico 1932–33, and in turn I wrote him letters of the same character; he wrote me loving and affectionate letters from Washington and Boston in 1934 after leaving Ft. Sam Houston by order for Boston. We were happy and harmonious in Boston and Colonel Burleson was kind and affectionate to me until…[143]

The 1927–29 marital crisis proved to be a tame precursor to the eruptions that shook the Burleson marriage from 1935 to 1937.

A Reassignment Under Protest

Orders were issued from the War Department on February 24, 1933, for Lieutenant Colonel Richard Coke Burleson to be relieved of his duties at Fort Sam Houston and report for duty in Boston with the training program for officers in the Organized Reserve.[144] This was a reassignment that Colonel Burleson most definitely did not want, and he made strenuous efforts—assisted by his wife—to have those orders rescinded and, failing that, to have the orders delayed.

The first approach was to request, as an alternate, an assignment that he did want, namely to the Historical Section of the Army War College in Washington. A letter dated March 10 from a U.S. senator from Texas, Morris Sheppard, was sent to George H. Dorn, secretary of war, nominating Colonel Burleson for assignment to the War College. The senator indicated that he was writing on his own initiative, without the colonel's knowledge, but the letter almost certainly was sent at Mrs. Burleson's request.[145] The senator received a polite reply, thanking him for his interest, but stating that there was no vacancy in the section, and due to budget cuts, none was anticipated.[146]

Next, the War Department and the adjutant general were bombarded with letters and telegrams from Colonel Burleson, Mrs. Burleson, both U.S. senators from Texas and a member of the House of Representatives, also from Texas, requesting that the reassignment orders be revoked. In his letter to the secretary of war, Senator Tom Connally wrote:

> *From the information furnished me, such a move at this time would entail a great deal of expense not only by the Government but by Colonel Burleson. Furthermore, it is hardly possible that the station at Boston calls for such specialized services that they may not be performed by some other officer in that vicinity without putting Colonel Burleson to the inconvenience and huge expense of transporting himself and family across the country.*[147]

The senators and the congressman received respectful, detailed responses, pointing out that Colonel Burleson had served nearly five years with troops at Fort Sam Houston (an unusually long assignment) and then explaining the reasons for the choice of the colonel to serve in Boston.[148] Mrs. Burleson wrote Brigadier General Andrew Moses in the Personnel Division of the Army General Staff. He referred her letter, as well as a telegram from her husband, to the adjutant general's office and, after discussion with that office, advised Mrs. Burleson that the reassignment order would not be revoked.[149]

Colonel Burleson was on duty in Boston by April 3, 1933.[150]

A MARRIAGE DETERIORATES

When Colonel Burleson left Fort Sam Houston to begin his duties in Boston, Mrs. Burleson, who had returned earlier in the year from archaeological work in Mexico, remained in Texas. She moved from the quarters that she and Colonel Burleson had occupied at Fort Sam Houston to a residence in San Antonio and, from there, continued her myriad social and civic activities until early May, when she departed to spend about a month in Mexico. After that, she sailed to New York to meet her husband, and they took up residence in Cambridge, Massachusetts. Mrs. Burleson took a summer course in archaeology at Harvard University and considered plans for another lengthy visit to the Yucatan that fall.

Mrs. Burleson, in fact, spent much of the winter of 1933–34, including January and February, on archaeological expeditions in Mexico. After she returned to her husband, matters marital appeared to go smoothly for a time, but strains erupted on a number of occasions in the summer and fall of 1934.

The details of these strains will be discussed in the next section on the divorce proceedings that occurred in the two-year period from fall 1935 through fall 1937. The underlying cause, however, was that Richard Burleson had become romantically involved with another woman who lived in the Boston area. By January 1935, Richard and May were living in an apartment on Pinckney Street in Boston, but he was spending less and less time at home at night. According to May, he was becoming increasingly hostile to his wife. An incident in February ended their time together as a married couple.

THE 1935 INCIDENT IN BOSTON
AND ITS IMMEDIATE CONSEQUENCES

Matters culminated on Saturday, February 16, 1935, when Colonel Burleson arrived home late at night and, according to Mrs. Burleson, threatened to kill her. She called the police, and three police officers arrived about 12:30 a.m. on Sunday, February 17, 1935. The report by the lead investigating officer is given below.[151] The report writer, Patrolman Byrnes, mistakenly referred to May as "Mary."

CITY OF BOSTON

POLICE DEPARTMENT
DIVISION No. 2.
February 26, 1935
Thomas M. Towle
Captain Commanding Division 2.

Sir—

With reference to the communication from the Superintendent relative to a case that I investigated at 15 Pincney [sic—Pinckney] Street, Suite 5, on February 17, 1935, I respectfully report that with Patrol Gorman in response to a radio message we went to the above premises.

Mrs. Mary Burleson who occupies the above mentioned apartment with her husband Richard Burleson complains that she was having trouble with her husband and that he had threatened to kill her several times during the past week, she said that the night before he had threatened her again and that she wanted a report of that fact made by the police, so that if it were necessary for her to kill him, the police would know that it was in self defense, she also said that she wanted no newspaper publicity as this would cause a scandal that would effect [sic] her husband's standing in the U.S. Army where he holds the rank of Lieut. Col. I asked her to leave the house and go to a Hotel for the night and to meet me in court in the morning and complain of him for threats, this she refused to do, saying I will not leave my own home and I do not want to go to Court.

We then went into the bedroom where her husband was asleep, she woke him up saying, Dick, there is someone here to see you, Patrol. Shaw asked him if he had threatened to kill his wife, he said Yes, but I won't do it tonight, I will wait until to-morrow.

I asked her if there were any revolvers or pistols in the house, she answered No. I asked her if he had been drinking, she said, No. I asked her again to meet me in court in the morning and she refused, again saying that she wanted no scandal in the Army.

Respectfully submitted,
(Sgd) DANIEL P. BYRNES

Patrolman Division 2.

The three officers who responded were Daniel P. Byrnes, William T. Gorman and Clarence P. Shaw. Mrs. Burleson was terribly agitated and upset by this incident. One of her first actions the following Monday was to go by the police precinct to ensure that an official record of the affair appeared on the police blotter. She then began to discuss the incident with the army officers who were Richard's colleagues as well as with his superiors, including Major General Fox Conner, commanding general, First Corps Area. She also discussed her marital problems with the wives of some of his fellow officers.

General Conner appointed Lieutenant Colonel L.B. Moody to investigate the incident and directed him to prepare a full report. Colonel Moody solicited information (by interview in most cases) from the following groups and individuals: the army officers who worked with Colonel Burleson, the

Burleson landlord, physicians who had treated either or both of the Burlesons and the investigating police officers. The Boston Police Superintendent was assured that the U.S. Army had no interest or concern with any civil action or charge associated with the affair; the military investigation was solely to determine if Colonel Burleson had brought "discredit" to the service and, if so, what action(s) his superior officers should take. Although some army officers stated for the record that they regretted having to participate, the cooperation and candor of everyone approached by Colonel Moody was secured. Colonel Burleson was interviewed. Mrs. Burleson, in spite of her long sessions with many others, declined to be interviewed by Colonel Moody.[152] Attached to the Moody report were pages of illustrations and documentation, largely transcripts of interviews conducted by Moody himself.

Moody's interview protocol is illustrated by some excerpts from his session with Colonel Albert W. Foreman, chief of staff, Ninety-Fourth Division, U.S. Army, to which Lieutenant Colonel Richard Burleson was assigned:

> *MOODY: Colonel, with reference to this matter of Colonel Burleson, will you please state, in your own words, anything which you believe you should state to enable us to get at the bottom of the matter and reach fair conclusions?*[153]
>
> *FOREMAN* [after description of a visit from Major Hitchcock, who alerted Foreman about the problem and referred Mrs. Burleson to Col. Foreman]...*Last Tuesday evening, February 19, Mrs. Burleson came to my apartment about 9 o'clock and remained until 12:15. She told me the entire story of his infidelity with at least three other women; stated these women, or at least one woman, Mrs. Knowlton, of Weston, Mass., was trying to steal her husband and break up her home. Furthermore, that Colonel Burleson had threatened her life and that it was necessary to call the police. This recital of the wrongs inflicted on her covered a period of over three hours.*

At this point in the session, Colonel Foreman indicated that he had "strongly recommended" that if the "worst came to the worst" she should pack up and go to her mother in Texas:

> *She stated that she would not desert him because he was mentally incapacitated and was a paranoic* [sic]. *She wished me to see General Conner and ask him to have him* [Burleson] *placed under medical supervision in Washington, because Col. Brooke had treated him two years*

ago in San Antonio, Texas, for a cerebral hemorrhage and that another doctor (I don't recall the name) had stated that he was a paranoiac.

During the course of the conversation she alluded to certain articles which he was writing in the magazine called "Today." She had purloined from his effects copies of the alleged article or articles and they are now in my possession. I have read portions of them but have not read the entire complement of articles.

Colonel Foreman concluded his response about his conversation with Mrs. Burleson as follows:

She seemed to me to be suffering from a menopause condition, very hysterical, weeping and sobbing, talking loudly, very nervous and attempted to smoke two cigarettes at the same time, which indicated to me that she was laboring under a very nervous and mental strain. Following that conversation of Tuesday night, she has called me twice on the phone and came to my office again on Thursday, February 21st*, after she had been to see General Conner. The conversation every time was along the similar strain which had been repeated before. I have never taken up the subject with Colonel Burleson, nor discussed any feature of his wife's mental condition.*[154]

Among the ten army officers interviewed by Moody was Colonel Brady G. Ruttencutter, U.S. Army, retired. He and his wife were resident in the area and knew Richard and May Burleson. Colonel Ruttencutter had met May and Richard at training camp at Fort Logan H. Root in Little Rock, Arkansas, in May 1917, when both men were part of the U.S. forces that soon would be shipped overseas. The two officers also worked together as members of a Presidential Court Martial from October 1919 until January 1920. They returned to the United States on the same date, and Ruttencutter recalled that Mrs. Burleson remained in Europe for several months. The two families had not crossed paths again until they saw each other in the summer and then again in the fall of 1934. Excerpts from the record of Colonel Moody's interview with Colonel Ruttencutter are provided here:

RUTTENCUTTER: Up until this time [fall 1934] *they appeared to be a happy married couple. A few days before Colonel Burleson left for Europe last fall on a leave of absence, Mrs. Burleson came to our apartment and stated that her husband would not take her to Europe with him and that she was convinced that he was having an affair with another woman—his third offense. From this time on until she went to the hospital at Fort Banks she had been a constant caller at our apartment....*

She stated that her husband was neglectful and very cruel to her and that she was most unhappy and that she believed that her husband's actions were due to the effect of a stroke that he had several years ago. She stated that in January she had lunch with a Mrs. Coombs of Boston, who gave her the name of the woman in whom her husband was supposed to be interested and that when she told him of learning the name of the woman in question, a Mrs. Knowlton, that he stated that he wished to divorce her and marry Mrs. Knowlton....

Sometime after February 17, the date she had called the police to her apartment, Mrs. Burleson called at our apartment and showed me a box of cartridges she had just purchased. I told her to get rid of the pistol or at least get a permit from the police to keep it and that in my opinion she was in no danger of her husband killing her or doing her any bodily harm. By this time she was apparently in great mental distress and worried about his threatened suit for divorce....

I do not know whether the things she said about her husband are true or not. I have never seen him with any woman other than his wife, nor has he ever discussed his family affairs with me. She further stated that she hoped her husband would have another stroke, with loss of speech so that she could torment him until he had a final stroke and died....

In my opinion Mrs. Burleson's mental state is not what it should be, in all probability due to her mental worries, real or imaginary and realizing her state of mind, my wife and I prevailed upon her finally to go to the hospital for rest and treatment.[155]

Mrs. Burleson, as shown by her reactions when she discovered the affairs or liaisons of her husband with other women in the 1920s, was not one to stand idle when she felt that her marriage was threatened by another woman. Once she was sure of Mrs. Knowlton's identity, she asked her friend Mrs. Ruttencutter to accompany her to confront Mrs. Knowlton at her home in Weston. Mrs. Knowlton was not at home, but they learned from an indiscreet maid that Colonel Burleson was there often—and that he felt sufficiently at home to act as host at parties, sometimes mixing the drinks. This visit added to Mrs. Burleson's distress, and against the advice of Colonel Ruttencutter, she immediately posted four letters, one to Mrs. Knowlton and one to each of her sons. The purpose was to demand that Mrs. Knowlton cease and desist from the pursuit of Colonel Burleson, but the letters were sharply critical of her. The fact that letters were sent to her sons, one of whom was a child under twelve years old, outraged Mrs. Knowlton. Mr. F.H. Nash, who had been a law partner of Mrs. Knowlton's late husband, was shown the letters and advised Mrs. Burleson that he was preparing to file charges against her for violation of the federal laws relating to the use of the U.S. mails as well as libel. He requested Mrs. Burleson to call on him at his office and bring her counsel.[156] By this time, however, Mrs. Burleson was in the military hospital at Fort Banks, Massachusetts, into which she had sought admission at the urging of the Ruttencutters. On the advice of Colonel Ruttencutter, she signed a legal retraction document (shown below), and in return, she received a letter from Mrs. Knowlton and her sons stating that they would not proceed with charges as long as Mrs. Burleson honored the promises made in her statement of apology and retraction:

Fort Banks
Mar. 4, 1935

I hereby apologize for the letters which I wrote in January 1935 to Mrs. Frank Knowlton and to her sons, and for the messages which I sent to her and for the statements which I have made to others, all imputing to her dishonorable conduct and a desire to steal the affections of my husband. It is not true that my husband had admitted or confessed any impropriety or undue intimacy with her.

My statements, charges, and innuendoes are not based upon fact but were inspired solely by anger. I retract them utterly. I regret them deeply. I will never again repeat them or make similar assertions.

This is written and signed by my own free will and in the presence of my advisers.

[Signed] *May Walker Burleson*

Witnesses:
<u>*B.G. Ruttencutter*</u> [Signed]
Col., U.S.A., Rt'd.

<u>*Paul L. Freeman*</u> [Signed]
Colonel, Medical Corps.[157]

The story told by Mrs. Burleson to the many army officers she spoke with after the incident on February 16–17, 1935, varied little from officer to officer. Mrs. Burleson usually got upset when telling her story. In so far as the incident in February is concerned, the information from others, such as the landlord, the police officers and even Richard Burleson, supports her story. The outcome that she desired was not clear, and Mrs. Burleson's ambivalence is evident throughout the aftermath of this incident. On the night in question, she told the investigating officers that she did not want a public scandal because she did not wish to harm her husband's interests in the army—as a scandal certainly would do. Yet a day after the incident, she was at the police precinct to insist that there be a record of the incident on the police blotter. She said in several conversations, including one with Colonel Ruttencutter, that she would stick by Colonel Burleson because he was a "paranoic." She also expressed to Ruttencutter, however, her grim desire that her husband suffer another stroke, with speech loss, so that she might "torment" him until he died.[158] This attitude foreshadowed her behavior during the divorce proceedings that her husband was soon to initiate.

Colonel Moody's Report

Other Issues

Unfortunately for Colonel Burleson, the scope of Colonel Moody's investigation was broadened to include several instances in which Richard Burleson's actions and/or behavior were alleged to violate accepted behavioral norms for army officers. These matters bore no relation to the incident on the night of February 16, 1935, or to his marital troubles in general, but it was Mrs. Burleson who triggered the expansion of Colonel Moody's purview.

As indicated by Colonel Foreman when he was interviewed by Colonel Moody, Mrs. Burleson had gone through her husband's private papers at some point and had located manuscripts for several articles that she claimed Colonel Burleson had prepared with a view to having them published anonymously in the magazine *Today*. She had the manuscripts copied by a stenographer, and the copies were transmitted to Colonel Foreman. These articles were highly critical of the U.S. Army General Staff, the U.S. Military

Academy at West Point and other units that were part of the U.S. Army. Mrs. Burleson offered them as evidence that her husband was capable of extreme opinions and wild statements, and she felt that the views expressed justified having her husband placed under medical observation. She also felt that the articles supported her contention that her husband was capable of both exaggerated and baseless allegations.[159]

These draft articles, however, had not been published and had been taken from Burleson's private papers without his consent—and could not serve as the basis for any action against him by U.S. Army authorities—but the existence of these papers did lead Colonel Moody to gather information that reflected unfavorably on Richard Burleson.

Moody's findings were basically that (1) Colonel Burleson held extreme views that he at times voiced intemperately and (2) he on occasion gave criticism in ways that were not only unhelpful but also destructive. These findings were supported by a seven-page report with twenty-three numbered summary statements or observations. The first nine points pertained to the incident at the Burleson apartment on February 16–17, 1935, and the remainder concerned Colonel Burleson's actions or behavior in other contexts.[160]

Colonel Moody's report was forwarded to Major General Fox Conner, commander, First Area Corps, who sent to Lieutenant Colonel R.C. Burleson on May 14, 1935, a memorandum headed: "Administrative Admonition." This admonition opened with the statement that a recent investigation had shown beyond a reasonable doubt

> *that you have been so intemperate in your criticism of official matters and in your expression of personal views on official subjects as to raise a serious question in the mind of the Commanding General as to your fitness to continue on duty with the Civilian components of the Army of the United States.*[161]

General Conner cited three points from Colonel Moody's report to highlight the justification for admonishment of Colonel Burleson, to wit:

The first concerned February 15, 1935, when Colonel Burleson spoke before an assembly of reserve officers at the City Club in Boston. At one point in his address, he picked up a glass of water as if to make a toast and said, "Here's to war." According to Colonel Foreman, who was present, Colonel Burleson proceeded to say, "What this Country needs is war. We need virility; we are too soft."

The second matter pertained to the following response from Colonel Burleson when he was asked to criticize the correspondence courses offered to officers in the Organized Reserve: "The correspondence courses are so poorly drawn that at least six months' work would be required to prepare constructive criticisms of them."

The third incident involved Burleson's observation of a mobilization test at Fort Ethan Allen by a regiment under the command of a Colonel Barnes. Burleson conducted the test, and his evaluation of the exercise concluded with these observations: "The physical condition of the officers and men is unsatisfactory for field service," and "The commanding officer, 7th F.A., is not qualified to command a regiment of field artillery under war conditions."[162]

Colonel Burleson exercised his right to respond and appeal. He wrote a ten-page response, to which was attached a list of twenty-two officers, including ranks from major through major general. Those on the list, at Burleson's request, had each provided a letter asserting his value and effectiveness as a training officer for officers in the reserve. All respondents spoke highly of Colonel Burleson and his work.[163] The matter was closed on August 7, 1935, however, when it was communicated to Colonel Burleson by letter from the War Department that the secretary of war had reviewed both the admonition and the appeal and had decided that no further action would be taken.[164] The appeal was dismissed.

Neither Richard nor May was satisfied with the outcome resulting from the Moody investigation. Richard received an administrative admonition that he saw as an undeserved blight on his record for matters unrelated to the incident at the Burleson apartment in February—the admonition was a byproduct of the investigation. For May's part, she was distressed that the investigation that was established to explore the February incident did not include any recommendation(s) concerning Richard's behavior toward May. May felt that the admonition should have included an order that Colonel Burleson not initiate a suit for divorce, and she was disappointed that her pleas appeared to have been ignored. She would continue to press for help from the U.S. Army as the crisis in her marriage to Richard Burleson continued to develop.

3

PROTRACTED DIVORCE PROCEEDINGS

Overview

The court trials that resulted from the divorce suit brought by Richard Coke Burleson against his wife, Jennie May Burleson, rank among the most bizarre proceedings in the annals of marital litigation in the United States.[165]

Among the elements were two continuances, a jury verdict set aside by the judge, a sudden cross action that reversed the roles of plaintiff and defendant and a bill of review filed by counsel on behalf of the party whose cross action plea had been *granted* by the judge, asking that the judge's ruling be set aside. The courtroom antics were augmented by two periods of hospitalization for mental problems on the part of Mrs. Burleson, the abrupt dismissal of several of her attorneys and a violent out-of-court physical confrontation between the contending parties during one of the continuance periods. The case came to trial three times and culminated with court action on a bill of review six months after the court ruling rendered at the third trial. The litigation process, from the filing of the original suit to affirmation of the verdict after consideration of the bill of review, required over two years.

THE DIVORCE SUIT ANNOUNCED

The following notice appeared in the *San Saba News* on September 5, 1935, and was republished in the same newspaper on September 12, 19 and 26 of the same year.

Citation by Publication

The State of Texas

To the Sheriff or any Constable of San Saba County, Greetings:

You are hereby commanded to summon Mrs. Jennie May Burleson by making publication of this Citation once in each week for four consecutive weeks previous to the return day hereof, in some newspaper published in your County, to appear at the next regular term of the District Court of San Saba County, to be holden at the Court House thereof, in San Saba, on the third Monday in October, A.D, 1935, the same being the 21st day of October A.D, 1935, then and there to answer Plaintiff's First Amended Original petition filed in said court on the 22nd day of July A.D. 1935, in a suit numbered on the docket in said Court as No. 3007, wherein Richard C. Burleson is plaintiff and Jennie May Burleson is defendant, and said petition is alleging that plaintiff and defendant were lawfully married on or about the 8th day of December 1908, and continued to live together as husband and wife until about the 25th day of February 1935 when by reason of the cruel treatment and improper conduct of the defendant towards plaintiff, he was forced to permanently abandon her since which time they have not lived together as man and wife.

Plaintiff alleges that defendant's action and conduct towards him generally have been of such a nature as to render their further living together as husband and wife insupportable. That on various occasions during the time that plaintiff and defendant were married, defendant, without any excuse or justification, would leave him for a long period of time and that on or about the 15th day of November 1934, defendant without just cause or excuse became greatly enraged at your plaintiff and attacked him, hitting and striking him with her fists and bit him severely on the right cheek; that defendant upon the slightest provocation and without any excuse or justification made serious charges to his superior officers and that, amongst other things, on or about the 15th day of February 1935, told plaintiff's commanding officer that he, plaintiff, was mentally unbalanced and thereby charging plaintiff as being of unsound mind and unfit to hold office. That the treatment of the defendant towards plaintiff generally caused him to suffer great humiliation, mental and physical pain and anguish.

Plaintiff prays that the bonds of matrimony existing between plaintiff and defendant be dissolved and that they be divorced, for cost of suit, and for general and special relief.

Herein Fail Not and have you before said Court, at its aforesaid next regular term, this writ with your return thereon, showing how you have executed the same.

Given under my hand and the Seal of said Court, at office in San Saba, Texas, this the 3ʳᵈ day of September, A.D., 1935.

36-4x Eddie Williams, Clerk
District Court, San Saba County[166]

THE NOVEMBER 1935 TRIAL

Mrs. Burleson did not want to be divorced and was present with her attorneys to contest her husband's suit when the case finally came before the District Court in San Saba County, Texas, on Tuesday, November 19, 1935. She was represented by J.W. Conger and J. Franklin Spears of San Antonio and Carl Runge of Mason. Colonel Burleson was represented by Newman C. Walker of San Saba. District Judge Lamar Thaxton presided.[167]

The case created a sensation from the beginning, and the *San Antonio Light*'s coverage of the trial's opening day began by noting that the divorce suit brought by Colonel Richard C. Burleson against Jennie May Burleson had stirred "the little town of San Saba" and reflected itself "in army and social circles from Texas to Paris, France." The article continued:

> *The recital of the marital difficulties of the couple shifted in scene from Paris to San Antonio to Boston to Denmark to Italy and back to Texas.*
>
> *Mrs. Burleson, daughter of a wealthy Galveston family, wept Tuesday as letters from women Colonel Burleson knew were read to a jury of farmers.*
>
> *The Burlesons, formerly stationed at Fort Sam Houston, are widely known here. Mrs. Burleson was active in politics when a resident here.*[168]

Colonel Burleson reaffirmed from the stand that he was seeking a divorce from his wife on grounds of cruelty. His testimony included examples both of physical cruelty to him by Mrs. Burleson and of causing him "embarrassments" with his superior officers that were a "detriment to my progress in the army." He cited being bitten on the cheek by her in November 1934 as one of the numerous occasions on which she had resorted to violence when they argued. The colonel also told the court that his wife had gone to his commanding officer to ask that her husband be sent to Walter Reed Hospital for mental observation and treatment.

A defense attorney then read in court love letters exchanged by Colonel Burleson and Mrs. Nellie Kemp von Ee. The colonel signed one of his letters to her with the Greek letter pi (π), and after that, von Ee referred to her lover as "pie." Colonel Burleson admitted on the stand to having committed adultery with von Ee in 1927. He also testified, however, that once he and his wife were reconciled, he discontinued his relationship with Nellie Kemp von Ee.

Letters to Mrs. Burleson from her husband were read as well—letters that apparently were written during periods when the relationship between husband and wife was a happy one. One of the letters in question was written while she was touring Denmark, and the other was sent while she was touring Italy. Colonel Burleson was stationed in Europe when his wife visited Denmark, and Mrs. Burleson toured several European countries, including Italy, in 1920, after Colonel Burleson had returned to the United States following World War I.[169]

Finally, Colonel Burleson had to acknowledge that after the reconciliation with his wife that followed the affair with Mrs. von Ee, he had written love letters to Mrs. William M. Roberts of Hampton, Maryland.

Having taken the stand and provided a record of her residence and other information required by the court, Mrs. Burleson was eager to testify, feeling that the introduction of her husband's amorous correspondence with other women had weakened his case. Colonel Burleson's lawyer must have shared her belief; he asked for a continuance until the April term of court, apparently to make plans to deal with that tactic. The judge granted his request.[170]

A Request for Intervention

On November 25, Mrs. Burleson wrote to General Malin Craig, chief of staff, U.S. Army.[171] The main purpose of her five-page letter was to try to convince General Craig to use his influence to get Colonel Burleson to withdraw the divorce suit. She first gave a detailed account of the history of her marriage to Colonel Burleson that focused on his affair with Mrs. Nellie Kemp von Ee and his correspondence with Mrs. William Roberts.[172] She then identified the cause of the current problem in her marriage:

> We were happy and harmonious in Boston and Colonel Burleson was kind and affectionate to me until he came under the wicked and evil influence of Mrs. Frank Knowlton of Western [Weston] Massachusetts and demanded a divorce from me in order to marry her. As I declined to file suit for a divorce he treated me with the utmost cruelty and brutality while he was frequenting Mrs. Knowlton's house at Weston, Mass. and was constantly in her company unknown to me....Colonel Burleson told me he filed this suit for divorce against me to get rid of me so that he could marry Mrs. Knowlton on several occasions.[173]

Mrs. Burleson then proceeded to launch into her appeal for help:

> If Colonel Burleson reenters this suit at law next April at the next term of court, San Saba, Texas, all of this will be proved, attested to by documents, and will be exposed in court. The newspaper report that the defendant Mrs. Burleson made motion for continuance is not true. I wanted the trial to go on, I felt sure I would win the suit. Colonel Burleson exercised the legal right he had and withdrew his suit for a continuance at the next term of court in April 1936. If Colonel Burleson reenters this suit, letters will be read in which Colonel Burleson calls the Army a "stink pot" and speaks of his superior officers as "paranoyacs" [sic] and "morons" and says "he is going to kick them in the face." Colonel Burleson has turned against the Army as he has turned against me.
>
> I ask you to influence Colonel Burleson to drop this suit at law and come to his senses, for my sake, for his own sake, and for the sake of the Army. I was brought up in the Episcopal Church and I am opposed to divorce on principle. All my life I have had a horror of it, and now after 27 years of marriage, I do not think that I should be divorced so that my husband can marry Mrs. Frank Knowlton of Weston, Mass. or any other woman.[174]

The next day, Mrs. Burleson sent a second letter to General Craig, in which she requested that Colonel Burleson be reassigned "far from Boston, so he can get away from the influence of Mrs. Frank Knowlton." If removed from Mrs. Knowlton's constant designs upon him, Mrs. Burleson believed that he might "repent that he has not listened to me and has allowed her to dominate him."[175]

Mrs. Burleson again wrote General Craig on January 9, 1936, to remind him that her letter of November 25, 1935, "remained unanswered" and to seek his help on another issue, namely that of the financial hardship being imposed upon her by her husband's decision to discontinue financial support. She advised General Craig that when her husband abandoned her in Boston in February 1935, he had agreed to provide $200 per month for her support from his salary. These payments to her had come in the months March through October, but Colonel Burleson was now $600 (three months) in arrears, checks having not come to her for November, December and January. General Craig was asked to direct Colonel Burleson to pay the $600 and to resume the monthly payments immediately. May wrote that she was "destitute" and that her mother had paid legal costs associated with defending the divorce suit as well as the medical expenses due to her breakdowns and other illnesses caused by Colonel Burleson's desire to divorce her. Referring to that situation, she wrote:

> *It is not right that after twenty-seven years of marriage my husband should be allowed to throw me upon her for support because he wishes to discard me in order to marry Mrs. Knowlton. I cannot go to work because of my advanced age and permanently impaired health that Col. Burleson and Mrs. Knowlton are responsible for. I, therefore, ask that this money be paid to me by Col. Burleson because I am his wife and intend to remain so if there is any justice in this land, and I ask support on the basis that I am his wife.[176]*

Mrs. Burleson then returned to one of her favorite themes when pleading her case with army authorities, arguing that her husband had been guilty of "conduct unbecoming an officer." She cited the current case in which her husband had hit her with a low blow when she was sick and down emotionally. She alluded to such conduct early in and even before their marriage and noted that Colonel Burleson had had liaisons with "unprincipled, designing" women at times throughout their union. In the same paragraph, however, she expressed her faith that redemption still would come to Colonel Burleson. She would give him yet another chance.

This time, Mrs. Burleson got a brief but immediate and substantive reply from General Craig: "The matter appears to be one over which the War Department has no jurisdiction and should be adjusted by the civil courts."[177]

Mrs. Burleson found this reply unacceptable and on January 23, 1936, wrote a two-and-one-half page response, in which she demanded yes or no answers to a series of five questions that simply rephrased the issues put to General Craig in earlier correspondence. The matters of restraining Colonel Burleson from continuing the divorce suit and of compelling him to provide support to his wife were built into questions, but the basic issue remained: "Cannot the War Department demand and require that his conduct be that of a gentleman?" Her letter closed with the following request: "I beg that you will address me as Mrs. Richard C. Burleson. I am not a widow, grass or sod."[178]

General Craig did not respond directly, but on January 28, 1936, a letter came from Major General E.T. Conley, the adjutant general, advising her that her letters of November 1935 and those of January 1936 all "have been forwarded for appropriate action to the Commanding General, First Corps Area, Boston, Massachusetts, who has jurisdiction over this officer." General Conley's letter was addressed to Mrs. Richard C. Burleson.[179]

THE SPRING 1936 TRIAL

Of all the events in the lengthy legal proceedings generated by Colonel Burleson's divorce suit, the spring 1936 trial, which opened in April of that year, shed the most light on the Burleson marriage. Testimony about several incidents that occurred in the twelve months preceding the trial revealed a stark picture of a crumbling relationship.

Two testimony segments extracted from different points in the trial concerned a car ride taken by Colonel and Mrs. Burleson in mid-November 1934 from downtown Boston to the dispensary of a local military base. The first segment deals with a trip taken by Mrs. Burleson to the Yucatan, and the second focuses on the cheek-biting incident that Colonel Burleson alleged to have occurred on that ride.

Expedition to the Yucatan

As discussed earlier, Mrs. Burleson had spent several months with archaeological expeditions to the Yucatan in Mexico just before her husband was reassigned from Fort Sam Houston to duty near Boston, effective April 3, 1933. She did not accompany her husband to Boston at first, but remained behind, returning to Mexico for most of the month of May, after which she visited with her mother in Galveston. Finally, she joined her husband in Boston in the early summer of 1933.

Mrs. Burleson testified during the spring 1936 trial that they were happy together in Boston at first. She noted that she took a summer course in archaeology at Harvard and cooked Richard's breakfast before he went to work each morning. Warnings of trouble, however, soon began to occur. Colonel Burleson began not coming home as frequently and, according to her testimony, "absented himself from our apartment and bed." He told her that he was "doing some research." Mrs. Burleson testified that she "suspected nothing," even when "about this time, the colonel asked me to return to the Yucatan to study. I told him that I did not want to go but he insisted."

Mrs. Burleson said that she went to the Walter Reed Hospital for an examination required for the Yucatan trip. She testified that Colonel Burleson paid her expenses for her trip to the Yucatan and that she suspected nothing when she left Boston, but the colonel's letters to her became indifferent and cold.[180]

Mrs. Burleson's testimony that she did not want to go to the Yucatan seems disingenuous in view of her participation in previous expeditions and her enrollment in a course in archaeology at Harvard, but it also became clear from other testimony that her husband indeed was pleased to have her away from Boston.

Their relationship deteriorated after she returned from the Yucatan in late winter or early spring of 1934. She was asked on the witness stand by Colonel Burleson's attorney about an incident in July 1934 when the Colonel stopped the car in which she and he were riding in order to search her handbag for a gun. She denied ever threatening to shoot her husband, but admitted, "He had a habit of opening my bag and looking through it all the time. I don't know why."[181]

Colonel Burleson was granted a leave of absence from his military duties for a period beginning in the third week of September 1934 and concluding near the end of October. He went to France alone, even though his wife had expressed interest in accompanying him. When he returned, however, Mrs. Burleson met his ship in New York, after which he went on to Boston where they had been living since the summer of 1933, and she remained for a week in New York. She testified that when she got back to Boston, "I found him barricaded in the bachelor's quarters of the University club."

She said she met Colonel Burleson on a Boston street one morning and got into his automobile with him. He said he was going to the clinic for treatment of a cold. She said, "I asked him what was the matter and asked him to explain his strange attitude toward me, and asked him to be himself. I told him I couldn't understand it; that I had gone to Yucatan and studied archaeology as he wanted and had made a success of it and was making some money." Mrs. Burleson wept and continued, "Then he told me he wanted me to go to Yucatan so he could be in Boston with Mrs. Knowlton." She continued pleading with the colonel and reported his response as "I am going to break you body and soul." Mrs. Burleson reacted, "I felt like a beast had jumped at me. I threw my arms around him."

In the courtroom, Mrs. Burleson collapsed, wept bitterly and slumped over in a chair. Her head sagged, and she waved her arms desperately. A nurse, who had been in constant attendance, rushed to her side, and Judge Lamar Thaxton ordered the jury removed.[182] Colonel Burleson added to the hullabaloo by shouting to a newsman who was present in the courtroom: "Why don't you take a picture of her now?"

The Cheek-Biting Incident

The citation announcing the divorce suit being brought by Colonel Burleson included a charge that the defendant, Mrs. Burleson, on or about November 15, 1934, while in the passenger seat of a car with the plaintiff, Colonel Burleson, in the driver's seat had attacked the plaintiff and bitten him on the right cheek.[183] This incident occurred on the same car ride as did the Yucatan issue just described. When asked about this allegation in court, Mrs. Burleson denied having bitten her husband. She said, "I remember the incident. We were driving in a car on the government reservation on our way to the dispensary. When we got there, I asked the medical officer about a slight wound on my husband's face, probably got from shaving."

Mrs. Burleson then testified that shortly after that her husband obtained a bachelor's room at the University Club in Boston, and she obtained a room in the married couples' part of the club.[184] She asserted, "He wouldn't move into the married couples' part, but he would come to my room all the time and stay late at night."[185]

Colonel Burleson's testimony was quite different: "As soon as we got into the car she began to row. She turned on me and started to scratch me. I grabbed her wrist and she bit me on the cheek. I first considered turning her over to the police for assault, but wanted to avoid the unpleasantness."[186]

He added a sentence about their living arrangements, testifying that one night in Boston, Mrs. Burleson induced him to come to her room and talk with her.[187]

Testimony Reconciliation

The relationship between the Yucatan and cheek-biting incidents is clouded by the timing of and the manner in which testimony about them was elicited. Although both incidents occurred on the same day in mid-November 1934 and during the same car ride from downtown Boston to the military dispensary used by Colonel Burleson, the *testimony* about these two incidents occurred at different times in the trial. One consequence was the discrepancy in Mrs. Burleson's testimony regarding when the living arrangements at the University Club began. These arrangements (she rooming in the married couples section and he in the bachelor's section) were in place *before* the car ride occurred, as she testified in discussing the Yucatan trip. In her testimony about the cheek-biting incident, she incorrectly has these arrangements being made after the car ride.

This discrepancy, though a source of confusion, does not alter the important facts about either incident. The way the testimony was collected, however, obscured the relationship between the Yucatan discussion and the cheek-biting affair and facilitated some slanting of testimony by both parties. The sequence of events almost certainly was as follows: once May was in the car and brought up her trip to the Yucatan and Richard had told her why he had wanted her to go there, she attacked him physically and bit his cheek.

A Washington Trip

Later in November 1934, not long after the car ride during which the two incidents just described occurred, Mrs. Burleson went to Washington, D.C., for a stay of four weeks.[188] The reasons for her trip, which were not related to her marital problems, were reported in the *Galveston Daily News* that December and had to do with attendance at a function at the White House and two conferences.[189]

Marital difficulties confronted her immediately upon her return, however. She testified as follows:

> When I got back to Boston the Colonel did not meet me. I left a message for the clerk at the hotel to call me. At 1 a.m. the clerk told me that the colonel had returned. I called him to say: "Richard, I'm sorry you did not meet me at the station." He told me he did not want to ever see me again and wanted me to stay away from him.

Mrs. Burleson added:

> I was surprised that he took that attitude, because I got a letter from him in which he said: "My Dear Muggins girl: It made me proud of you the way you walked out in the night alone."[190]

According to Mrs. Burleson in her letters to the army chief of staff and in her talks with other officers, not only did Colonel Burleson not meet her when she returned from Washington but he also absented himself from her for days thereafter, including Christmas Day. Further, although they began living together in an apartment on Pinckney Street in Boston, Mrs. Burleson wrote that her husband rarely was home and that he treated her with indifference and hostility.

Culminating Incident

The incident that occurred in the Burleson apartment in Boston on February 17, 1935, that involved a police investigation was the subject of trial testimony by both the defendant and the plaintiff.[191] The two were in agreement that the police were called, talked to both parties and left without taking any action. Colonel and Mrs. Burleson disagreed sharply, however, on the cause or motivation for the incident. Mrs. Burleson testified as follows:

> In the early part of 1935 when we were living in an apartment in Boston, the colonel came home one morning at three o'clock. He was in a cruel mood and told me he was going to murder me. He told me if he didn't do it then,

he would do it the next day. The following morning he came home at two o'clock and threatened to murder me again. I called police. Two policemen came to the apartment. They took the Colonel into a room and talked to him. When they came out, the officers said that it would be all right.[192]

Colonel Burleson, for his part, denied that he had ever seriously threatened to take the life of his wife:

In the early part of 1935, when she was nearly driving me crazy with rowing, rowing, rowing, I jokingly said something like that. I knew she held her body more precious than anything in the world. In an effort to have a little peace, I said to her, "You're always threatening to kill me. It would be strange if I got a crazy spell and killed you."

The colonel continued:

Whereupon, Mrs. Burleson rushed into the kitchen and returned with a large butcher knife. She dramatically cut circles in the air with the knife and said, "I am ready for death."

Colonel Burleson also testified that Mrs. Burleson continued her rowing and that one night she called the police to their Boston apartment. He said that he took the policemen into the next room and "they laughed about it."[193]

Regardless of which version was closer to the truth, the Burlesons never lived together again, and Richard proceeded with plans to file for divorce.[194]

Fundamental Issues

The incidents described above were symptoms of the deterioration of a marriage, but the major themes underlying the testimony and arguments in the spring 1936 trial and other court sessions for this divorce case were the following. For the plaintiff: (1) Mrs. Burleson had been cruel both to her husband and to his family; (2) she also had been neglectful of her husband and often absent from him throughout their marriage, such that simple companionship, not to mention intimacy, had been rare. For the defense, the themes were (1) Colonel Burleson's affairs with other women, which on occasion had led him to ask for a divorce, were the root cause of all problems in the marriage; (2) when he had not been involved with another woman, the marriage had been a happy one.

The following discussion of the remainder of the trial is organized to reflect these strategies on the part of the defense and the plaintiff and begins with Mrs. Burleson on the witness stand describing and documenting her husband's involvement with other women.

The Defendant: Affairs of the Colonel

Mrs. Burleson opened the defense's case by testifying that her husband had wished to divorce her on three separate occasions in the prior six years, each time to marry another woman—and the woman was a different one each time. She then said on the witness stand that she had lived with her husband twenty-seven years, during which time he had been "unfaithful, treacherous, and deceptive." She also testified that Colonel Burleson had come back to her twice and predicted he would come back to her again after his current affair with the third woman had blown over.[195]

When she was asked for the names of women the colonel proposed to marry, Mrs. Burleson replied, "They were Mrs. William Roberts, Mrs. Nellie Kemp von Ee, and Mrs. Frank Knowlton. My husband has told me that he now wants a divorce in order to marry Mrs. Knowlton of Weston, Mass., a suburb of Boston."[196]

The first of these relationships had been with Mrs. Nellie Kemp von Ee, for which an overall account of this affair was given earlier.[197]

On April 30, 1936, the third day of the continued trial, Mrs. Burleson read letters written by Mrs. Nellie Kemp von Ee to Colonel Burleson in Paris, beginning with one dated August 31, 1927: "Your Nellie wife is rocky tonight. Needs her husband to rub her back and hug her a bit. Darling I love you so. Kiss my spark of love. Your devoted Nellie wife."[198]

Mrs. Burleson proceeded to read from another letter that revealed that Mrs. von Ee had bought the colonel a lounging robe and twelve shirts. Mrs. Burleson volunteered that she had the shirts as evidence. She then read from some of the colonel's letters. The following excerpt was one of several that were read from letters written by him in Paris to Mrs. von Ee in Baltimore during the spring of 1927:[199]

> *My dear little Nellie Frances: Monday night. Just one such as we spent sweet moments together. I love you. Love you. Love you.*
> *Your darling pudding.*
> *Your Pi.*

During the same period that the colonel was sending love notes to Mrs. von Ee, he was also writing his wife that he loved her. His communications included a Valentine's Day card written in French and a note on March 16 that opened: "My dear, darling, sweetheart, peach." Later, on April 27, he saw Mrs. Burleson in person and told her that he loved her. On that very same day, according to Mrs. Burleson's testimony, Colonel Burleson wrote to Mrs. von Ee: "Your cable came this morning. It was a ray of sunshine."[200]

Mrs. Burleson concluded her readings with excerpts from late July 1927 letters written by Colonel Burleson to Mrs. von Ee, in which he addressed the status of his relationship with his wife. An excerpt from one such letter, written on July 20, is provided here:

> *Soon I think I will have some good news for you. The break should come within two weeks. I wish you could be here so we could show the world the true situation, but I think it is best to keep the situation under cover. It would be divine to hold you in my arms.*[201]

Mrs. Burleson then testified: "At that time we were living in the same room, in the same bed, and were living as husband and wife. He was rude, unkind, and hostile, but I didn't know why."[202]

A little later in the trial, on May 1, Mrs. Burleson read from letters that she had found in their quarters from Mrs. William Roberts of Baltimore, Maryland. Mrs. Roberts referred to the colonel as "her adorable boy." One notable excerpt was from a letter dated April 25, 1930: "My precious darling. You are not in and I had called you. Your darling letter came. Take care of yourself because I love you. Don't let any Mexican Senoritas run off with you."[203]

The letters from Mrs. Roberts were found after Mrs. Burleson had returned to her husband in 1930, but as noted earlier, the discovery did not derail the Burlesons' reconciliation.[204]

The Plaintiff: The Colonel Presses His Case

After the reading of and the testimony regarding the letters, the question "Who should be seeking to divorce whom?" might well have flashed across the minds of members of the jury. Colonel Burleson and his attorneys, however, pressed their case for his being granted a divorce strongly when they had the floor.

Colonel Burleson charged his wife with cruelty, involving mistreatment not only of him but also of his family. The cruelty to him was manifested in periodic desertion, irresponsible spending and derogatory remarks about him—some of which were made to his superior officers and had undermined his military career.

The testimony that follows was heard on May 2, 1936. The context for the first excerpt is that at one point Colonel Burleson was stationed at Camp MacArthur near Waco, Texas, and his wife was living at Leon Springs. His wife had refused to join him at the post:

> *She refused to come to me because my sister, Mrs. J. W. Price, lived there. She said no one was quite as low as my family. I called her long distance and tried to get her there and she said a lot of insulting things. The wires got pretty hot. I called her back later. When I finally got the bill, it was $46.*

Judge Lamar Thaxton rapped for order when laughter occurred at this point—the first time since opening of testimony the previous Saturday.[205] Colonel Burleson then turned to the personal abuse he endured from Mrs. Burleson and the constant financial difficulties that she created:

> *She talked about me to her friends and told them that I was worthless and lazy. She ran up expensive debts. I had to deny myself everything so I could pay them. One year she went to Galveston for nine months. I sent her half of my salary, then $350 per month. That was about ten years ago. When I got down to Galveston, I found that she had borrowed $1200. She said that she needed it for a social campaign among Galveston socialites. She became one of the social dictators of Galveston.[206]*

The colonel testified briefly at the trial on May 2 about the issue of having children and the intimate side of their marriage, as follows:

> *I talked to her many times and told her that it was our duty to have children. That we came from good families and were healthy and intelligent and owed it to our country and posterity....From the day we were married until February 20, 1928, my wife and I did not live as husband and wife in such a manner that we might have children.[207]*

At points throughout the trial, Colonel Burleson testified that his wife had damaged his military career by criticizing him before his superiors

88

and fellow officers. The colonel's attorneys placed in evidence on May 2 a series of signed depositions that were read to the jury to document this charge. A brief summary of the depositions was included in the account of that day's court session, and excerpts from that summary are provided below. Several of these depositions made reference to Colonel Burleson's mental health. In early 1933, Colonel Burleson was in the station hospital at Fort Sam Houston, having suffered a slight stroke. He was there several months, with symptoms suggesting arteriosclerosis and neurosis or psychoneurosis. Mrs. Burleson had corresponded with Colonel Roger Brooke of the U.S. Army Medical Corps concerning this matter, and this part of the colonel's medical history clearly influenced her perspective on her husband's mental health.[208]

Excerpts from Summary Depositions
Submitted by Attorneys for Plaintiff[209]

Maj. Nathan F. McLiver, Caribou, Me., in his deposition, said Mrs. Burleson told him the colonel was not responsible for what he did and that he had been a mental case for years. Mrs. Burleson, he said, told him she took a course in psychiatry in order to understand the colonel.

The deposition of Maj. Harry H. Baird, Newton, Mass., stated that on July 20, 1934, Mrs. Burleson visited his office and that of Capt. M.M. Pharr and drew an inference that her husband had been in a hospital for a mental derangement.

Depositions signed by Maj. General Fred T. Austin, retired, and Col. Rene E. DeRussey Hoyle, stated that Mrs. Burleson called on them in 1929 and made derogatory statements and used bad language concerning her husband.

On May 3, Colonel Burleson made a sharp reference to the matter of his wife's impact on his army career, when he testified that "when he was transferred from Fort Sam Houston to Boston he was informed at Washington he could never obtain an important army mission as long as he was with Mrs. Burleson."[210]

The Defendant: Counter Depositions

Although Mrs. Burleson did testify to instances of cruelty to her by her husband, the main thrust of her defense against his divorce petition was his alleged infidelity and its consequences. When Colonel Burleson was not being pursued by other women, she contended, their marriage was a happy one. Near the trial's end, in the late afternoon of May 4, 1936, her attorneys introduced a barrage of depositions to support this contention. Typical depositions, as summarized in the *San Antonio Light* on May 5, 1936, are provided here.[211]

Senator Sam Sheppard, chairman of the military affairs committee of the U.S. Senate, said:

> *In my opinion, Mrs. Burleson has not retarded the progress of her husband in the Army. On several occasions, because of Mrs. Burleson's requests, I intervened and assisted the colonel on army matters.*

Dr. Mary King Robbie, a member of the San Antonio Board of Education, added in her deposition:

> *I have known Colonel and Mrs. Burleson for about five years. On one occasion I attended an entertainment in San Antonio at their home in honor of Frank Kent,* Baltimore Sun *political writer. Mrs. Burleson appeared to be a good wife, made no derogatory remarks about her husband and was a charming hostess. I thought that they had a lovely home.*

Mrs. Beluah B. de Castillo of San Antonio was placed on the stand by the defense and testified:

> *I met the Colonel and Mrs. Burleson in Mexico in 1932 and they seemed to be an ideal American couple. While there Mrs. Burleson wanted to buy a picture of a saint, but the colonel asked her not to because it was too expensive. Later the colonel came in with the picture under his arm.*

A Contrast of Positions

In spite of Mrs. Burleson's willingness to leave her husband for long periods, and her awareness of his infidelity, she wanted to remain married to him. In her view, all that was needed for her marital happiness was to keep designing women such as Mrs. Knowlton away from her husband. The colonel, however, had a different view; although he regretted his romantic liaisons, he saw them as symptoms of their marriage problems, not as the cause.

Near the end of the proceedings, just before the various depositions were read into the record, while under cross-examination by defense counsel, Colonel Burleson gave perhaps the most poignant and straightforward testimony of the trial. He was asked, "Have you any affection for Mrs. Burleson?" and responded, "I have no affection for her now and have not since 1928." He proceeded to expand on his answer:

> *Mrs. Burleson destroyed me, body and soul. All I ask now is a mind and love of my country and family. I don't think I am capable now of ever loving anyone. I had the opinion when I married Mrs. Burleson in 1908 and had the thought for 20 years that I loved her.*[212]

Colonel Burleson had long given up on his marriage. At Mrs. Burleson's insistence, they had no children, and the intimate side of their life together had been rare to the point of being almost nonexistent. They had lived apart more than they had lived together, and except for those times when he was a necessary or useful adjunct to her social activities, there had been no companionship. Although he and his wife reconciled in 1930 and lived together peacefully for several years, their relationship apparently remained loveless. He felt guilty about his affairs, but in his view, it was long past time to end the misery of marriage to Jennie May Walker.

THE VERDICT

Colonel Burleson had filed a petition in which he as the plaintiff prayed that "the bonds of matrimony existing between plaintiff and defendant be dissolved and that they be divorced, for cost of suit, and for general and special relief." Trial Judge Lamar Thaxton, however, did not ask the jury for a simple yes or no verdict on the question: "Should a divorce be granted to Richard C. Burleson?" Instead, the judge directed the jury to render a verdict in the form of answers to the following special issues or questions submitted by the court:

Special Issue No. One:

Do you find from a preponderance of the evidence that the defendant has been guilty of excesses, cruel treatment or outrages toward the plaintiff as alleged in the plaintiff's position, of such a nature as to render their living together insupportable?

Special Issue No. Two:

Do you find from a preponderance of the evidence that such act or acts of excesses, cruel treatment or outrages, if any, were condoned by the plaintiff?

Special Issue No. Three:

Do you find from a preponderance of the evidence that said excesses, cruel treatment, or outrages, if any, found by you in answer to Special Issue Number One, were reasonably provoked by any act or acts on the part of plaintiff towards defendant?

Special Issue No. Four:

Do you find from a preponderance of the evidence that such act or acts of excesses, cruel treatment or outrages, if any, found by you in answer to Special Issue Number One, were caused by the mental or physical condition of the defendant at the time occasioned by her state of health?[213]

The Jury retired on May 5 and returned the verdict on the following day:

Special Issue No. One	*Answer: "Yes"*	*"J.H. Huffstetler, Foreman"*
Special Issue No. Two	*Answer: "No"*	*"J.H. Huffstetler, Foreman"*
Special Issue No. Three	*Answer: "Yes"*	*"J.H. Huffstetler, Foreman"*
Special Issue No. Four	*Answer: "No"*	*"J.H. Huffstetler, Foreman"*

Immediately following the jury verdict, Judge Thaxton issued a ruling:

And it appearing to the court from the said answers of the jury to said Special Issues Nos. One and Three that said jury has found that the cruel treatment, excesses and/or outrages of the defendant towards plaintiff were reasonably provoked by acts on part of plaintiff towards the defendant, for which reason the said plaintiff is not as a matter of law entitled to a divorce from the defendant, it is therefore considered, ordered, adjudged, and decreed by the court that the prayer of the plaintiff, Richard C. Burleson for a divorce from the defendant, Jennie May Burleson be and the same is hereby in all things denied.[214]

Three days later, however, this verdict was set aside by Judge Thaxton, and the official court record had the following entry under Cause No. 3007, *Richard C. Burleson v. Jennie May Burleson*:

On this 9ᵗʰ day of May, A.D. 1936, came on to be heard in the above entitled and numbered cause, plaintiff's motion for a new trial filed in this cause and the court having heard said Motion read and presented and action urged thereon, and having heard the evidence adduced thereon, and the argument of counsel for plaintiff and defendant thereon, and having duly considered same, is of the opinion and finds that plaintiff is entitled to a new trial herein.

It is therefore considered, ordered, adjudged, and decreed by the court that the plaintiff Richard C. Burleson be and is hereby granted a new trial herein.[215]

This stunning development came about after Colonel Burleson's attorneys, Newton Walker and Clay MacClellan, charged that the jury had been guilty of misconduct.[216] In particular, the jury said "Yes" to Special Issue No. 1 (Had determined that the defendant had been guilty of acts toward the plaintiff that would render their living together "insupportable"), but the jurors also said "Yes" to Special Issue No. 3 (Had determined that the plaintiff had provoked the acts of the defendant that had led to the affirmative answer for Special Issue No. 1). The jurors' intention, however, was that the affirmative for No. 3 would serve as a "rebuke" to the plaintiff—but that he would get his divorce.

This jury room scenario was revealed in detail when Judge Thaxton held a hearing to consider a motion for a new trial by the colonel's attorneys. Three jurors, including the foreman, testified about the jury's deliberations and what they thought would be the result of their verdict.

Judge Thaxton ruled immediately after the jurors' testimony that the jury had been guilty of misconduct because "their verdict did not reflect their true intentions," and he proceeded to grant a new trial. The judge had instructed the jury to answer "Yes" or "No" after each special issue—and not to consider the impact of their answers on the ruling on the divorce, which would be made by the court. The jury's decision to use an answer to Special Issue No. 3 as a reprimand of the colonel was a clear violation of the judge's charge.[217]

The new trial was placed on the docket for the October 1936 term of court. The outcome, especially given the intention of the jury, was not pleasing to Colonel Burleson—in that it meant further delay. The impact of setting the verdict aside on Mrs. Burleson ultimately was to prove catastrophic, but her immediate problem was a financial one caused by the drawn-out divorce proceedings—and her husband's refusal to continue the financial support he had promised while the case was pending.

Interim Support

In August 1936, Jennie May Burleson filed with the court an application that began with the following background information: (1) that the plaintiff, Richard Burleson, had deserted the defendant on February 26, 1935, and (2) shortly thereafter wrote to the defendant that he would provide her with $200 per month "during the pendency of this suit and thereafter until applicant should be able to support herself." Further, Richard Burleson was a colonel in the U.S. Army, with a salary of $600 per month, and the applicant thought that the sum provided was reasonable, given that "plaintiff and applicant had no children and plaintiff has no one depending upon him for support except this applicant."[218]

Colonel Burleson, however, had not adhered to his promise. From March through October 1935, he had, in fact, sent his wife the promised $200 per month, but for the next four months, November 1935 through February 1936, he had sent nothing. Then, from March through July, he had sent $100 per month. For August 1936, he had sent Mrs. Burleson only $38.50. For the time already elapsed during the pendency of the divorce suit, the colonel already was $1,461.50 in arrears on payments he had promised.

The applicant stated that she was heavily in debt and "penniless," requesting that the plaintiff be required to pay her the unpaid balance and "compelled to continue the payment of said sum of $200 per month during the pendency of this suit."[219]

The court responded by setting September 7, 1936, as a hearing date for consideration of the applicant's request. The judge ordered that the plaintiff be notified of the hearing. The hearing was postponed, however, and before a new date was set the terms of settlement of the divorce suit made this matter irrelevant.[220]

Mental Health Issues

Richard Burleson

Mrs. Burleson's frantic concern about Richard's desire to divorce her led her to believe that her husband's mental health might be at the root of his behavior.

Some five days after February 17, 1935, during the early morning of which Mrs. Burleson had called the Boston police from the apartment in which she lived with Colonel Burleson, she sent a handwritten note to Major General Fox Conner, commanding general for the First Corps area:

15 Pinckney Street
Boston, Mass.
February 22, 1935

Dear General Conner,

If Lt. Colonel Burleson could be ordered to Washington for duty in some department where he could be observed unknown to himself while in the office with other officers, as to professional reactions, utterances, remarks, opinions, writings, etc. and at the same time be under observation from the medical department, specialists, such as are on duty in Washington, I believe it would be for the best interests of all. Can you not use your influence to this effect?

[signed] *May Walker Burleson*[221]

Undoubtedly, Mrs. Burleson recognized that such an assignment would have the great advantage of separating Colonel Burleson and Mrs. Knowlton, but she was concerned as well about the actions of her husband that had triggered the recent incident in their Boston home. In fact, her concerns about his mental health went back to the period of late 1932 through early

1933, when he had spent a few months in the station hospital at Fort Sam Houston. She thought that what appeared to be incipient mental difficulties at that time might have worsened and could be a factor in what she now saw as bizarre behavior on the part of her husband.

Mrs. Burleson sought out one of the physicians who had treated him at that time, Dr. Roger Brooke, seeking information from him both by letter and by telephone. Dr. Brooke had been on the U.S. Army Medical Corps staff at Fort Sam Houston in 1933 and was presently associated with the Office of the Surgeon General in Washington, D.C. Colonel Brooke was contacted also by Colonel G.M. Ekwurzel, a member of the medical staff at General Conner's headquarters, who was investigating on behalf of General Conner. Ekwurzel's letter to Brooke began by noting, "A rift in the marital happiness of Lieut. Col. Richard C. Burleson has appeared." His letter then stated that Mrs. Burleson thought her husband to be "mentally unsound" and had "begged" that he be sent to Walter Reed Hospital "for observation." Ekwurzel was gathering information about the backgrounds of both Colonel and Mrs. Burleson and would appreciate any information—or opinions—that Brooke could offer. Colonel Ekwurel indicated that Mrs. Burleson wanted Colonel Brooke contacted because he (Brooke) had treated Colonel Burleson for a "brain hemorrhage."[222]

Colonel Brooke responded immediately. He told of his understanding that the Burlesons had been "temporarily alienated" in the past but had "always made up." He confirmed that Colonel Burleson had been in the Station Hospital at Fort Sam Houston for several months about two years earlier. He added that "at one time consideration was being given to retirement," but the colonel had been returned to duty. The section of Colonel Brooke's letter dealing with Colonel Burleson's symptoms is provided here verbatim:

> *As I recall, he had several fainting attacks, dizzy spells, and other symptoms that suggested cerebral arteriosclerosis. I have heard, but have no direct evidence, that in the past he has had several episodes of neurosis or psychoneurosis. If there is any doubt about his condition, I would strongly suggest observation at Walter Reed Hospital under most favorable circumstances. I have not at hand the disposition board proceedings of the Station Hospital, as they are filed in the War Department. Whether he was thought to have a small thrombosis or only symptoms due to arteriosclerosis, I am unable to recall at this time.*[223]

Colonel Burleson's personality and attitudes at times did cause him difficulty during his military career, but the investigations in 1935 did not reveal any sign or evidence of an underlying mental health issue that would justify his commitment for observation.

May Burleson

Although there was no record or evidence of mental imbalance earlier in her life, once it became clear to her that her husband actually intended to seek a divorce, episodes of emotional illness, some requiring hospitalization, began to occur. The onset of this problem and the impact of some early episodes on the divorce proceedings are noted below. Mental problems continued to affect May Walker Burleson's life for the next five years.

On February 25, 1935, three days after sending her letter to General Conner recommending that her husband be reassigned for "observation," Mrs. Burleson was admitted to the hospital at Fort Banks, Massachusetts, suffering from nervous exhaustion and worry about a possible divorce petition to be filed by her husband. In March, she was admitted to Walter Reed Hospital in Washington. The attention of Colonels Brooke and Ekwurzel, who had corresponded concerning Colonel Burleson, shifted from the colonel to Mrs. Burleson. Her condition was deemed serious and resulted in an urgent appeal by telegram for help from Colonel Brooke at Walter Reed Hospital to Colonel Ekwurzel at the First Area Army Base in Boston:

> MRS. BURLESON HERE VERY NERVOUS AND DEPRESSED MUCH
> WORRIED ABOUT DISPOSITION OF HUSBAND NOW BLAMES HERSELF
> FOR ENTIRE MESS. WILL TRY AND ADMIT HER TO HOSPITAL
> TOMORROW. IS IT POSSIBLE TO WRITE ME PROMPTLY ABOUT
> PROBABLE ACTION IF ANY AGAINST HER HUSBAND. ANY ASSURANCE MAY SAVE
> COMPLETE NERVOUS COLLAPSE.[224]

Colonel Ekwurzel responded promptly with the information that the Boston incident was under investigation, but at present, there were no plans afoot for action against her husband by the army.[225] Colonel Brooke replied that things were improving with Mrs. Burleson. When she was released from Walter Reed, she took Colonel Brooke's advice, which was not to return to Boston, and traveled instead to Galveston.[226]

There, however, her problem struck again, as was made clear at the spring 1936 trial when a deposition, signed by Dr. Titus H. Harris, a specialist, professor of neurology and psychiatry at the University of Texas and staff member at the John Sealy Hospital in Galveston, was introduced by Mrs. Burleson's attorneys.

Dr. Harris's deposition set out that he had Mrs. Burleson under his care from May 2, 1935 until August 12, 1935, and that for a part of those months she was in the "disturbed division of the John Sealy Hospital."[227]

May Burleson did not cope well with the delays and setbacks that marked the legal proceedings. Her frustration with the continuance granted on the day that the trial opened in November 1935 showed in a letter to the U.S. Army Chief of Staff.[228] Her collapse on the witness stand during her testimony at the spring 1936 trial also reflected her fragile mental state, but those frustrations were dwarfed by the devastating impact of the outcome of the trial in 1936. To have victory snatched away by the judge and simultaneously be told that she must face the entire ordeal again at the October term of court was too much for her. She managed to file her application for support from her husband during the trial proceedings, but her mental condition deteriorated as the new trial date approached.

Petition for Continuance

Sam D.W. Low, attorney for Jennie May Burleson, decided on November 4, 1936, after the October 1936 term of the district court in San Saba, Texas, was underway, to file a petition asking that Cause No. 3007, *Richard Coke Burleson v. Jennie May Burleson*, not be heard at that term of court but be deferred until the April 1937 term. Low's eleven-page petition opened with reasons why the defendant could not participate in a trial at the October term and the reasons why it was imperative for her to participate when the trial was held:

> *That the defendant, Jennie May Burleson, is now suffering from a complete mental and physical breakdown, and a complete disability of her nervous system, and is, at this time, confined for rest, treatment, and observation, in the Neuropsychiatric section or ward of the base hospital at Fort Sam Houston, Texas; and that, in view of her present mental and physical condition, it will be impossible for her to be present or to testify, or to give such information and assistance to her attorney as would be essential to the*

proper defense of the action filed against her; and that any attempt on her part to so participate in the trial of said cause, would be extremely dangerous, and would probably result in the permanent disability, and derangement of her mind, and the permanent impairment of her health....[229]

Defendant, through her attorney, further alleges that her testimony, on the trial of the pending cause, is pertinent, material, and absolutely necessary to her defense, in that her testimony will directly contradict many of the allegations contained in the plaintiff's petition, and that her testimony is vitally necessary to further show that every act of cruelty charged by the plaintiff against her, except those which she would specifically deny, was brought about by the unbridled ambition of the plaintiff.[230]

In support of the petition, there were three sworn statements by physicians. One was submitted by Dr. Mary King Robbie, who had known Mrs. Burleson for several years, the two having worked together on the founding of the Alamo City Woman's Democratic Club. It must have been difficult for this physician to see how her friend had deteriorated. Dr. Robbie began with this observation: "I am of the opinion that her nervous disorder is so acute that any severe emotional strain might result in the permanent impairment of her nervous system and her general health," and she proceeded to recommend hospitalization.

Dr. P.S. Madigan, a major in the U.S. Medical Corps and chief of the neuropsychiatric section, Station Hospital, Fort Sam Houston, certified that Mrs. Burleson was a patient at his hospital. Dr. Thad Shaw, a physician practicing in San Antonio, who had examined Mrs. Burleson, submitted the third statement. Both Dr. Madigan and Dr. Shaw supported Dr. Robbie's findings and recommended that hospitalization be continued.[231]

A remarkable part of the petition was the description of Mrs. Burleson's treatment of the lawyers who had served her during the spring 1936 trial. Lead attorney J. Franklin Spears and attorneys Carl Runge and James Hoyt Baker had been terminated by Mrs. Burleson during the period between the final outcome of the April trial and the opening of the October term of court. They were accused of "selling her out" (Spears), "gross failure to prosecute her defense" (Runge) and "laxness of duty" (Baker) as well as various other forms of improper conduct.[232]

The continuance sought for Mrs. Burleson by means of this petition was granted. The new trial of Cause No. 3007 was placed on the docket of the spring 1937 term of the district court in San Saba, at which Judge F. Raymond Gray was to preside.[233]

Violent Hiatus

As noted above, Mrs. Burleson's request in November 1936 to have the divorce suit against her continued to the spring 1937 session of court was approved. In that the grounds given in her petition were that she was confined in hospital suffering from a "complete mental and physical breakdown, and a complete disability of her nervous system," she certainly would have been expected to avoid to the extent possible stressful situations before the spring court proceedings. Instead, as soon as she was released from the hospital in December, she made plans to visit her estranged husband. Colonel Burleson had fallen behind in the monthly support that he had promised to send her during the divorce proceedings, and she wanted to secure the missing payments. Another reason for her visit was to arrange to have returned to her some boxes, now in her husband's possession, that contained her personal papers, including correspondence, as well as some items of personal property.[234]

In late June 1936, Colonel Burleson had received orders to report to Fort Bragg in North Carolina. He was to serve there as brigade executive for the Thirteenth Brigade from August 1936 until September 1937.[235] On January 4, 1937, his wife arrived at Fort Bragg in order to visit him.

Mrs. Burleson went first to see the commanding officer at Fort Bragg, Brigadier General Manus McCloskey. She wanted his assistance in dealing with Colonel Burleson. General McCloskey had secured a check from Colonel Burleson for three months of support payments, but when she asked the general to meet with Colonel Burleson and her regarding the matter of her correspondence and other private papers, General McCloskey refused. Clearly, Mrs. Burleson wanted to secure her husband's word that he would return all of her papers—and she wanted that done in the presence of a superior officer to whom she could turn later if need be.

Mrs. Burleson put her recollection of what happened from that point on in the letter that she sent to the secretary of war in February 1937:

> *General McCloskey declined to allow me to confer with my husband in his office and told me to go see him in his quarters; called his driver, and in my presence ordered him to take me to Colonel Burleson's quarters in the General's official car. Shortly after I arrived at the quarters of Colonel Burleson, General McCloskey telephoned to Colonel Burleson and told him he had not sent me to his quarters, thereby insulting me by the insinuation, if indeed he did not tell Colonel Burleson that I had appropriated his*

official car. A deplorable situation followed this duplicity of General McCloskey. Because of General McCloskey's double-dealing, Colonel Burleson fell upon me, struck me in the face, threw me on the floor and kicked me with his feet out of the house; slamming the door on my legs so violently that they were injured and bruised. My face and arms were badly bruised. These bruises are attested to by a doctor. Colonel Burleson sent for a Captain of the Military Police, who attempted to eject me from the Post. At that juncture, Mrs. McConnell observed me and offered me refuge. Colonel Burleson then sent for her husband, Major McConnell, and made false statements to him that I was armed with a gun and intended to kill him, Colonel Burleson, and also Mrs. McConnell. This attack on me of which General McCloskey and Colonel Burleson are guilty, is known to all Fort Bragg and to many persons in Fayetteville, the nearby town. I have been informed it has been reported to the War Department by the Department of Justice.[236]

A Procedural Resolution

Mrs. Burleson also filed an affidavit with the U.S. commissioner in Fayetteville, North Carolina, soon after her visit. The substance of that affidavit was transmitted to the secretary of war from the attorney general. The secretary of war and the attorney general exchanged letters, and the following proposal was made by the secretary of war:

> *There is in the War Department considerable correspondence in connection with the marital difficulties of Colonel Burleson. In view of this fact and the circumstances under which the assault is alleged to have occurred, it is believed that the matter is one which may be handled best by the War Department. If such action meets with your approval, the military authorities will investigate and dispose of the case.*[237]

The attorney general replied that this arrangement was "entirely satisfactory" to him and proceeded to advise the U.S. attorney at Wilmington, North Carolina, that proceedings should not be instituted in the civil court.[238]

After an internal review of procedural options, the War Department, through the adjutant general, referred the entire matter (the Fort Bragg incident and related marital difficulties described by Mrs. Burleson in her letter to the secretary of war) to the commanding general, Fourth Corps Area, "for his attention and necessary action, and direct reply" to Mrs. Burleson, who was notified of this referral. No record of any action by the commanding general could be located in Colonel Burleson's official military record file.

MRS. BURLESON'S PERSPECTIVE

Although the only matter that could have been acted upon by either the War Department or the civil authorities was the allegation of assault having occurred in Colonel Burleson's quarters at Fort Bragg, Mrs. Burleson viewed that incident as being subsumed under the larger wrong of her husband's effort to seek a divorce on grounds that she believed were false and unjustified. She felt that the army had the obligation to stop Colonel Burleson from continuing to press his suit for divorce. Further, in her mind, the basic fault lay with Mrs. Frank Knowlton, whose influence was the cause of the colonel's cruel behavior, and if Colonel Burleson could be removed from Mrs. Knowlton's influence, he would revert to being the loving husband that he had been in the early 1930s. Finally, if her husband were freed from Mrs. Knowlton's tentacles and stood ready to resume his life and marriage with his wife, she very much wanted him back.

This perspective was implicit from the beginning in her strong resistance to the divorce suit and her correspondence with high-ranking army officers during the early stages of the trial. Most strikingly, as will be shown in excerpts below, it was explicit in her February 1937 communication to the secretary of war—which was written over a month after her ordeal at Fort Bragg. Her viewpoint held even after the spring 1937 trial got underway. Her perspective then suddenly altered but, incredibly, began to build back in the aftermath of the divorce.

The first excerpt from Mrs. Burleson's February 1937 letter to the secretary of war refers to the period when she had to seek a continuance because she was unable to participate in a trial of the divorce suit that had been scheduled for fall 1936:

> *I was in Fort Sam Houston station hospital, suffering another severe nervous breakdown due to the unjust and harsh treatment I have been subjected to since my husband began his attentions to Mrs. Frank*

Knowlton of Weston, Massachusetts, while living with me in Boston in 1934–35. Since I have been in Fayetteville, N.C. I have reestablished my conviction that the Knowlton woman is the only reason why my husband has so ill-used me. The case will be called again at San Saba, Texas this coming April. I hereby request you to keep Colonel Burleson out of the court against me.... The affair is already disgraceful and the Army will only be again embarrassed if Colonel Burleson is allowed the license he is now enjoying.

In 1927 Colonel Burleson attempted to divorce me in order to marry a Mrs. Nellie Kemp von Ee. Later he sought to divorce me in order to marry a Mrs. William H. Roberts. Now he seeks to divorce me in order to marry Mrs. Frank Knowlton of Weston, Massachusetts. Having defeated the Kemp von Ee and Roberts women in their evil designs upon my husband, there is no reason why I should allow the Knowlton woman to dislodge me and take the fruits of the twenty-eight years of my married life.[239]

Mrs. Burleson had much more to say in her six-page letter to Secretary Woodring, including sharp condemnation of General McCloskey's role in the Fort Bragg affair and criticism of the army for not stopping officers with long marriages from casting aside their wives to marry other women.[240] Her perspective—and primary goals—however, are reflected in the excerpts provided earlier.

APPEAL TO THE HIGHEST LEVEL

The U.S. Army had one more level in its chain of command, scilicet the commander in chief. Mrs. Burleson wrote a desperate appeal to President Roosevelt and enclosed a copy of her communication to the secretary of war.

Hotel Millbrook
Fayetteville, North Carolina
February 23d 1937

TO
The President of the United States
Hon. Franklin D. Roosevelt

My dear Mr. President:

As you are the Commander in Chief of the U.S. Army, I appeal to you in despair. I am enclosing a copy of a letter that I have forwarded to the Secretary of War, which is self explonitory [sic]. I appeal to you because I am a woman alone. I am completely at the end of my resources, physical and financial. I have made a valiant fight to preserve my home. I came here to try to influence my husband to withdraw his unjust suit-at-law against me from the court. I have met with violence and abuse. What a pity, that a Colonel of the U.S. Army should be so brutal, and that a Brigadier General should show himself so little the gentleman. As you recently spoke to the Army, urging decorum, honor, high principle and right living among the officers, will you not interest yourself in my behalf and help me? I have suffered almost beyond endurance, and feel as if I cannot stand it anymore.

I am utterly crushed; all available funds have been exhausted in my defense; my health is broken. With your great heart and sympathy for the abused and mistreated protect me I beg.

With all expressions of loyalty and respect,
Sincerely yours,
   May Walker Burleson
   (Mrs. Richard C. Burleson)[241]

SPRING 1937 TERM OF COURT

Cause No. 3007, *Richard C. Burleson v. Jennie May Burleson*, was taken up again on April 21, 1937, by the district court in San Saba, Texas. On the second day, Jennie May Burleson was given leave to file a cross action, wherein she prayed that "plaintiff's suit for divorce be denied and that she be granted a divorce from plaintiff." In that up to that point she had fought bitterly her husband's petition for divorce, this was a stunning development.[242]

On the stand, Mrs. Burleson said that "further cruelties suffered since the last term of court" had resulted in her not wishing to live with Colonel Burleson any longer. She also claimed that during the previous trial, her husband had said that he felt like "he had been in a house of prostitution after spending an evening with his wife." In contrast to her behavior during her testimony in November 1935 and in the spring 1936 trial, when she wept on the stand—and collapsed on one occasion—her demeanor was calm, and she testified unemotionally on both direct and cross-examinations.[243]

The judge's decision came quickly. Colonel Burleson's suit for divorce was denied. Jennie May Burleson's prayer for divorce on her cross action was granted. The official court record of the divorce was brief but comprehensive:

It is therefore ORDERED, ADJUGED, and DECREED by the court that plaintiff's suit be denied and that, on the cross action of the defendant, Jennie May Burleson, the bonds of matrimony heretofore existing between the plaintiff, Richard C. Burleson and the defendant, Jennie May Burleson, be and the same are severed and dissolved forever, and that she be in all things divorced from him, and

It appearing that the pleadings of the parties place at issue herein the partition of the estate of the parties, and the right of defendant to the recovery of back alimony and attorneys' fees, and the court having heard and fully considered the evidence relating to these issues is of the opinion that the following is a just and equitable disposition of these issues:

And, therefore, orders that the estate of the parties be partitioned so that there is set apart and delivered to defendant all of the personal estate of the parties being the only property owned by the parties save and except the personal effects of plaintiff now in his possession (including his automobile) and save and except certain property given to defendant as gifts by the plaintiff's mother, and except certain books received by plaintiff as gifts, which said property defendant has agreed in open court, to deliver forthwith to plaintiff: and further in full adjudication and settlement of defendant's claims for alimony and attorneys' fees it is ordered that plaintiff shall, within a period of ninety days from the date of this judgment, pay unto the defendant the sum of Five Hundred ($500.00) Dollars, in default of which payment defendant shall have her execution.

It is further ordered that plaintiff pay all costs in this behalf incurred, for which execution may issue, as by law in such cases provided.

Announced in open court and entered as the decision and judgment of the court, this 22nd day of April, A.D. 1937.

RAYMOND GRAY, Judge[244]

The lead-in to the judge's decision made clear that settlement terms took into account the court's consideration of the petition that Mrs. Burleson had submitted in August for support payments that were in arrears of what Colonel Burleson had promised.

Given the two continuances that had occurred earlier for this case and the length of the 1936 trial, the rapid resolution in April 1937 must have pleased attorney Sam Low. The case really wasn't over, however, and Mrs. Burleson was to give Mr. Low a dose of the same treatment she had meted out to three of his colleagues who had served her earlier.

PETITION FOR A BILL OF REVIEW, OCTOBER 1937

On September 27, 1937, Jennie May Walker Burleson, now represented by attorney John D. Hartman of San Antonio, filed a petition in the District Court at San Saba, Texas, for a Bill of Review of Suit No. 3007, which had been decided by a judicial decree that granted a divorce to her and stipulated a property and financial settlement. A citation reflecting that petition was issued that same day and served on Colonel Richard Coke Burleson at Fort Bragg, North Carolina, on October 1, 1937. The first paragraph of Mrs. Burleson's petition concluded with the request that the judgment rendered in Suit No. 3007 "be set aside, or in the alternative a new trial be given, because of fraud, deceit, conspiracy, intrigue, collusion, duplicity, deception, perjury, and error, practiced during the trials of this case, especially during the April 1937 trial."[245] This request was reaffirmed and explicated at the end of the petition, as follows:

> *Therefore, this plaintiff prays the court for reasons set forth in the petition to set aside the decree of divorce awarded her in April 1937 and in the alternative a new trial where fair play and justice can be administered, this having been denied her in former proceedings. And this plaintiff prays that her former conjugal rights be restored to her.*
>
> *This plaintiff prays that the defendant, Richard C. Burleson, be cited to appear and answer this bill of review and upon a hearing the judgment heretofore entered in this case be set aside and held for naught, and that a new trial be granted this plaintiff, and this plaintiff further prays for such other and equitable relief as under the facts she may be entitled to have and receive.*[246]

This astonishing petition was filed in spite of the facts that (1) Mrs. Burleson had been granted a divorce in response to a cross action motion filed by *her* attorney; (2) the divorce had been decreed as final; and (3) she had charged her estranged husband with brutality for his treatment of her at Fort Bragg.

Her reasons were delineated in the petition document, which was eleven legal-sized pages in length. She began when the divorce suit first appeared in court in November 1935, noting that the plaintiff had withdrawn his announcement of ready for trial after the first day. Plaintiff (Colonel Burleson), she argued, "should have been forced to a non-suit" but instead was granted a continuance without the knowledge or consent of the defendant. Her analysis of the spring 1936 trial and its outcome needs to be read in her words:

> *Upon the trial of this case, April 1936, J.M. Conger, who had prepared the case with this plaintiff, failed to notify this plaintiff that he had fallen ill and would not be able to try the case. J. Franklin Spears undertook the trial of the case without any conference with the plaintiff or without examining her evidence although he had promised her that he would be in San Saba the evening before the case was called in order to confer with her.*[247] *This plaintiff was thrown unto a state of panic upon the ill treatment of her prior to this trial by J. Franklin Spears, Carl Runge, and James Baker, her attorneys. Mr. Spears told her Jesus Christ himself could not make any headway in that crooked and corrupt court; that Judge Lamar Thaxton was a fool and prejudiced against this plaintiff's cause, and that the jury was fixed. This statement to her by her attorney and the abuse and harsh treatment of this plaintiff by her attorney, J. Franklin Spears, so completely unnerved her that she went to pieces on the witness stand, damaged her case before the jury and her lack of control, hysterical weeping on the stand caused the jury to discuss whether a divorce should be granted, against the charge of the Judge, which resulted in the judgment divorce denied being set aside, and a new trial granted to the plaintiff, Richard C. Burleson. The bad demeanor of this plaintiff in the court room was the result of the ill treatment of her by her attorneys and she claims that they willfully prevented her from conducting herself so that the jury would not have discussed whether a divorce would be given against the charge of the judge and would not have been guilty of misconduct, which they were held to be and which act gave a new trial to the plaintiff, Richard C. Burleson.*[248]

In brief, Mrs. Burleson contended that the favorable verdict of the April 1936 jury had been vitiated by her court room behavior, which, in turn, had been caused by her attorneys' mistreatment of her. Hence her attorneys were the root cause of her not winning the case at that term of court.

Mrs. Burleson said in her petition that when Cause 3007 came back to trial in April 1937, she was convinced by her attorney, Sam Low, that her cause was lost and that the judge was determined to grant Colonel Burleson a divorce. Low advised her to file a cross action, in which she sought a divorce from the colonel. Thus she would avoid the humiliation of having her husband winning the divorce. She reluctantly agreed but noted in her petition that Low had agreed to request a continuance that would give the time to assemble the needed documentation and witnesses needed to provide an account of Richard's affairs with other women. She also wanted to bring in as evidence her husband's actions during the Fort Bragg incident. Mrs. Burleson thus desired to have her "day in court," presenting the full story of her husband's infidelities and cruelties.[249]

Incredibly, however, she also expected—and wanted—her cross action to fail. Mrs. Burleson therefore had her attorney file a cross action for divorce believing that after a continuance was granted, giving her attorney time to assemble the required documentation and witnesses, that a "fair" trial would result in the denial of a divorce either to her on the basis of her cross action or to Colonel Burleson on the basis of his original divorce suit.[250] This strategy (filing a cross action that she hoped would fail) was unrealistic, if not bizarre—and certainly doomed to backfire—and it exploded before it got off the ground when her attorney failed to file for continuance. Considering the arguments put forth by both parties, a divorce to end this marriage was inevitable, and that fact probably did result in a meeting of the minds of the attorneys on both sides with the judge, so that Mrs. Burleson's influence on the divorce settlement was minimal. The divorce was quickly granted, but the resultant financial settlement for Mrs. Burleson, in her judgment, was inadequate.[251]

On the surface, it appears mystifying why Mrs. Burleson and her attorney in the April 1937 trial did not focus on the settlement terms and still more puzzling why, even in October 1937, when the only approach with any chance of success was to try to alter the financial arrangements, Mrs. Burleson still clung to the hope of restoring her marriage. It may have been an obsession rooted in her mental problems, but Mrs. Burleson felt entitled to—and wanted—her home and husband, not just monetary security. She made this clear in the following statement in her petition for a bill of review:

> *The plaintiff fully realizes the cruelties and brutalities inflicted upon her since the plaintiff, Richard C. Burleson, filed a suit for divorce against her but she finds divorce insupportable. Since the divorce her state of utter financial destitution is cruel and humiliating, the loss of her home and her husband's protection is unbearable.*[252]

On October 19, 1937, the district court in San Saba considered the petition by Jennie May Burleson for a bill of review of the April 1937 court decision. Mrs. Burleson, new attorney John D. Hartman and the defendant Richard Burleson and his attorneys all were present.

The court ordered that "this cause be dismissed and that plaintiff take nothing by this suit and pay all costs of the suit and the defendant go hence without day."[253]

An appeal was considered by the court of civil appeals in Austin, Texas, and a decision was rendered on March 15, 1939: the decision of the trial court was affirmed.[254]

SUIT FOR DAMAGES

On the same day that the district court in San Saba dismissed the cause presented in her petition for a bill of review, Mrs. Burleson filed in that court a suit for damages against Colonel Richard Burleson. Her petition was based upon the January 1937 incident at Fort Bragg and stated that she, the plaintiff,

> *is entitled to $100,000.00 damages for assault and battery upon her person at Fort Bragg, N.C., by Richard C. Burleson, the defendant, and bodily injuries done her by him and damage to her health and well being, and for indignities upon her, causing her grief, shame, humiliation, illness from which she is totally unable to recover....Her tranquility and peace of mind has been totally destroyed. She is injured and damaged to the extent that her life is ruined.*[255]

This suit did not move promptly onto the court docket. On October 26, 1939, some two years later, there was an ironic entry in the *San Saba News* at the end of a story under this headline, "DIST COURT GRINDING OUT CASES": "Suit for damages brought by Mrs. Jennie May Burleson vs. Richard C. Burleson, continued for service."[256] This author could not determine if any action ever was taken on the suit, but Mrs. Burleson was never awarded damages.

4

IMPACT OF THE DIVORCE

A Death and a Marriage

The devastating impact of the divorce on Mrs. Burleson was compounded
by the death of her mother, Clara Walker. Mrs. Walker died on October
20, 1937, the day after the court in San Saba dismissed May's petition
that the judgment rendered after the April 1937 divorce trial be set aside.
Funeral services were held the next day at the Walker residence, with the
rector of Trinity Episcopal Church in Galveston, the Reverend Edmund
Gibson, as the officiant. Survivors listed in the obituary were son Richard C.
Walker, daughter May Walker Burleson and granddaughter Carol Walker,
all of Galveston, and brother Judge William H. Wilson, prominent Houston
attorney. Burial was in the Glenwood Cemetery in Houston.[257] Although
Mrs. Walker was eighty-two and in poor health, her daughter came to believe
that the drawn-out proceedings that culminated in her April 1937 divorce
from Richard Burleson were a contributing cause of her mother's death.

Another blow followed six months after Mrs. Walker's funeral and was
featured in the society section of the *San Antonio Light*:

Colonel Burleson Is Married in Honolulu

*Announcements have been received of the marriage of Colonel Richard
Burleson, and Mrs. Isabel Knowlton of Weston, Mass. The marriage*

took place Wednesday, April 27 in Honolulu where Colonel Burleson is stationed at Schofield Barracks.[258]

This marriage in April 1938 had occurred just over a year after the court in San Saba had decreed that "the bonds of matrimony heretofore existing between the plaintiff, Richard C. Burleson and the defendant, Jennie May Burleson, be and the same are severed and dissolved forever."[259] To May Walker Burleson, who had learned in 1934 that her husband was involved with Isabel Knowlton, the marriage announcement constituted confirmation that Mrs. Knowlton had intended to steal May's husband, and May vowed that Isabel would not go unpunished.

SPRING 1936: A FORESHADOWING

Mrs. Burleson's mental health problems, including hospitalizations, in the fall of 1936 and the episode at Fort Bragg in early 1937 were discussed earlier. These were among Mrs. Burleson's reactions to the setting aside of the spring 1936 trial verdict. That action by the judge, however, also had an impact on her relations with other family members, especially her brother, Richard, and her uncle Judge Herbert Wilson.

Immediately after the court ruling that Richard Burleson was entitled to a new trial, May Burleson began to travel and incur fiscal obligations that she could not meet. Herbert Wilson, who served as his sister's attorney and financial advisor, wrote May's brother, Richard, in May 1936 to inquire about May's whereabouts and to recommend that Richard urge her to return to Galveston to "resume a normal life." Uncle Herbert expressed the fear that May was mentally "off." He also advised Richard that Mrs. Walker could not afford to pay May's overdrafts at the bank and asked Richard to explain the situation with May to Mrs. Walker.[260] Richard replied that he had paid a $100 overdraft on an Oklahoma bank and that Mrs. Walker had paid a $50 overdraft, but went on to say that his sister was back in Galveston and was no longer running around the country spending money. On the other hand, he noted,

She will have nothing to do with me as a matter of fact she hardly spoke to me when I saw her. I understand that she is telling around town unpleasant stories about you and me, as a matter of fact she has

even made threats against our families. Of course I pay no attention to those things however I think the girl is sick and should be cared for accordingly.[261]

FALL 1937–SPRING 1939

For May Walker Burleson, the period beginning in November 1937 through February 1939 was one characterized by bouts of depression, real or perceived financial difficulties, uncertainty about what she should do with her life, conflict with her brother, Richard, and constant changes in mood and plans. Her comings and goings were no longer chronicled by newspapers, but family correspondence in those years, especially that between May and her brother, provides a record not only of her activities but also a series of snapshots of her thoughts and feelings.

Embittered by the outcome of the divorce proceedings and depressed by her mother's death, May Burleson's moods and mental health were erratic for over a year. Richard Walker and his uncle Herbert corresponded about May, and Judge Wilson was distressed not only about May's condition but also about the growing need for May's financial situation to be stabilized. He urged Richard to visit him in Houston to discuss the matter at length.[262] Important as they were, however, these concerns took a backseat at the end of October 1938, after May had spent twenty-five days that month in the John Sealy Hospital in Galveston.[263] Richard retained Mrs. J.A. French, a nurse at that hospital, to accompany his sister to Baltimore to seek psychiatric help. After a consultation at Johns Hopkins hospital, May was admitted on November 2, 1938, to the psychiatric ward of Pratt Hospital in Towson, Maryland. During her stay there, she discussed with medical staff the fact that one of her trips between April and October 1938 had been to Honolulu, where her ex-husband and his new wife were living and that she found the visit very upsetting. She remained at Towson for two months, departing on January 4, 1939, returned to Galveston and was readmitted to John Sealy Hospital.[264]

A Change in Attitude

By mid-March, this long "down" period for Mrs. Burleson finally ended and was followed by a spell in which she appeared to have an upbeat attitude. In April 1939, Mrs. Burleson went to Puerto Rico and wrote Richard from the Condado Hotel in San Juan to say that she was seeking work at the hotel and "going in search of seafood." She added that she was going to speak at the Rotary Club when she got back.[265] In early May, she wrote that she was under consideration for a "big job."[266] On May 23, she wrote again from San Juan, indicating that she did have a "tourist job" but that it might be discontinued soon—though another job might come. She indicated that she would leave soon and then return in September. May also noted that she wished that she had gone to Honolulu. She does not elaborate, but this comment strongly suggests that she felt that she had unfinished business with Richard and Isabel Burleson in that city. This was a long letter, and parts of it will be quoted in order to show her mood shifts in her own words:

Dear Richard:

I was glad to get your letter. I am sorry you are going to California.[267] I wish that you could stay in Galveston at least another year. I don't know what I shall do. I shall have to sell some property, then decide whether to bum around the world or stay at home. In the words of the old woman of Voltaire's Candide,

"I should like to know which is worse, to be raped a hundred times by negro pirates, to have a buttock cut off, to run the gauntlet among the Bulgarians, to be whipped and flogged in an auto-da-fé, to be dissected, to row in a galley, in short to endure all the miseries through which we have passed, or to remain here doing nothing."

She noted that many prominent people were in Puerto Rico and also wrote:

All the <u>best</u> people know of me and my charming little house here. Will have a write-up in the leading newspaper soon. Julian Platome Adriono Sevillas Cousiee is here, married to a girl from Brosos Bottom who had a position in the Woddy Bank. They are taking me [to a] dance at the country club. Had a cocktail party last week.

3 o'clock in the morning!

Have just returned from a grand ball at the Governor's Palace in honor of an Argentine battleship in port. It was something worth going to. For the first time since I have had them the jewels flashed in a brilliant company at a grand event.[268]

May did return to Texas in June, and she and her brother, Richard, were able to get together to discuss property matters. Richard returned to California and wrote to Uncle Herbert in July as follows:

May and I executed our deeds to most of the property and the bank closed the Estate and delivered the property of John C. Walker and I am glad to say we had a very peaceful settlement.[269]

As indicated in this letter, May and Richard had agreed on how the bequeathed property would be divided between the two of them. Proof of ownership of a piece of property (and any buildings thereon), though, had

Mrs. Richard Burleson and her brother, Richard Walker, in a car by trees in front of the Walker home, mid-to-late 1920s. *Walker Family Collection.*

to be reflected in a valid deed, and preparation of the deed had to reflect a current survey. What was not stated in Richard's report to his uncle was that a survey of the various properties was not done before the agreement was made. The fact that the decision to proceed this way was done at Richard's urging (most likely because he was eager to return to his home in California) is implicit in subsequent correspondence between May and her brother.

A Matter of Deeds

There were cases in which lots that had devolved to May bordered lots that had become Richard's, and when the required survey was done, two instances of overlap were revealed, in one of which a building on land belonging to May was shown by survey to be partly on land belonging to Richard, and the other involved a roof overlap on the adjoining property. Both overlap issues were ones of "feet and inches" but had to be resolved before deeds could be drawn up. In order to sell or refinance or engage in any transaction involving a piece of property, an owner had to hold a valid deed, and May Burleson wanted to refinance some property as soon as possible, including the lot affected by the "building overlap" issue.

Although a nuisance, the problems were really trivial and should have been easy for sister and brother to resolve, but months of wrangling, including some very harsh exchanges, ensued. Much of the conflict was over process and assignment of blame, not over the resolution of the basic problems. Finally, May's anger against her brother boiled over. The following excerpt is from her letter to him of July 27, 1939:

> *Again, I have allowed you to misuse me for your own purposes. After my former experience with you, I was worse than a fool not to stand my ground against you. It is now perfectly clear why you pushed and hurried Bleeker and Marion so violently.*[270] *You know how I demanded a survey of the boundary between my property and yours and you were determined to force my signature to the deed and get away before a survey could be made, which you did….After all it is my fault for believing you to be honest.*[271]

The letter from which this excerpt was taken was one of several letters written close together that aroused Richard's ire. He responded on July 29:

Dear Sister:

Your three insulting letters received. I have written to you and to your attorney stating that I was willing to correct the deed to you for that part of lot 3 Blk 22 in order that the fence will be boundary front and rear between your property and mine and requesting that your attorney advise me what could be done as to the overlap of the garage roof, also requesting that I be furnished with a map of the survey, which I certainly am entitled to and must have in order to properly authorize any corrections.

To date I have had no reply from your attorney Mr. Morse nor have I received the map.

I will not tolerate your insulting letters, so if you cannot treat me with ordinary courtesy through the mail I prefer to have all communications come through your attorney,

Your brother[272]

On August 9, Richard wrote a detailed response to May's request for authorization to have a new deed prepared. He began with a reference to May's letter of July 27, in which she had "abused" him "in regard to the mistake made in the deed between ourselves relative to the boundary line," and suggested a correction. He proceeded to outline a detailed set of adjustments that he was sure were right and fair—and that would satisfy May's concerns. He sent a copy to May's attorney Bleeker Morse and requested a reply concerning whether a correction to the old deed or a new deed would be better.[273]

It was, in fact, necessary for a new deed to be drawn up, but the process required over three months more. Part of the delay was caused by May's tardiness in providing the old deed to her attorney.

Near the end, although a solution to the deed controversy seemed near, perhaps the nadir of May's relationship with her brother was reached on November 6, 1939, when she wrote the following terse letter:

Dear Richard,

Bleeker is sending you that deed for you to sign. I have been obliged to accept it the way Marian and he have prepared it. I want it signed and returned at once. I have only a few dollars and can't wait any longer. I am living like a dog and have reached the end of my endurance. I can't wait for you to come to Galveston. If you don't sign that deed and return it at once after what you have done to me, I will never speak to you again so help me god.[274]

May

Richard did sign and return the deed, and though some harsh words remained to be written, the issue was resolved. During the months when angry letters were exchanged, there did not appear to be a single attempt at nuncupative communication between brother and sister—either by arranging to meet or by use of the telephone.

May's letter of January 4, 1940, written from the Hotel Cavalier in Galveston, was more civil but reflected considerable residual bitterness toward Richard. The letter also communicated uncertainty and desperation as well as sadness about her situation. Still, she offered assistance to Richard on his upcoming trip to Texas, and there were hints that she might begin to take an interest in things again:

Dear Richard,

Thank you and Caroline and Carol so very much for the beautiful basket of fruit you sent us for Xmas. We certainly did enjoy it and I appreciate the thought of me. Xmas was a sad time for me but I managed to get thru fairly well. The Yamadas asked us to dinner. There was a grand turkey and plenty of good cocktails and wine. Margaret drove us around town at night to see the lights and took us to her apartment for supper. I got many cards and a telegram from friends. New Years Day was miserable. The Harris had a grand ball on the 27th Did not have much of a time...Did not go to Uina's ball.

At last the business with the bank is done. McCollough would not give me one cent more than the $2500, out of that he took the money for the taxes, $400 for interest and when I pay what I owe only $200 will be left. I am going to save money, all my jewels, and go to San Francisco and try to get some work. Though my nerves are so bad there is no chance for me to [illegible word] anything. I am quite sure I will blow off my head, but that is so much better than having to live like those in misery and humiliation. My morale is completely broken for the last time. If I could have had that money in July and got away, my board and rent money would *have paid the taxes. By now I would have been working some variety in California. It is my own fault for being a ___ ___ fool to sign that deed without a survey I was entitled to before signing You can just thank yourself for the utter misery I have suffered since I allowed you to impose on me in that matter.*

Bleecker has promised me he will do everything he can to refinance in Houston at once. McCollough told him he wanted to get rid of me as soon as he possibly could. Will you please write me at once and let me know if you intend to come back and when. If you want to be here in your 2 story house, you can have all the furniture you need of mine stored in the [illegible word] part of the attic. I have everything there for the whole house. All you have to bring is your linen and silver. It will save you paying rent in Houston. You can get my two domestic oriental rugs…and use my bedroom rugs for upstairs.

I am going to make every effort to leave within the next 10 days.…I can't see anything ahead of me but certain death unless I can get that Houston refinancing within the next two months.

Lovingly

May[275]

Richard Walker responded on January 10, 1940, to his sister's letter, first acknowledging her thanks for the fruit basket and then noting, "We did very little over Christmas." They had been, however to see *Gone with the Wind*, the Rose Parade and the Rose Bowl game. His response to May's perception of his role in the deed affair was brief, but sharp:

I do not thank you for jumping me about your inability to raise more money. You knew all along that I was prepared to give you that deed but you refused to accept it for some cockeyed reason and raised a scene in the bank, so I was told.[276]

Richard proceeded to offer May some unsolicited but calm financial advice and requested that she cooperate with him on some matters concerning separate property tracts of hers near some tracts of his—tracts that might be sold separately or together in the near future. Richard, for example, had declined to lease his property in Houston for grazing cows and hoped that May would do the same for her property there.[277]

He thanked her but declined her offer of furniture, indicating that when he came he would stay in Houston. He also advised her strongly against coming to California to seek work, pointing out difficulties with distances and traffic and noting that they did not have room for her to stay with them. He closed by asking May to keep him informed of her whereabouts.[278]

February 1940: Hopeful Attitude but Unrealistic Plans

May wrote Richard three times in February 1940. The plans outlined in these communications seemed to be jumbled and unrealistic at times, but the tone was entirely different from all her other letters since July 1939. The outlook expressed by May Burleson in February was optimistic—and future-oriented. The first, a letter written from San Antonio, expressed delight that she had departed Galveston at last. She was still concerned about getting loans on the land she owned in Houston, but the thrust of her letter is a gallimaufry of future plans. First, she had decided to stay in Texas for the rest of her life, but not in Galveston, where she could not be happy; she wanted to sell everything there and put her money into a small ranch house in San Saba County. She also wanted to maintain a little apartment in San Antonio. On the ranch where her house would be located, she would raise sheep, goats and furs. She described her plans for the ranch in some detail:

The Country around San Saba is full of foxes, skunks and bob cats and rabbits. They are caught and sold at 8 cents and resold for 1 dollar. I am going to [Texas] A&M and get a course on breeding and feeding and develop these wild animals into fine furs, and then I am going into produce, buying and selling pecans, turkeys, and all other products of the country. I want to put up ware houses and a cold storage plant. There is a big future in this West Texas country and whoever goes in now is going to get rich within the next ten years. I went to San Saba and talked to a man and his wife in the produce business who have already begun to corner the fur trafficking. I want to form a partnership with them and have to begin next summer if I am going to get in on the ground floor.[279]

In the same letter, she tells Richard that she wants to join him in the development phase for their lands. In fact, they should open an office for that purpose in Houston. In her closing paragraph, she writes that she plans a trip to Washington, New York and other cities when she leaves San Antonio.[280]

Ten days later, she wrote again from San Antonio, but said that she was leaving that day for Pinehurst, North Carolina, to visit her friend Miss A. Hilton. May's plans to go to Washington and New York had been canceled because she did not have sufficient funds. She planned to spend two weeks with Miss Hilton, move to a "cheap place" in Pinehurst and remain there until she had to return to Galveston in June. She then returned to the topic of her overall plans:

> *I have to stay there until June when I have to go back to Galveston (if you and Bleecker haven't refinanced for me) to raise that money for my note. I ought to be there anyhow to work with you in getting the land on the market, or starting a development whichever you decide to do. I think we should open a real estate office in Houston, Walker and Walker. We could pick up some money on deals not our own. I will handle rents—apartments and houses along with sales.*
>
> *I am certainly going to sell out in South Texas and put the money in a ranch near here. The west Texas produce is a clean up. I won't be able to get out of the state for ten years, but I am going to make my money make money for me; and will have a big job to do. That is what I need.[281]*

She concluded by asking Richard to think over plans for a real estate office in Houston and to write to her soon. Five days later, May sent a picture postcard to Mr. and Mrs. Richard Walker. The card was postmarked February 28, 1940, in San Antonio and featured a Texas Longhorn on the obverse. The message read:

> *Texas for me forever.*
> *May[282]*

On March 8, 1940, in Columbia, South Carolina, May Walker Burleson was arrested and charged with murder.

5

HOMICIDE

Texas to South Carolina

May Walker Burleson finally began her journey from Texas to North Carolina at the end of February 1940. She left San Antonio with thirteen pieces of luggage, traveling by bus to Atlanta, where she stopped over for a quick visit with a friend at Fort McPherson and then continued to Pinehurst, North Carolina, where she remained for several days. Her mood when she left San Antonio, however, was not as upbeat as her letters of February 13 and 23 to her brother, Richard, and her postcard appeared to suggest.[283]

A friend and resident of San Antonio, Mrs. John H. Means, testified later that "Mrs. Burleson appeared particularly morbid when she left Texas to come to South Carolina."[284] Another Texas friend, Claudia C. Dodd, also testified later that she received a letter from Pinehurst postmarked March 3, 1940, in which Mrs. Burleson said, "This is a beautiful place. I think that I'll stay here three weeks." In the same letter, Mrs. Burleson wrote that she planned to tear down her Galveston home (an enormous beautiful stone residence) and move it to Houston. Then she said that she thought she would start a fox ranch in Texas. "But I'll never be happy, never, never," she concluded.[285]

From Pinehurst, Mrs. Burleson went to Fort Bragg, where she said that she learned that Colonel Burleson was stationed at Camp Jackson near Columbia, South Carolina. She took a bus from nearby Fayetteville and arrived with her luggage in Columbia on the night of Wednesday, March 6. She telephoned a boardinghouse and went there to spend the night. She called Camp Jackson the next day and was told that Colonel Burleson was staying at the Jefferson Hotel in Columbia. She then proceeded to register at the Jefferson at 5:30 p.m. under a fictitious name and address but left most of her luggage at the boardinghouse.[286] She saw her ex-husband and his second wife in the hotel lobby that evening; they did not see her, and she did not approach them.[287] May Walker Burleson spent the night and checked out the next morning (Friday, March 8) at 6:40 a.m.[288] Beginning about 11:00 a.m., she sat in the hotel lobby, hoping, she later told the police, to catch Colonel Burleson when he came in from Camp Jackson for lunch. After a while, she ate lunch in the cafeteria, then returned to wait in the lobby. Her ex-husband did not appear, but Isabel Reece Knowlton Burleson, whom Colonel Burleson had married in April 1938, did come to eat lunch in the cafeteria.

The Scene of the Crime

After their marriage in Honolulu in April 1938, Colonel Richard C. Burleson and his second wife, Isabel Knowlton, remained in Hawaii, where he was on duty, until July 1939. Then, after a brief assignment to Fort Lewis in Washington State, the Burlesons came to Columbia, South Carolina, in November 1939 for the colonel to serve as artillery advisor to the Sixth Division at Camp Jackson.[289] They took up residence at the Jefferson Hotel.

The Jefferson had been Columbia's leading hotel since it opened in 1913. Many members of the South Carolina House and Senate stayed there when the legislature was in session, and there had been times when legislative actions had been settled at the hotel, in advance of a formal session at the capitol. Famous guests included Jack Dempsey and Eleanor Roosevelt, and the hotel's ballrooms and dining areas were favorite places for social affairs and informal business interactions in Columbia. A dark spot in the Jefferson's history had occurred in 1925 when a bridegroom took a fatal dose of poison pills in the honeymoon suite, shortly after he and his bride arrived.[290]

The Jefferson was a seven-story building with the front of the hotel and main entrance on Main Street, at the intersection with Laurel Street. Adjacent to this hotel entrance, toward Richland Street, was a street entrance to the hotel cafeteria. The hotel ran along Laurel toward Assembly, and in

This page: The Jefferson Hotel in Columbia, South Carolina. *Russell Maxey Photograph Collection, Richland Library, Columbia, South Carolina.*

the photograph of the exterior, the Laurel Street entrance is visible. In the photograph of the lobby, one is looking from the registration desk toward the Main Street entrance. The Laurel Street entrance that was near the registration desk is not shown. Some stairs near the registration desk led into the cafeteria, and from those stairs, one is looking toward the street entrance to the cafeteria. The mezzanine floor was above the registration desk and could be accessed from stairs (not shown) in the lobby.[291]

The Shooting

Frederica Atlee, assistant to the clerk at the Jefferson Hotel, came to work at noon on Friday, March 8, 1940. About one o'clock that afternoon Atlee spoke with a smartly dressed woman whom she did not know, unaware that the woman was May Walker Burleson. The two women observed a young mother with a baby. In response to Mrs. Burleson's question, Atlee replied that she did not know the young woman with the baby. Mrs. Burleson asked rhetorically, "I wonder if that is her first baby?" before walking away toward the front of the lobby and the mezzanine, where she sat down and began to smoke cigarettes.

After a while, Isabel Reece (Knowlton) Burleson, Colonel Burleson's second wife, entered the lobby from a street entrance to the hotel and came to Frederica Atlee at the hotel desk. "Do I have any mail?" she asked Atlee, who responded, "No, but you have a phone call." Isabel Burleson indicated that she did not have her glasses and asked Atlee to read her the message. After thanking Atlee, Isabel departed to go into the cafeteria.[292]

Moments afterward, May Walker Burleson came to the desk to speak with Atlee, and the following conversation ensued:

> "Is that Mrs. Burleson?" Mrs. Atlee was asked.
> "Yes."
> "In the green coat?" In that Mrs. Richard Burleson was wearing a green coat, Mrs. Atlee responded "Yes."
> May Walker Burleson then told Mrs. Atlee: "I used to know her several years ago," and walked into the cafeteria.[293]

Mrs. Atlee soon heard something that "sounded like a fire cracker." An eyewitness to what happened inside the cafeteria, Jefferson hotel clerk Frank

Andrews, described the shooting later when questioned at the coroner's inquest into the death of Mrs. Richard C. Burleson.[294]

Q   Mr. Andrews, describe to us the part of the cafeteria in which you were sitting.

A   At the first table on the right as you go in from the lobby of the hotel.

Q   Then, sir, as you go in the cafeteria, you turned to the right, and sat at the first table?

A   Yes, sir.

Q   Had your lunch been served?

A   I had just sat down.

Q   While you were seated there, did some [one] come in that you knew, and occupy a table ahead of you?

A   When I sat down, in front of me directly, possibly four feet, Mrs. Burleson was sitting down eating, with her back toward me.

Q   Did you know Mrs. Richard C. Burleson well enough to recognize her sitting down there?

A   Yes, sir.

Q   And she was sitting at the table just ahead of you?

A   Yes, sir.

Q   Go ahead, and tell us what actually happened.

Jefferson Hotel Cafeteria in Columbia, South Carolina. *Russell Maxey Photograph Collection, Richland Library, Columbia, South Carolina.*

A   Well, she was sitting there eating, and I had just sat down to eat, and I noticed a woman, very neatly dressed, and, I imagine, about six feet, one inch tall, come in,

Q   Describe how she was dressed.

A   She was dressed in black, with a little black hat, and she wore a corsage—a bunch of violets—in front of her, and she carried—what attracted my attention to her was her height, and in front of her she carried a black bag.

Q   Go ahead, Frank.

A   This lady dressed in black came in past me, and went up to where the second Mrs. Burleson was sitting, and as she did, she laid her hand on the back of this chair, leaned over, and at the same time shoved her bag right in the back, of Mrs. Burleson, I would say, halfway between her waistline and her neck—I'll show you—about right here [indicating]. Mrs. Burleson was eating. And she glanced up like this [indicating]—naturally, somebody punched her in the back—and she screamed, and at that moment, I saw as well as heard the report of a pistol. Then, after the first shot she came to the side of the table; looked at her; nodded her head; and, cocked the gun, and shot again, and meant to shoot her here [indicating], but I think that the bullet went through her arm and into the wall. At that time I tried to get to where the gun was, but some gentleman in front of me approached her from the back, and grabbed her. When I saw this other party this gentleman—I think, it was Professor McCall—after he had wrested this gun away from her, I went to where Mrs. Burleson was still sitting in her chair slumped over like this [indicating], and finally helped her down on the floor, and when I laid her down, after she was down on the floor, I went to this gentleman—and I told him—Professor McCall who had the other Mrs. Burleson—I told him, "I am a clerk in the hotel, and if you don't mind, I will take care of the lady." I went up to this Mrs. Maizie [sic] Burleson, and told her who I was, and asked her if she would escort me back to the manager's office; that I would like to talk with her; and, she readily and at once went off with me. We went through the lobby of the hotel back to the office where Mr. Crout, the assistant manager at the time was sitting, and I said, "Mr. Crout, here is the lady that did the shooting," and he looked up very much surprised. The only thing she said when we got back to the office was she said she was tired, and could she sit down. I told her, "Yes, Ma'am," and pulled up a chair and she sat down in it, and I immediately left the office, and went back to the cafeteria where Mrs. Burleson was, and she was still living when I got back—probably that was a period of not over two minutes—and I was kneeling over feeling her pulse, and they were beating, but you could just feel them, and Dr. Bauer happened to come in the cafeteria, and I called to him and said, "Doctor, here is a lady that has been shot. I believe, she is dying." I said, "Will you come over here?," and he walked over and knelt down by her and felt her pulse, and he looked up at me and said, "She is dead," and just as he pronounced her dead, the ambulance drove up, and Mr. Dunbar came up, and I said, "Mr. Dunbar, this lady is dead." He said, "Let's carry her out to the Columbia Hospital for examination." So, I immediately went back to the Manager's office, where I talked to Mr. Crout, and Mr. Crout advised me then to go to the hospital to meet Colonel Burleson who had been notified at Camp Jackson to meet me at the Columbia Hospital. So I immediately got in the car—in the police car with Sargeant, I believe his name is Sargeant Gnatt. In the meantime, I asked Detective Wescott, who arrived on the scene, could he carry me, and he said he would get me a way so I went with Sargeant Gnatt.

Q   Do you remember Officer Broom coming into the main office of the hotel while Mrs. May Walker Burleson was being detained in the office.

A   No, sir.

Q   You had left before that?

A   Yes, sir.

Q   After you went back into the cafeteria, did you find where the second bullet struck?

A   No, sir.

Q   You never looked around to see if you could find it?

A   No, sir.

Q   When Mrs. May Walker Burleson passed you going toward Mrs. Richard C. Burleson, did or not you see the bag and gun?

A   I saw the bag, and I saw the gun before it was fired.

Q   Would you be able to identify it?

A   I can.

Q   Well, sir. Is that the bag?

A   This is the bag.

Q   All right, sir. How much of the gun did you see before it was fired?

A   I saw this much [indicating] of the gun; about two inches of the barrel.

Q   Sticking through the bag or out in her hand loose?

A   Punched through the bag.

Q   Punched through the bag?

A   *That's the right.*

Q   *And there is a hole in the bag, isn't there?*

A   *That's right.*

Q   *Now, sir, I believe you say that when she came up behind her, she put the gun to her back, and she put one hand on the chair, is that correct?*

A   *Yes, sir.*

Q   *Looked around in her face, and as she screamed, she fired a shot in her back?*

A   *Mrs. Burleson looked around, and recognized her, and screamed, and as she screamed, she pulled the trigger.*

Q   *Was Mrs. Richard C. Burleson dressed in a green dress?*

A   *Yes, sir.*

Q   *Would you be able to identify the dress?*

A   *Yes, sir.*

Q   *Does that* [indicating] *look like it, sir?*

A   *Yes, sir.*

Q   *That's the dress?*

A   *Yes, sir.*

Q   *Tell us where a pistol bullet is in that dress.*

A   *In the back, right here* [indicating].

Q   *Just where the doctor described the bullet as being fired?*

A   *That, right; she shook her head like this* [indicating]

Q   *She nodded her head before she fired the second shot?*

A   *That's right.*

Q   *Did or not the lady who fired the shots, at the time she nodded, immediately before, or just afterwards, say a word or make any expression?*

A   *If she did, I couldn't hear it, sir.*

Q   *You didn't hear it?*

A   *No, sir.*

Q   *After she fired the second shot, when Professor McCaw or McCall took charge of her and the pistol, and you stepped up to her and requested that she go with you to the manager's office, did she make any statement then?*

A   *No, sir.*

Q   *She didn't say a word?*

A   *Not a thing.*

Q   *Did she appear excited and nervous at all?*

A   *No, sir; she was just as calm as she could be.*

Q   *She was just as calm as she could be?*

A   That's right.

Q   Well, when you went on down to the desk or to the office of the main building in the Jefferson Hotel, and made your statements, which you have told us about, to someone else with regard to the shooting and the death of this lady, did this lady who fired the shots say anything then?

A   When we got to the manager's office, the only thing she said was that she was tired, and could she have a chair; that she would like to sit down.

Q   And that's all she said there?

A   Those are the only words she said.

Q   Did she still appear calm and cool?

A   She certainly did. I didn't stay in the office thirty seconds.

Q   Did or not, on reflection, she ask for a cigarette or something?

Mr. Andrews did recall that Mrs. (May Walker) Burleson asked him for a cigarette when the two of them reached the hotel manager's office, and he replied that he was sorry, but he did not smoke. This exchange and the one over her desire to sit down comprised their only conversation in the office.

University of South Carolina professor William McCall was in the cafeteria and heard, but did not see, the shooting. He did not identify the first noise as pistol fire, but after the second explosion, he saw a tall woman holding a bag with a pistol barrel protruding who was standing beside a seated woman. She seemed to be cocking the gun to fire again. He grabbed her from behind and wrested the pistol away, which she did not relinquish willingly. She moved away after he gained control of the weapon—but then asked that he return it. He refused, and then Andrews came to escort her from the cafeteria.

Three other people were in the cafeteria at the time: J.I. Lenoir of Rembert and A.H. Sanders of Hagood, who were having lunch together, and Mrs. E.C. Barker, the cafeteria cashier. Mrs. Barker witnessed the incident from the beginning. The two gentlemen heard the first shot, and Mr. Lenoir saw the second shot fired.

Later testimony by Dr. Henry F. Hall, who performed the autopsy, revealed that the first pistol bullet "entered Mrs. Isabel Reece Burleson's back and lodged just beneath the anterior skin, severing the life artery of the chest, causing a massive hemorrhage and death." The other bullet, Dr. Hall reported, merely grazed the woman's arm.[295]

THE ARREST

At 2:25 p.m., police headquarters in Columbia was notified by telephone of the incident. The first law enforcement officer at the crime scene was Patrolman J.P. Broome, who had thirty-seven years of service on the police force and was on duty in front of city hall just across the street from the hotel. He found the victim lying on the floor, saw no weapons near her and proceeded to the hotel manager's office, where he advised May Burleson that she was under arrest. He remained there for only a few minutes until releasing her into the custody of Detective C.K. Wescott, who had been dispatched to the hotel with his partner Detective L.C. Williams. Detective Wescott secured the black bag and pistol used by May Burleson from a member of the hotel staff. The law officers and May Burleson then departed the hotel to get into a police car. With Williams in the backseat with the suspect and Wescott driving, the car sped off to police headquarters. Twice, when he took her into his custody and when they arrived at headquarters, Wescott asked the woman to give her name. She did not answer, saying only, "I don't care to make a statement until I see my lawyer." The three were joined at police headquarters by Chief of Police Rawlinson, who led the questioning of the alleged killer of Mrs. Richard C. Burleson.

May Walker Burleson After Her Arrest for Murder in Columbia, SC (*San Antonio Light*, March 10, 1940, p. 7)

May Walker Burleson after her arrest for murder in Columbia, South Carolina. San Antonio Light, *March 10, 1940.*

FUNERAL SERVICES

On the afternoon of March 8, the body of Mrs. Richard C. Burleson, who had been pronounced dead at the Jefferson only minutes after being shot, was taken to Columbia Hospital. The fatal bullet was removed during examination of the body, and Colonel Burleson made arrangements for a brief funeral at Dunbar's Funeral Home the next afternoon. *The State* described the service on Sunday, March 10, in an article that focused on May Walker Burleson's account of her actions and thoughts en route to and in Columbia in the forty-eight hours just before the shooting.

The account noted that Colonel Burleson had remained in seclusion since the tragedy and then continued:

> *His face drawn with grief, the colonel sat with members of the family while services were conducted by Lieut. Col. James L. McBride, Chaplain of the Sixth Division.*
>
> *Banks of flowers lined the wall behind the casket. Attending the services were a number of army officers and a number of Columbians. The Burlesons have been very popular in Columbia society and have made many friends since the Sixth division came here last fall.*
>
> *The second Mrs. Burleson, the former Miss Isabel Reece, was a member of a prominent Boston family. Prior to her marriage to Colonel Burleson, she was the widow of Frank W. Knowlton, a Boston attorney.*
>
> *Besides three sons, Frank W. Knowlton of Boston, Robert A. Knowlton, a Washington newspaperman, and Cadet William A. Knowlton of the United States Military Academy, Mrs. Burleson is survived by a brother, Albert Reece of Boston, and a sister, Mrs. Horatio Bigelow of Boston and Virginia.*[296]

Colonel and Mrs. Burleson had spent Christmas at West Point with Isabel's son Cadet William Knowlton and then visited in Washington with her son Robert and his wife. The colonel returned after New Year's Day to duty, but Mrs. Burleson had remained with her son and daughter-in-law until January 19.[297]

Following the rites at Dunbar's, Colonel Burleson accompanied his wife's body to Weston, Massachusetts, for another service, held at 2:30 p.m. on Monday, March 11, at the First Parish Unitarian Church. Mrs. Burleson was buried in Lynwood Cemetery beside her first husband, a Boston attorney who had died in 1932. The lead pallbearer was Major General James A. Woodruff, commanding officer of the First Corps area.[298]

THE EARLY QUESTIONING

Day One: Friday, March 8[299]

The first questioning session of May Walker Burleson, which began at police headquarters soon after her arrest on March 8, yielded nothing of value. It was already clear that the basic facts of the incident—what happened and who did it—could be documented by several eyewitnesses. What was missing was the reason why the shooting had occurred, namely what had motivated the shooter and what were her thoughts as she proceeded, as well as the details of her planning. Direct answers to questions about these matters could be given only by the perpetrator, but "I do not remember" responses or equivalent answers were all that the chief of police and his detectives were able to extract on the afternoon of March 8.

For example, Chief Rawlinson used telephone calls to Galveston and other places during the afternoon and evening to construct an overview of May Burleson's trip to Columbia and what she had done after her arrival, but when asked questions about her activities before she entered the cafeteria, May replied, "I cannot tell you where I was."

She was willing to talk about other matters, including her home in Galveston, and thanked Chief Rawlinson for the considerate way in which she was treated. She was polite to all questioners but firmly continued to decline to answer their queries.

Mrs. Burleson declined to see Claud N. Sapp, the Columbia attorney that the mayor of Galveston had arranged to represent her, saying, "I dislike lawyers and army men." She then explained, with an obvious reference to her perception of what occurred during the divorce proceedings, "Lawyers were so mean to me in the past." She also added that she liked "police and detectives."

Finally, at a little past 8:00 p.m., Chief Rawlinson terminated the questioning, and Mrs. Burleson, accompanied by a nurse, was escorted to her room in the jail by Marian P. Kramer, the jail matron. She declined a sedative, remarking, "I shall sleep well tonight."

The State article about the interrogation session began what became a tradition of reporting on Mrs. Burleson's appearance, a topic that seemed to fascinate the public:

> *The alleged slayer, blue-eyed and portly, but neat-figured, was clad in an expensive wool crepe dress. A black sailor hat, a beautiful black coat, black*

Left: Gold locket kept by Mrs. Burleson until her death. Inside were head shots taken at the time of her marriage to Richard Burleson, captain, U.S. Army. *Walker Family Collection.*

Below: Inside the gold locket: Captain and Mrs. Richard Coke Burleson at the time of their marriage. *Walker Family Collection.*

silk hose, and neat pumps of patent leather and satin completed her outfit. Accessories included a black pocketbook, black earrings, a pearl stickpin holding lifelike imitation violets on her breast, and a golden chain with locket—bearing an old picture of herself and the present Col. Richard C. Burleson, her divorced husband—and on the third finger of the left hand an emerald ring with clustered diamonds. The ring was a gift from her mother, she said.[300]

Day Two: Saturday, March 9[301]

Late in the evening of the next day, Mrs. Burleson began to talk to Chief Rawlinson and other police officers about her actions leading up to the shooting. She claimed that her goal was to reach a "financial settlement" with her former husband and that she had come to Columbia after learning that he was stationed at Camp Jackson. She had posted herself late Friday morning on the mezzanine of the Jefferson Hotel, Mrs. Burleson said, after finding out during a telephone call to Camp Jackson that Colonel Burleson was staying at the Jefferson. She recalled making a decision to leave the hotel when the colonel did not come to lunch. Before she could leave, however, the appearance of her husband's second wife triggered a memory of her mother's death.

She said that the pistol she was carrying had belonged to her father and that she had practiced shooting it at the beach in Galveston. The black silk bag used to conceal the pistol had belonged to her mother.

Mrs. Burleson talked without reservation about her movements prior to the killing of Isabel Burleson, but "as for the shooting, I do not remember—perhaps I shall recall something later."

Other topics covered in the questioning were Mrs. Burleson's mental health and her artistic talent. She confirmed that she had been in mental health institutions three times in recent months, a fact that Colonel Simon B. Buckner, chief of staff of the Sixth Division, had shared with reporters after talking by telephone with people in Galveston.

She downplayed her artwork, saying, "I'm no good at it" and "I'm punk." At the same time, she spoke with enthusiasm about painting.

Day Three: Sunday, March 10[302]

On Sunday afternoon, the first wife of Colonel Richard Burleson finally confessed to shooting her ex-husband's second wife, Isabel Reece Knowlton Burleson. Under questioning, May Walker Burleson reviewed her thoughts and actions prior to entering the cafeteria, including what happened when she saw the colonel's second wife. "When that woman passed me while I was sitting in the lobby of the mezzanine, the vision of my mother came before me and with it the thoughts of my wrecked home and my mind went blank." She then said that she fired two shots into Mrs. Richard Burleson without removing the pistol from the black bag. She was adamant, however, that she was in front of the victim and fired both shots from that direction. This contradicted the statements of eyewitnesses who saw the first shot fired into the second Mrs. Burleson's back. In that the autopsy had revealed that the fatal shot was fired into the back, Coroner Sargeant was not concerned about the discrepancy. He advised newsmen that his investigation, including the questioning of the alleged shooter, was complete.

In talking with reporters, Chief of Police Rawlinson noted that she (May Walker Burleson) had demonstrated with a rubber paper weight how she held the pistol in the black bag. Chief Rawlinson also said that they had carried the first Mrs. Burleson to the apartment that she had rented when first arriving in Columbia and that they also had stopped at the Jefferson Hotel. They had given May Burleson the opportunity to go into the cafeteria to reenact the shooting, but she had responded, "No, no!" "We didn't press the point," the chief said.

After May Burleson told Chief Rawlinson that she had known former South Carolina governor Robert Cooper "very pleasantly," she was driven by the governor's mansion and allowed to view the grounds.[303]

May Burleson met with attorney Claud N. Sapp after her questioning session ended on Sunday. Sapp noted that "she told me that she doesn't have any independent recollection of the shooting" and was not certain if the suggestive nature of the questions the officers asked triggered her confession or if the confession had resulted from her actual memory of doing the shooting. Mrs. Burleson returned to her cell and was attended by the jail matron and a nurse. *The State* reported, "She continued to smoke cigarettes in a fast, nervous manner and dip generously from her box of cough drops." The paper's readership was advised also she was wearing the same black dress that she had worn since her arrest and that her fingernails were mauve-tinted.[304]

May had a visitor on Sunday, a male cousin who was a resident of South Carolina and who at one time had visited her at her home in Texas. The name of the visitor was not released, but Chief Rawlinson indicated that seeing in her present circumstances, a family member who visited her in happier times upset her. Jailer M.P. Kramer advised the police chief that Mrs. Burleson continued to be extremely upset after returning to her quarters in the jail.

TRANSFER TO SANITARIUM

A reporter from *The State* was granted access to a paper found in May Walker Burleson's luggage, and the newspaper published an article titled "Mrs. Burleson Highly Nervous at City Jail," from which the following excerpt was taken:

> *Had the first Mrs. Burleson, an artist, observed the warning in her March horoscope, she would not have been in the jail today.*
>
> *Found among her baggage, it said "Domestic and family matters are stressed. Problems connected with relatives will perhaps make difficulties and misunderstandings until after the eighth as you incline to be somewhat touchy." (It was on the eighth that she shot the second Mrs. Burleson, whom she blamed for "wrecking" her home.)*
>
> *A few sentences farther down, the horoscope warned: "Be extremely cautious about sudden and spectacular ideas and distrust things that arise unexpectedly."*
>
> *(Mrs. Burleson has steadfastly maintained that she went to the hotel only to arrange a financial settlement with her husband, from who [sic] she was divorced two* years ago. It was while sitting in the hotel awaiting him that she saw the second Mrs. Burleson and "saw red.")*[305]

*Actually, it was three years ago; the Burleson divorce was granted in April 1937

The days of March 11 and 12 were not good ones for May Walker Burleson, who was struggling to come to terms with her circumstances.[306]

Although she had confessed to firing the fatal shot, she continued to insist that she had done so while facing her ex-husband's second wife, despite the autopsy finding that the bullet came from behind. She responded to that finding and the eyewitness accounts stridently: "No Walker ever shot a person in the back." Chief Rawlinson, however, indicated that there was no need to question her further. "As far as I am concerned, the case is closed," he said.[307]

On March 11, she received the news from her Columbia counsel, Claud N. Sapp, that her brother had collapsed in Los Angeles and was in "serious condition." Richard had been planning to come to Columbia but now would not be able to do so. Sapp told newsmen that Richard Walker's collapse had been triggered by his sister's plight. May Burleson had become increasingly nervous and upset since Sunday, when Chief Rawlinson had a physician called to examine her (and provide any treatment needed) after she had the visit from a relative who lived in South Carolina. Her personal mail was placed in the care of her attorney because she indicated that she was "too nervous" to read it. The nurse retained to be in attendance for her reported that May had intermittent crying spells.

Finally, at 8:15 p.m. on March 12, Dr. P.E. Payne, city health officer, was called in to examine May Walker Burleson. Dr. Payne's report was unequivocal: "This is to certify that I have examined Mrs. May Walker Burleson and find her suffering from psychosis, depressive type, and she should immediately be confined to an institution for treatment."[308]

By 8:48 p.m., Mrs. Burleson had been transferred to the Waverly Sanitarium, a private facility on Forest Drive in Columbia. Chief Rawlinson, who authorized the transfer, said that she would have a nurse with her as well as a twenty-four-hour police guard. Rawlinson explained his decision to call in Dr. Payne and proceed with the transfer: "She can't sleep, wouldn't eat, and was in a terribly nervous condition. We were afraid she might harm herself." The chief was supported by counsel Claud Sapp, who was present when the decision was made. Sapp noted that "Mrs. Burleson had not slept for two days or nights and was in a delirious state."[309]

Chief of Police Rawlinson denied a request from Mrs. Burleson to have her luggage shipped to the sanitarium, telling her that she could take any clothes desired, but he had to have her bags searched. He asked about "firearms, drugs, etc." that might be in the baggage. "Well, to be fair," she answered, pointing to a black handbag, "I have an automatic pistol in that bag—loaded too."[310]

Police Chief Rawlinson drove Mrs. Burleson to the sanitarium in a scout car; she was in the front seat with him, and Officer P.H. Thornton, who came to serve as the police guard for Mrs. Burleson at the Waverly facility, rode in the back. Her attorney also accompanied her to the sanitarium. Rawlinson made a stop along the way, at which cigarettes were purchased for the prisoner. Although Mrs. Burleson did not talk during the trip, she seemed in good spirits. Before parting from her entourage at the sanitarium, she placed cut flowers in the buttonholes of Chief Rawlinson and her attorney, Claud Sapp. The flowers were from a bouquet that she had received as a gift the day before.

Mrs. Burleson also had received a corsage of violets from a Columbia resident and, according to her attorney, numerous telegrams from well-wishers and friends who expressed sympathy for her plight.

Back at headquarters, Chief Rawlinson asked two detectives to search the black handbag that she had identified and some other pieces of luggage. They did find a .32-caliber Colt revolver, and though the pistol was unloaded, an army cartridge case found in the same bag contained twenty-three cartridges. The pistol was new, but it was not an automatic. A small box—from a Galveston drugstore—that was labeled "poison" was found in a different piece of luggage. It contained a black powder.

Columbia attorneys Claud Sapp and Patrick Cain indicated to reporters that they had not constructed a plan for Mrs. Burleson's defense and would await the arrival of Bleeker Morse, the Galveston attorney who was expected to arrive that day (March 13). Sapp did say that he had heard from Morse and others in Galveston that Mrs. Burleson had undergone treatment for mental problems during the past year.[311]

THE INQUEST

The inquest into the death of Isabel Knowlton Burleson was held on March 14, 1940, in the Richland County courthouse, beginning at 7:00 p.m.[312] Given how her death occurred and the eyewitnesses, the outcome for this required step in the legal process was never in doubt. Nevertheless, the process was thorough. The following persons were called to testify: Dr. Henry F. Hall, Richland County physician, who presented the autopsy results; Frederica Atlee, assistant clerk at the Jefferson Hotel registration desk, who spoke with both Mrs. Richard C. Burleson and May Walker Burleson, separately, just before the incident and who witnessed the first Mrs. Burleson enter the cafeteria shortly after the second Mrs. Burleson had done so; Frank Andrews, Jefferson Hotel registration desk clerk, who was seated at the table in the cafeteria just behind the one at which the second Mrs. Burleson was having lunch, and who witnessed the shooting and its immediate aftermath;[313] William McCall, University of South Carolina professor, who wrested the pistol from the first Mrs. Burleson after she had fired the second shot; J.I. Lenoir of Rembert, who was seated at a table with A.H. Sanders of Hagood in the cafeteria when the shooting began; Columbia police officer James P. Broome, the first law officer to arrive after the shooting and who placed May Walker Burleson under arrest; Detective C.K. Wescott of the Columbia Police Department, who secured the pistol used in the shooting from a member of the hotel staff and who, assisted by Detective L.C. Williams, transported May Walker Burleson from the Jefferson to police headquarters; and Mrs. E.C. Barker, cashier at the Jefferson cafeteria, who witnessed the fatal shot.

Questioning of witnesses commenced at 7:10 p.m. and concluded at 8:00 p.m. The case went to the six-man coroner's jury at 8:10 p.m., and the verdict was returned fourteen minutes later:

> *Coroner's Verdict: That Mrs. Richard C. Burleson came to her death by pistol shot wounds inflicted by the hands of Mrs. May Walker Burleson, and so said the jurors aforesaid, do say that the aforesaid Mrs. May Walker Burleson did kill and slay the said Mrs. Richard C. Burleson, against the peace and dignity of the State at the Jefferson Hotel Cafeteria, Richland County, S.C., on March 8th 1940.*[314]

This verdict meant that May Walker Burleson's case was to be held for general sessions court in Richland County.

Attendance at the inquest was high, and at least half of those who came to observe the proceedings were women. Surprisingly, Bleeker Morse of Galveston, because of whom the inquest date was changed from Tuesday to Thursday, did not arrive in time to attend.

Given the purpose of the inquest—to determine at whose hands Isabel Burleson had died—the testimony heard was restricted to events and actions in the Jefferson Hotel just before, during and just after the shooting. Chief Rawlinson was present but did not testify, and in fact, no testimony that concerned questions asked of May Walker Burleson subsequent to the shooting or any post-shooting investigative results was heard. The defense attorneys present, Claud Sapp and Patrick L. Cain, did not ask any questions of the witnesses.

After the verdict, Coroner Sargeant drew up papers that would serve to commit Mrs. Burleson to confinement in the Richland County jail, where persons charged to appear before the county court were held. Sheriff Heise said, however, that the prisoner would remain under police guard at Waverly Sanitarium until "further arrangements can be made." The nature of these arrangements was clarified the next day.

SOUTH CAROLINA STATE HOSPITAL FOR THE INSANE

At 3:20 p.m. on Friday, March 15, the day after the inquest, a court order was issued by Judge G. Duncan Bellinger of the Fifth Judicial Circuit.[315] Bellinger's order provided for the immediate transfer of May Walker Burleson to the South Carolina State Hospital for the Insane, where she was to remain for a thirty-day period in order that she be examined and observed. Further, the medical staff at the State Hospital for the Insane was to report any findings to the court at the end of the thirty-day period. The judge's order followed a motion by Claud N. Sapp and the law firm of Pinckney and Cain, which represented May Walker Burleson. Their motion, in turn, was based on an affidavit issued by Dr. D.E. Payne, who had examined Mrs. Burleson and certified that he found her to be of unsound mind. A.F. Spigner, solicitor for the Fifth District, gave his consent to the order. Attorney Bleeker Morse of Galveston, who also represented Mrs. Burleson, arrived late Thursday night (after the inquest) and conferred Friday with Attorneys Sapp and Cain before they made the motion that triggered Judge Bellinger's action. Morse departed for Texas on Saturday.

At 6:20 p.m., in compliance with the court order, Sheriff T. Alex Heise escorted Mrs. Burleson from the Waverly Sanitarium to the admissions office of the State Hospital for the Insane. Sheriff Heise reported that Mrs. Burleson appeared calm and had no comments about the transfer.

Police Chief William Rawlinson told newsmen that the officer on guard duty at Waverly Sanitarium on Friday, P.H. Thornton, had reported that "Mrs. Burleson had been sleeping regularly and had chatted in normal fashion on various subjects."

The grand jury hearing for Mrs. Burleson was set for April 15, immediately after the examination period stipulated by Judge Bellinger expired. In the event that Mrs. Burleson were to be declared insane, however, the expectation was that she would be confined in a state hospital rather than put on trial, but attorneys questioned by *The State* did not know if that confinement would be in South Carolina or in Texas.

JUDGE WILSON'S STATEMENT

William Herbert Wilson, Mrs. Burleson's maternal uncle, an attorney in Houston and former judge, had arrived in Columbia on March 14. For many years before her death, Judge Wilson had served as attorney and financial advisor for Mrs. Burleson's mother, and the relationship between niece and uncle had not always been smooth, especially during the divorce litigation and its immediate aftermath, when Mrs. Burleson had placed financial demands on her mother.

Judge Wilson did not attend the inquest, but he had visited his niece at the state hospital, conferred with her attorneys and indicated a willingness to testify if her case came to trial. On the night of March 18, he issued a statement that appeared in the next day's *State* newspaper. It is not known if he consulted with Mrs. Burleson's Columbia attorneys specifically about a press release before giving the statement, but it seems almost certain that he did so.

Judge Wilson noted that Mrs. Burleson's grandparents on her mother's side had been residents of Newberry County, South Carolina, and that some of her relatives still lived there.

Although his avowed purpose in issuing a release to the press was "to let her South Carolina relatives know that in my opinion the terrible act by Mrs. May Walker Burleson would be shown by the evidence to be the act of a demented person," his more basic purpose must have been to circulate widely the message that his niece was not mentally competent to stand trial. The timing of a statement on his part—just as Mrs. Burleson was being committed to the State Hospital for the Insane to undergo observation and diagnosis—certainly supports that motive. His statement opened as follows: "Mrs. May Walker Burleson for quite a number of years has given at intervals evidence of being of unsound mind and this condition in the last five years has been intensifying and growing rapidly worse and assuming at times a threatening and dangerous aspect." He went on to list several psychiatric facilities at which she had been treated and continued, "She has been at times quiet and without violence, though giving evidence of mental unsoundness, but has been subject to occasional violent spells in which she became dangerous, those spells resulting from her brooding on her marital troubles."[316]

The heart of his statement was the presentation of the affidavit by Dr. Edward Randall Sr., a distinguished physician and president of the hospital board of John Sealy Hospital in Galveston, Texas:

> *I have known Mrs. Burleson intimately since her birth....There is a history of mental trouble in her family. Her Grandfather Walker was a distinguished Texas lawyer and a member of the state supreme court. He lost his mind and died in an asylum. Mrs. Burleson has threatened in my*

presence to kill her brother and her brother's wife. They were so alarmed that they left town [Galveston] *for several weeks.*

In the suit for divorce filed by her husband when her lawyers told her that a divorce would be granted upon his plea she filed a cross action and was granted a divorce upon the cross action This preyed upon her mind continuously and became an obsession.

Mrs. Burleson gives way to violent bursts of anger which at times I have considered dangerous. These attacks have been followed by profound depression, which after a time passes off and her mind seems to become normal. I have thought for a long time that she was suffering from manic depressive insanity, characterized by violent obsessions which render her dangerous.

I believe she should be confined in an institution for an indefinite period of time and if she should be released she would be a menace to society. She has been confined three times in a psychopathic hospital here [at Galveston] *and her wild outbursts had to be quieted by submersion in a tub of hot water for four hours at a time.*[317]

Report from State Hospital and Next Legal Steps

On April 15, Dr. C. Fred Williams, superintendent of the South Carolina State Hospital for the Insane, submitted the following report to Judge Bellinger:

In compliance with the order of the Hon. G. Duncan Bellinger, presiding judge, court of general sessions, committing Mrs. May Walker Burleson to the South Carolina State Hospital for 30 days' observation to determine her mental status, you are informed that the medical staff after observation and examination of Mrs. Burleson find her to be not insane. You are respectfully requested to have the sheriff come for her.[318]

At six o'clock the same afternoon, Sheriff Heise dispatched officers to transfer Mrs. Burleson from the hospital to the women's quarters of the Richland County jail. She joined several other women already incarcerated in that section of the jail and was to remain there until her trial was called.

Mrs. Burleson enjoyed the dogwood that was in bloom along the transfer route and appeared to be feeling fine physically but was upset by the transfer, the officers noted. Her request to have the Richland County physician see her was granted.[319]

Receipt of Dr. William's report was followed immediately by action of the Richland County Grand Jury, which returned a true bill, with jurors swearing that

> *MAY WALKER BURLESON the said ISABEL REECE BURLESON did feloniously, willfully and of his* [read "her"] *malice aforethought did kill and murder against the form of the statute, in such case made and provided, and against the peace and dignity of the state.*[320]

Given the inquest findings and the report from the state hospital, the grand jury action on the indictment was essentially a formality. Solicitor Spigner wanted to proceed with a trial immediately during the April term of court, but Mrs. Burleson's attorney succeeded in having the case deferred to the May term. Sheriff Heise had Mrs. Burleson's luggage moved from the state hospital to the county jail. The trial would open in just over a month.

6

THE TRIAL

OVERVIEW

The trial of May Walker Burleson, charged with the murder of Isabel Reece Burleson, opened at the Richland County courthouse in Columbia, South Carolina, at 9:30 a.m. on May 22, 1940, with the Honorable G. Duncan Bellinger of the Fifth Judicial Circuit of South Carolina as the presiding judge. Attorneys for the prosecution were A. Fletcher Spigner, solicitor for the Fifth Judicial Circuit, lead counsel, and Clint T. Graydon, a prominent Columbia lawyer who had been retained by Colonel Richard C. Burleson to assist with the prosecution. Claud N. Sapp of Columbia, U.S. District Attorney, was the lead defense counsel, assisted by Galveston attorney Bleeker L. Morse and H.H. Edens of Columbia. The trial was in session on seven of the nine days from May 22 through May 30, sessions not being held on Sunday the twenty-sixth and Wednesday the twenty-ninth. A total of twenty-five witnesses testified at the trial, fourteen for the prosecution and eleven for the defense.

The trial attracted many spectators, most of whom were women, and Judge Bellinger instructed the bailiffs that they were to see that "order and dignity" were maintained throughout the proceedings. No standing was permitted—attendance was limited to seats available. Cameras brought into the courtroom were to be seized.

The strategies of the two legal teams were simple. The prosecution first offered evidence that the defendant had killed Isabel Reece Burleson. May

Walker Burleson's legal team did not challenge the witnesses presenting that evidence but built the defense case on testimony designed to prove that the defendant was insane. The prosecution then countered with a rebuttal that featured witness testimony designed to negate that of defense witnesses.

PROCEEDINGS DAY-BY-DAY

Day 1: May 22

The first order of business was selection of the jury, which required just over an hour. During the selection process, ten members of the jury pool were dismissed by peremptory challenges by the defense and five by peremptory challenges by the state; six were excused by Judge Bellinger.

Testimony began at 11:00 a.m. Colonel Burleson, wearing civilian clothes, sat behind the prosecution table with Robert Knowlton, a son of the colonel's second wife, the woman for whose murder his first wife was on trial. Mrs. Burleson's appearance and activities were described by a reporter as follows:

> *Mrs. Burleson wore a black ensemble, including a black hat, a black long-sleeved dress, black hose, and black slippers. Her jewelry included silver earrings, two strands of silver beads, a four-strand silver bracelet and also a large ring set with a green stone and diamonds on the middle finger of her left hand.*
>
> *In her hands she held a green Japanese fan and a white handkerchief. During the trial she frequently raised a lorgnette to scrutinize jurors and witnesses. Frequently during the day she looked at Colonel Burleson through the glasses.*
>
> *When she entered the courtroom she was wearing a silver fox fur. After the lunch period, she returned to the air-conditioned courtroom without the fan and was wearing gray gloves.*
>
> *Just as the hearing of testimony began, she opened a prayer book and read from it for a minute, then placed it back on the table.*
>
> *Mrs. Burleson made no show of emotion and only when she was standing in the prisoner's dock while the warrant was being read did she give any outward reaction to the proceedings. While Deputy Clerk of Court Charles Dahtzler pronounced the formal charge, she shook her head negatively each time he read the words, "with malice aforethought."*[321]

The following items of physical evidence were put on the record on the first day of the trial:

- the green dress worn by Mrs. Richard C. Burleson when she was killed while eating in the Jefferson cafeteria
- a telegram from May Walker Burleson to Mrs. Richard C. Burleson, dated December 9, 1939
- the pistol used to kill Mrs. Richard C. Burleson
- the black bag in which the pistol was concealed
- the bullet from the victim's body
- the bullet that grazed the victim's arm and was later found on the floor
- the empty cartridges found in the revolver.

Nine witnesses were called by the state:[322]

- Dr. H.F. Hall, who performed the autopsy on Mrs. Richard C. Burleson
- Mrs. Frederica Atlee, assistant to the clerk at the Jefferson Hotel
- Mr. Frank Andrews, clerk at the Jefferson Hotel
- Professor William McCall, University of South Carolina
- Mr. J.I. Lenoir, a resident of Rembert, South Carolina, who was having lunch in the Jefferson Hotel cafeteria at the time of the shooting
- Officer J.P. Broome, Columbia Police Department
- Detective C.K. Wescott, Columbia Police Department
- Mrs. Farey Belle Shaffer, Western Union Office, Columbia
- Mrs. E.C. Barker, cashier, Jefferson Hotel cafeteria

After the autopsy results were presented, Mrs. Atlee gave her account of May Walker Burleson's movements in the hotel lobby until she entered the cafeteria. Mr. Andrews testified regarding the actual shooting and immediate aftermath, and Professor McCall described taking the pistol away from the defendant. Officer Broome and Detective Wescott testified about the defendant's arrest.[323] The eyewitness accounts of Mr. Andrews and Professor McCall were corroborated and supplemented by Mr. Lenoir and Mrs. Barker, both of whom were in the cafeteria when the shooting occurred.

The accounts of what was observed by those who saw what happened just before, during and immediately after the killing of Isabel Reece Burleson were not challenged by the defense. What Attorney Sapp did challenge were judgments about the defendant's emotional state offered by Mrs. Atlee and Mr. Andrews in response to questions by Solicitor Spigner.

Mrs. Atlee was at the registration desk after the shooting when she observed the defendant being escorted to the hotel manager's office by Frank Andrews and George Crout, assistant hotel manager. "What was her condition?" Solicitor Spigner asked. "She seemed all right to me." Mrs. Atlee answered.

On cross examination, Claud Sapp, defense attorney, asked: "You are no judge of whether or not a person is normal or not normal, are you?" "No." Mrs. Atlee replied.

Similarly, Frank Andrews described May Walker Burleson's manner after the shooting in the hotel manager's office as "calm and not excited." When he took the witness, Sapp made the jury aware that Mr. Andrews was not an expert on whether or not someone had an "uncontrollable impulse."

The defense stayed on this point (distress or emotional dysfunction on the part of the defendant) in cross-examining Detective Wescott. The detective had transported May Walker Burleson from the Jefferson Hotel to police headquarters. When called to the stand by Solicitor Spigner, Wescott testified that he asked the defendant her name three times, but she declined to answer. He also said that she told him that "she did not care to make a statement until she had seen her lawyer." Attorney Sapp seized this last point to open his cross-examination:

> "She refused to see me, didn't she?" Attorney Sapp asked to open the cross examination.
> "Yes."
> "She was highly nervous?"
> "She smoked a lot of cigarettes and drank a lot of water."
> "She said she hated all lawyers and army officers, didn't she?"
> "She didn't like me. She asked me if I thought she was crazy and I told her 'No.'"

Detective Wescott said he had participated in the questioning of Mrs. Burleson at police headquarters.

"Did she not get so violent that the jailer and his wife had to lock her up in the Negro woman's cell?" Sapp asked. Detective Wescott said he had no knowledge of this.

The one piece of evidence that did not focus on the events of the day of the shooting was a telegram dated December 9, 1939, sent by the defendant to "Mrs. Richard C. Burleson, name for purpose of delivery only."

MRS. KNOWLTON, WITH ALL YOU TOOK BECAUSE I WAS TOO SICK TO DEFEND MY HOME AGAINST YOU AND EVEN THO YOU SENT MY MOTHER TO HER GRAVE IN GRIEF YOU COULD NOT TAKE THE MANY YEARS THIS DAY GAVE TO ME. YOU CAN NEVER TAKE THEM. THE WICKED FLOURISH LIKE THE GREEN BAY TREE. MAY GOD HAVE MERCY ON YOUR SOUL.

Mrs. Farey Belle Shaffer of the Western Union Office in Columbia was called to the stand to identify the telegram, which was read to the jury by Mr. Spigner, who put emphasis on the word *soul*. Court recessed after the telegram was read and moved on to the next (and final) witness after the recess.

This telegraphic communication, however, deserved more discussion. December 9, 1939, the date it was sent, would have been the thirty-first wedding anniversary of Richard Coke and May Walker Burleson, had they not been divorced. The penultimate sentence in the telegram reflects Psalm 35:37 in the King James Bible, "I have seen the wicked in great power and spreading himself like a green bay tree." The telegram reflects a deep anguish on the part of the sender, and it is difficult not to interpret this message as a warning of what was to come. The fact that May Walker Burleson knew in December 1939 that the colonel's second wife was staying at the Jefferson Hotel in Columbia also prompts a question about the motive for the itinerary of May Walker Burleson before she arrived in Columbia. Videlicet, did she take the steps to "find out" where Colonel and Isabel Burleson were staying (when she already knew) just to make her action in the cafeteria appear spontaneous?

Day 2: May 23

On Friday, May 23, the spectators in the filled courtroom, most of whom were women, saw Mrs. Burleson appear with a wimple or white nun's cowl on her head. She wore a black dress and a black jacket with white lining and white lapels, and on her left shoulder was a corsage of violets. Black stockings and black slippers completed her outfit. Colonel Burleson wore a gray civilian suit and seated himself behind the prosecution table in order to confer at times with Clint T. Graydon, assistant counsel for the state.

This was the first of three days used by Mrs. Burleson's legal team to present its "temporary insanity" defense. The four witnesses listed here, each one from Texas, were called to testify. Sapp handled direct examination of witnesses, and Graydon did the cross-examinations.[324]

- Judge William Herbert Wilson, a leading attorney in Houston and maternal uncle of Mrs. Burleson, who was seventy-four years old
- Sam D.W. Low, of Houston, forty-two, an attorney who represented Mrs. Burleson in her divorce proceedings
- Mrs. Claudia Dodd, of San Antonio, seventy, official court reporter of a Texas district court, a friend of the defendant
- Mrs. John H. Means, of San Antonio, friend of the defendant and longtime friend of the Walker family

Beyond proving that the defendant was insane at the time she killed Isabel Reece Burleson, the defense hoped to show a causal relationship between the deterioration of her marriage and May Walker Burleson's insanity.

Mrs. Burleson's uncle, Judge Wilson, was the first witness, and he indicated at the start of his testimony that he was the defendant's closest living relative except for her brother, a Los Angeles resident.

"Why is he not here now?" Mr. Sapp asked the witness.
"He is sick. Several years ago he suffered from insanity. He had the delusion that he had two heads and that people were plotting against him. He went to a private hospital and then to Johns Hopkins where his mind was restored."

The defense counsel then turned to Mrs. Burleson, asking about her mental health history, which led to the following exchange with Judge Wilson:

"The first time I saw her [Mrs. Burleson] violent, was in April 1935. She had just returned from Boston, where her husband was in the army. A month and a half later, I saw her in a psychopathic ward in a hospital in Galveston."
"Was she in a troublesome ward?"
"Yes, she was locked in. The room was barred."
"Do you know of any treatments given?"

"Only by hearsay. She was behind bars and she shook them. She had a wild look in her eyes. They let her come into another room so that her brother and I could visit her. She was wearing a single garment. She lay down on a cot, trembled and said nothing for an hour."

"How long was it before you next saw her?"

"It was some time previous to the first trial of her divorce case. In 1936, she came to my residence in Houston and wanted me to take her case. I would not represent her because of the close family connection. You know there's a saying, if a lawyer represents himself, he has a fool for a client."

"What was her attitude when she came to talk about the divorce?"

"She was highly excited but not violent like she was in 1935."

Sapp thus had informed the jury of a mental problem in the defendant's family and shown an early link between Mrs. Burleson's marital problems and her violent behavior. He proceeded to introduce records of the divorce proceedings in Texas that led to a divorce being granted, and the judge excused the jury while the admissibility of that evidence was debated. During the discussion, Sapp made explicit that it was his intent "to prove that Mrs. Burleson had been driven insane by her marital difficulties." In fact, he told the court before the jury returned:

> *The purpose of the defense is to show that acts of Colonel Burleson prior to or in 1935, while he was the husband of the defendant, drove her crazy. And also to show that the deceased, as co-respondent in the divorce case, having taken the love and affection of her husband, caused her to go crazy at intervals....We hope to prove that she* [the defendant] *was obsessed with the idea five years before* [the slaying] *that she* [Mrs. Knowlton] *was taking her husband and breaking up her home whether it was true or not.*[325]

Judge Bellinger denied admission of the court records from the Burleson divorce case. He cited as grounds for his decision the fact that the prosecution would not have the opportunity to cross-examine witnesses who testified at the divorce proceedings. Only the final divorce decree was admitted, and the decree did not mention Isabel Knowlton as a co-respondent. This ruling prevented the defense from bringing before the jury a mound of court papers pertaining to their client's marital difficulties and to instances of her bizarre behavior, but it did not prevent the Burleson lawyers from developing the "insanity defense"—which they proceeded to do.

Judge Wilson, when questioned further by Sapp, consistently emphasized that his niece was normal until the divorce suit brought by her husband in 1935. This is illustrated by the testimony excerpts below.

"While she was growing up," he testified, "she was bold, clear cut, bright, kind, amiable, very attractive, and lovely."

"She always liked to play to the grandstand, so to speak. When the women [suffragettes] marched on the capital while Woodrow Wilson was President, she led the procession on horseback. She liked to display herself."

"Was she an artist?"

"I've never considered her much of an artist."

"Did she lecture on archaeology?"

"Yes, she has."

"Was she a leader in woman suffrage?"

"She cut some figure in San Antonio. She interested herself in woman's suffrage"

"Did you notice anything about Mrs. Burleson's mental condition?"

"I did not notice anything until the latter part of 1935. She would repeat over and over again that her husband was divorcing her in order to marry Mrs. Knowlton."

"Did you see her in Galveston during the last and serious illness of her mother?"

"Yes, in May, 1937, Mrs. Walker had an attack. It was thought certain that she would die, but she survived. In October, Mrs. Walker, my sister, died."

"What about the conduct of Mrs. Burleson?"

"Irrational"

"What did she do?"

"Mrs. Walker had a day nurse and a night nurse. She had a limited income, but she owned property worth $150,000. She was a woman of means. However, Mrs. Burleson dismissed her nurses, saying that she would nurse her mother herself. If she had been rational, she would not have done that."

Graydon first used his cross-examination to highlight an activity pattern on Mrs. Burleson's part, namely spending time away from her husband, that could have been the root cause of her marital problems. Attorney Graydon then asked Judge Wilson about a series of places in which Mrs. Burleson had spent time unaccompanied by her husband:

"Do you recall that she spent some time in Norway with her mother?"
"I think she spent a month or two in Norway."
"Did she spend some time with an artist's colony in Italy?"
"I think that she spent some time in Italy."
"Did she go to Mexico with an archaeology expedition?"
"I was told she did."

Attorney Graydon then challenged the documentation that the defense was offering to support a plea of insanity. He asked the judge first if he considered Mrs. Burleson to be insane.

Yes, I think she is insane now. If she would meet any opposition, she would break loose and become violent and dangerous. I've felt that she has been that way since 1935. From then until this day I think she has been insane, but she was a lovely and attractive woman until then.

After the judge had conceded that Mrs. Burleson had not been confined to either of the Texas hospitals for the insane, Graydon asked him two questions together: (1) if an effort had ever been made by anyone to have Mrs. Burleson incarcerated for insanity and (2) if she had been declared in Texas to be insane. Judge Wilson simply responded, "No."

The next witness, Sam D.W. Low, had begun to represent Mrs. Burleson in the divorce proceedings in the fall of 1936. In the spring of that year, the case first had ended with a divorce being denied to Colonel Burleson, who had brought the suit, but almost immediately, the presiding judge found that the jury had disobeyed the verdict guidelines in his charge and set the decision aside, granting the colonel a new trial. Low testified that Mrs. Burleson came to his office that fall (1936) and "discussed her persecutions in an unintelligible way." He told her that she was in no condition to proceed and secured affidavits to support his request to the judge to have the case continued. Mrs. Burleson was admitted to the hospital at Fort Sam Houston for observation and treatment.[326] The judge granted a continuance.

Attorney Low noted that his client's condition was much improved by the time they were preparing for the April 1937 trial, but in visits to his office, after she had talked "intelligently for half an hour, her voice 'would rise into a crescendo of hysteria,'" and this happened frequently in the weeks just before the trial.

Low testified that his client caused frequent interruptions in the trial by her outbursts of excitement. The trial ended with her being granted a divorce based upon her cross action (that Low had advised her to file), and just after the trial, she seemed "supremely happy" and told her legal team that the case had been handled "wonderfully." Within a few days, however, she refused to speak to him and on one occasion stuck out her tongue at his wife and him when they passed on the street. She told someone (in Low's hearing) that "Sam Low double-crossed me and Colonel Burleson paid him off."

Claudia Dodd was a friend of the Walker family who had known Mrs. Burleson since she "was two hours old." Mrs. Dodd lived in Galveston until 1901 and spoke of young Jennie May Walker: "She was a normal, lovely, and beautiful child. She was very smart, like she is right today."

Later, Mrs. Dodd lived in San Antonio and knew Mrs. Burleson when she lived there also. "She was a very beautiful woman, a little high strung, and seemed to be happy with her husband. I lived in the neighborhood and would see her three or four times a week. I had never seen Colonel Burleson until yesterday."

Times had changed some years later, when they had a close association during the 1935–37 divorce proceedings:

> She and I stayed at the Crockett hotel at San Antonio. She would come to my room and yell and pull her hair and say Mrs. Knowlton had ruined her home. I had to nail down my windows. She threatened once to throw my radio out the window. The hotel complained because of the noise she made.

When asked by Attorney Sapp if Mrs. Burleson ever went to picture shows, Mrs. Dodd replied:

> She took me to see 'Gone with the Wind' in San Antonio. When the picture came to the part where a woman [Scarlett] was trying to take a married man [Melanie's husband, Ashley Wilkes], Mrs. Burleson stood up and yelled, "That's the way they'll do you!"

Mrs. Burleson had visited Mrs. Dodd for the last time in early January 1940, when, the witness said, "She walked the floor for hours at a time."

The final witness of the day was Mrs. John Means, a San Antonio resident who once had lived in Galveston and then lived in the Philippines, Japan, China and places in the United States. She had known the defendant when Mrs. Burleson was a child, and the two had remained connected over the years. A segment of her testimony is provided here: "I knew Mrs. Burleson when she was a little girl," she testified, "and again in 1920 to 1922. She and her husband seemed very happy. She was normal. Her mother had a refined, lovely home and all that went with refinement."

The witness confirmed that Mrs. Burleson told her she found some letters in Colonel Burleson's office in Paris and was disturbed because he wanted her to divorce him. "When she came back from Boston, she said Colonel Burleson wanted to marry Mrs. Knowlton."

She also said that Mrs. Burleson showed a reversal of personality after her marital troubles began and once expressed an antipathy for baths because they had given her so many at the hospitals. After Mrs. Burleson secured her divorce, Mrs. Means said, she asked her if she was glad.

"No," Mrs. Means quoted Mrs. Burleson as saying. "He is my husband. He will always be my husband. There'll never be another Mrs. Burleson."

"'I'm going to Italy,' Mrs. Burleson told me," the witness said. "Mussolini will give me a job. Or I'm going to Mrs. Daisy Harriman (ambassador to Norway). She's my friend and will give me a job as secretary or something."[327]

When she was quoted about there never being another Mrs. Burleson, the defendant "wrung her hands nervously" according to a *State* reporter who covered the trial.[328]

The first two days of the trial thus involved mostly lay witnesses—first, on Day 1, eyewitnesses at the scene of the shooting, followed on Day 2 by friends who had seen Mrs. Burleson before and after her divorce.

After the first day of the trial, when the state presented compelling, irrefutable evidence and testimony that May Walker Burleson had killed Isabel Reece Burleson, the defendant's legal team had begun building its insanity defense. Testimony by friends of the first Mrs. Burleson on the second day of the trial described behavior that the defense argued was clear evidence of insanity. The next two days of the trial featured defense witnesses who were healthcare professionals—a nurse, two psychiatrists and a physician who served as city health officer for Columbia. These witnesses all agreed that Mrs. Burleson was insane.

Day 3: May 24

The defendant was again dressed in black and wore a corsage of violets; many of the women spectators spent much of their time observing her, and when the trial adjourned, several women rushed to be by the exit through which she would depart.[329]

Witnesses for the defense are listed here:[330]

- Mrs. John Means (brief cross-examination only—continued from Thursday)
- Mrs. J.A. French, a nurse who had accompanied Mrs. Burleson from Galveston to Baltimore in November 1938
- Dr. Esther L. Richards, associate professor of psychiatry at Johns Hopkins Medical School, who had charge of outpatients at Henry Phipps Psychiatric Clinic at Johns Hopkins Hospital
- Dr. William W. Elgin, psychiatrist on staff of Sheppard and Enoch Pratt Hospital, Towson, Maryland
- Louis Youngren, manager of Cavalier Hotel in Galveston
- W.H. Eldrige, second cousin to Mrs. Burleson
- Mrs. W.H. Eldrige, second cousin by marriage to Mrs. Burleson

By late October 1938, it was clear to her brother and others close to Mrs. Burleson that she needed, at minimum, a psychiatric examination and possibly hospitalization for treatment. She was persuaded to seek help at Johns Hopkins, and a nurse, Mrs. J.A. French, was retained to accompany her on the trip to Maryland. After the cross-examination of Mrs. Means was completed, Nurse French was the first witness called by the defense. Her testimony provided insight into Mrs. Burleson's state of mind as well as an account of the train trip:

> *"I took her to Baltimore at the suggestion of her brother."*
> *"What did you do with her at Baltimore?"*
> *"First I took her to Johns Hopkins Hospital."*
> *"Whom did you see there?"*
> *"I met Dr. Richards."* [Dr. Esther L. Richards, psychiatrist, who was to take the stand later]
> *"What did you do with Mrs. Burleson?"*
> *"We had a consultation, and I took her to Sheppard and Enoch Pratt hospital at Townsend, Md."*
> *"Do they treat anybody there but the mentally affected?"*
> *"Not that I know of."*
> *"What happened on the way there* [to Baltimore]*?"*
> *"She was in favor of going to Baltimore, but did not want to go to the psychopathic ward in Texas. She wanted to go as she felt that she was going crazy, but she changed her mind on the way to Baltimore. She would not*

look out of the window. We traveled in a compartment. She jumped out of bed and ran into the car. I brought her back. She told me she did not know where she was going, that she was going to jump off the train. She smoked incessantly."

"Whom did you see at Sheppard and Pratt?"

"Doctor Elgin." [Dr. William H. Elgin, psychiatrist, who was to testify later]

"Did you talk with him?"

"He handled her case."

"How did Mrs. Burleson appear on the trip to Baltimore?"

"She was disheveled. She would eat with her hands. I ordered meals exactly like hers on the trip, but she would reach over and take food out of my plate. She had to be forced to bathe."

"What did she talk about?"

"She talked about Mrs. Knowlton. She said that she had once been prominent in Washington society, but had lost that prominence, and had lost her home and had nobody to turn to."

"Did you see her when she returned to Texas?"

"Yes, I saw her in the psychopathic ward of the John Sealy Hospital. She was admitted to the psychopathic ward there when she returned from Maryland."

"What was your conclusion as to her sanity?"

"From my experience I feel that Mrs. Burleson is normally unbalanced and psychopathic."

Solicitor Spigner handled the cross-examination. "She was raving when she returned from Honolulu where her husband was?" he asked:

"Yes."

"Was it on account of the divorce and her losing prominence?"

"Yes. She said that she loved her husband."

"Did she say she'd gone to Honolulu to kill Colonel Burleson?"

"No."

"The second Mrs. Burleson?"

"No."

"You failed to get her into a crazy ward [in Texas], *didn't you?"*

"Yes."

"Did she have suicidal tendencies?"

"Yes."

"But so far as you know, she has never harmed a hair on her head, has she?"
"No."

Sapp took the witness and asked, "Did Mrs. Burleson tell you why she did not want to go to the psychopathic ward at John Sealy hospital?" "She said that she had been there and did not want to go back. She wanted to go to Baltimore. When she got there, she wanted to go back to Texas."

The next witness, Dr. Esther L. Richards, was an associate professor of psychiatry at Johns Hopkins Medical School. She was in charge of outpatients at Henry Phipps Psychiatric Clinic, a unit of Johns Hopkins Hospital and was psychiatrist in charge of the psychopathic department of Baltimore City Hospital. She had first seen Mrs. Burleson in June 1931 when Mrs. Burleson brought her brother, Richard, to the Phipps Clinic for a psychiatric evaluation.[331] Dr. Richards testified that she did not see Mrs. Burleson again until Nurse French brought her to Dr. Richard's office on November 2, 1938, to seek an opinion with regard to Mrs. Burleson's mental condition, in accord with a request by telegram from her brother. When she was called to the stand, Dr. Richards described her interview with May Walker Burleson:

"What was her conduct at the examination?" Mr. Sapp asked.

"She was highly excited, her hair was disheveled her clothes spotty. She talked in quick, jerky sentences. She could not sit still long at a time, paced the floor and moaned, 'O, if I hadn't gone out west.' Then she threw herself on a cot."

"Her eyes would flash with anger when she told me of her fears and suspicions of the way people treated her. The most interesting part of the conversation was the general direction of the patient's thought.

She expressed supreme suspiciousness of Colonel Burleson, the late Mrs. Burleson [who was slain by the defendant], *her brother, her uncle, her lawyers, and her nurses. She seemed to feel that something had been put over on her in every possible way. She said her divorce had been granted because she had been tricked by lawyers and that her family was trying to get the property that her mother left. However, her memory and her ability to make simple intellectual calculations were excellent and showed no impairment whatsoever."*

The witness said she advised Mrs. Burleson on her condition and that Mrs. Burleson wanted to enter Phipps. As there were no vacancies there, she went to the Pratt hospital at Towson.

Doctor Richards offered the certificate of commitment [dated November 2, 1938] *in evidence and read it. In it she pointed out that Mrs. Burleson kept saying "If I only hadn't gone west. Why did I do it?"*

"She has threatened to kill herself and her former husband," Doctor Richards read from the paper. "Following separation from her husband and the final divorce in 1937, there have been many lawsuits—the patient suing or threatening to sue anyone who crossed her. She has had several breaks requiring rest cure hospitalizations. Her behavior has been conspicuous for its lack of self-control, indecisiveness and grossly poor judgment."

One month after May's admission to Pratt Hospital, Dr. Richards visited Mrs. Burleson there, such visit being made in response to a request for a report on Mrs. Burleson's condition by her brother, Richard Walker. When Attorney Sapp asked her the results of her examination, Dr. Richards read from a letter that she had written to Richard Walker following her visit with his sister.

She [Mrs. Burleson] *states that you and her "little lawyer" put her up to going to Honolulu with a gun to shoot her ex-husband and his wife. You and the "little lawyer" agreed that you would come on and get her out on a plea of insanity. She thinks that this plot was perpetuated by you to prevent her from living in the family home, which you coveted. Now that you are in possession of her finances you are in a terrible state of mental and physical health and really should be in an institution yourself....She feels she is being put away under control of her brother....I do not know whether this is part of her psychotic process or whether it has been a lifelong tendency to make* [up] *a good story and finally believe it.*

"What further connection with Mrs. Burleson did you have?" Mr. Sapp asked.

"March 3, 1939, I received a letter from Mrs. Burleson mailed from Galveston. She wrote: 'From advices I received from Washington, I am led to believe that you concerned yourself in my affairs there. I want you to let me know if you did.'"

Doctor Richards also read her reply:

"I've never had communications with anybody in Washington regarding you or your affairs."

Mrs. Burleson's letter was written in large handwriting on mourning stationery. It was introduced as evidence.

"From your observation and knowledge, what is your professional opinion as to Mrs. Burleson's mental condition?" Mr. Sapp asked.

"Her gradual and progressive change in personality, change in her personal behavior, increasing suspiciousness, persecution trends of something being done to her by people she formerly trusted and violence of emotional outbursts together with suicidal and homicidal threats made me feel her condition was one of paranoia. I thought that she was psychopathic and insane."

"Was she capable of knowing right from wrong?"

"She was incapable when I examined her."

"What kind of insanity is paranoia?"

"Paranoia is a form of mental disorder that is slow and insidious at the outset. The patient has a change in personality, has a feeling that people are against him and are trying to harm him. He is wholly unable to rectify any misinterpretation of illusions and suspicions. His emotions rise to meet his persecutory and grievance thoughts. He is associated as a homicidal risk."

In Attorney Graydon's cross-examination, he raised the issue of whether or not the mental condition of the defendant qualified her as "insane" under South Carolina law. The assistant counsel for the prosecution began by pointing out that South Carolina law defines insanity as "a person not knowing whether his act is wrong, legally or morally, or that it is criminal or punishable." He then asked Dr. Richards a series of questions.

"Do you consider that Mrs. Burleson would know what she is doing?"

"No."

"You knew that she wanted to kill the second Mrs. Burleson?"

"I considered her homicidal."

"You believe she went to kill her?"

"Yes."

Referring to Mrs. Burleson's trip "out West," Mr. Graydon asked, "Did she not say she became afraid out in Honolulu?"

"She said everything went black. She remembered little."

"Did she say she went into a night club, where Colonel and Mrs. Burleson were, stepped in the door and lost her nerve?"

"No."

The next witness was Dr. William Elgin, a psychiatrist on the staff of Sheppard and Enoch Pratt Hospital in Towson, Maryland, a facility at which nervous and mental disorders were treated. Dr. Elgin was in charge of Mrs. Burleson's treatment at Pratt and testified as follows regarding her initial interview.

> *"Mrs. Burleson came into my office reluctantly." Doctor Elgin said. "She was indecisive, loud, shouting at her brother, and criticizing him. She was restless and agitated, got up and down, paced the floor, talked constantly and went elaborately into irrelevant and useless details."*
>
> *"What did she say?"*
>
> *"She criticized nobody at the time except her brother and those admitting her."*

> *Doctor Elgin introduced a certificate setting forth that upon Mrs. Burleson's admittance to the hospital, she was "extremely depressed, apprehensive, and hopeless and felt that there was nothing in the future for her."*
>
> *Doctor Elgin said further on the stand that Mrs. Burleson related that she was unsuccessful in an attempt to arrange a reconciliation with Colonel Burleson, and that she had alternately asserted and denied that she "had gone to Honolulu" after they (Colonel Burleson and the second Mrs. Burleson) were there to "kill them."[332] She was so upset when she reached there, however, he continued to quote her, that she failed to achieve that object.*
>
> *The defendant was "fundamentally a paranoiac type" when she entered Pratt Hospital and that when she left (on January 4, 1939) she did so "definitely against our advice," Dr. Elgin testified. He also noted that a member of his staff had prepared a detailed report that included the conclusion that Mrs. Burleson was insane. This report began with the period when the defendant was a child and had described her behavior from that time forward. One excerpt stated: "Being the only daughter, she was catered to and spoiled....Throughout most of her life she appeared to be an impulsive spoiled child."*

Clint Graydon, assistant counsel for the prosecution, launched an aggressive cross-examination that picked up with the report:

> *"She was very forward, very dramatic—always in the limelight?" Graydon asked on cross examination.*
>
> *"I can't vouch for that, but that's in the record," Elgin answered.*

"She exhibited all the characteristics of a spoiled child; that's right, isn't it?
"Yes, sir."
"She was an actress in her dealings with people, wasn't she?" Mr. Graydon asked.
"That's right."

At this point, Mrs. Burleson made an outcry; "I can't stand his voice—he makes me nervous!" This did not interrupt the proceedings, however, because neither the witness nor the attorney doing the questioning took notice.

Events preceding the slaying of Colonel Burleson's second wife, the former Mrs. Isabel Reece Knowlton of Boston, Massachusetts, were described by Graydon, who then asked Dr. Elgin:

"Do you think that she knew what she was doing?"
"I don't think so," Dr. Elgin replied.
"And yet she followed the object of her scorn as straight as the dog follows the bird or the hound follows the fox," Mr. Graydon said.

A letter and postcard written by Mrs. Burleson to Elgin after she left that hospital (on January 4, 1939) were brought into the testimony and read in court. The letter (March 14, 1939) written from Galveston said she (Mrs. Burleson) had been informed by Dr. Harris that she had an "adult maladjustment" but that "no mental disorder had ever existed."

The postcard written (April 18, 1939) from San Juan, Puerto Rico, merely told that she was visiting there.

Three lay witnesses remained after the two psychiatrists had testified. W.H. Eldrige, a second cousin to the defendant, said he had known Mrs. Burleson for forty years and that the beginning of her mental problems coincided with the start of her marriage difficulties and testified that she was a "very normal person until that time."

Mrs. W.H. Eldrige testified that Mrs. Burleson had been a frequent household guest during the twenty years that they had known each other, but when May had come to visit in January of that year, she (Mrs. Eldrige) had refused to let her spend the night. She explained, "I heard the name Knowlton, Knowlton, Knowlton until I thought I would go crazy myself." When Solicitor Spigner cross-examined her, she told him that she had felt for some time that "May has not been right."

Louis Youngren, manager of the Cavalier Hotel in Galveston, testified that Mrs. Burleson arrived with a Puerto Rican woman companion at the hotel on October 10, 1939, having arranged to stay two weeks. Mrs. Burleson remained until February 6, 1940, however, and she became boisterous and disturbed other guests. Youngren testified that he considered Mrs. Burleson to be insane.

When asked in cross-examination by Spigner if he still would consider Mrs. Burleson insane if physicians declared her sane, he responded that he would.

Day 4: May 25

On Saturday morning, May 25, 1940, May Walker Burleson came to court wearing a flowered black-and-white dress. In addition to the corsage of violets, she had a black cross attached to a chain around her neck.[333]

The only witness heard during the twenty-five-minute court session was Dr. P. Eugene Payne, Columbia health officer, who testified concerning his examination of Mrs. Burleson at the city jail on March 12, four days after the defendant had fatally shot her former husband's second wife.

Dr. Payne said that he found her shaking the bars of her cell and pacing the floor. She wore only one ragged garment, and "her hair was all messed up." He also reported that her answers to his questions during his thirty-minute examination were "rather inconsistent."

Defense attorney Claud Sapp asked Dr. Payne what he concluded in regard to the defendant's sanity. The witness responded that he considered Mrs. Burleson insane. Dr. Payne noted that he had prepared the certificate stipulating that Mrs. Burleson was of "unsound mind" that led to her transfer from the city jail to the Waverly Sanitarium. This certificate also was considered by the court after the inquest in directing that Mrs. Burleson undergo a thirty-day observation at the South Carolina State Hospital before proceeding with a trial.

In his cross-examination, assistant prosecutor Clint Graydon elicited responses from the witness that confirmed that he (Dr. Payne) was a practicing physician and was not specially trained to deal with mental disorders—and that the state hospital did have experts in that area. Graydon also asked, in reference to the night Dr. Payne had examined Mrs. Burleson in her jail cell, "whether or not a person pretending to be insane could not have done the same thing she was doing that night to put on a show?" Dr. Payne responded candidly: "Why, I think so."

After determining that the trial could not be completed that day because the state had several witnesses to call in rebuttal of defense testimony, Judge Bellinger adjourned the trial until ten o'clock Monday morning.

Days 5 and 6: May 27 and 28

For three days, Thursday, May 23–Saturday, May 25, Spigner and Graydon had seen the defense go on offense as a plethora of witnesses took the stand to support a claim that the defendant, May Walker Burleson, was insane. Longtime friends, family members, a hotel manager, one of the lawyers who represented her in divorce court, a nurse, a physician and two prominent psychiatrists had bolstered the insanity defense with testimony. The prosecution had done its best by attempting to raise doubts in cross-examinations about the relevance and significance of that testimony, but on Monday and Tuesday, May 27 and 28, the state mounted a counterattack featuring healthcare professionals who had examined Mrs. Burleson and reported her as being sane. The witnesses involved were psychiatrists and other medical staff members from the South Carolina State Hospital for the Insane, where the defendant had been confined for thirty days for the explicit purpose of determining the state of her mental health.

These witnesses, with their positions at the state hospital, are:[334]

- Mrs. I. Parnell, nurse, receiving ward
- Miss Meta Quattlebaum, student nurse
- Dr. E.L. Horger, chief of medical staff
- Dr. J.E. Freed, medical staff (May 28)
- Dr. Fred Williams, superintendent of the hospital (May 28)
- Key evidence considered: a sixty-page report prepared by hospital staff.

Chronologically, at the trial on May 27, the two members of the nursing staff testified first, and then Dr. Horger took the stand. His testimony was interrupted when Spigner wished to read an excerpt from the hospital report on Mrs. Burleson (presumably from a section of the report that was related to an answer just given by Dr. Horger). Sapp quickly intervened, insisting that the entire report be read as opposed to excerpts that were selected by the prosecution. Judge Bellinger upheld the defense's demand, and the entire sixty-page, single-spaced document was read aloud, with the two attorneys for the state sharing the reading duty. Dr. Horger returned to the witness chair after the report had been read into the record. The hospital report contained transcripts of all staff interviews with Mrs. Burleson and accounts of her actions, behavior and treatments while she was at the state hospital. Also included was biographical information about Mrs. Burleson and her general health records while she was at the hospital.[335] This report stated in conclusion that the hospital staff who examined Mrs. Burleson did not find her to be insane, and some conversations with her were reported that indicated that she had attempted to deceive the medical staff into believing that she was insane.

In addressing the issue of deception, Nurse Parnell testified that "She [Mrs. Burleson] would be reading and when she'd hear the doctors' voices on the ward she'd throw down the magazine and start moaning....She would carry on a normal conversation and would listen to anything I told her to do." This testimony was augmented by a statement in the hospital report that noted that "she [Mrs. Burleson] would change her attitude from a normal one to a spell of crying and nervousness when an examiner would appear....She once asked the nurses if she were 'fooling' the doctors."

When Dr. Horger, who had served on the staff of the state hospital for twenty-five years, first took the stand, he was questioned by Solicitor Spigner as follows:

> *"You observed and studied her case?"*
> *"Yes."*
> *"Did you reach a conclusion?"*
> *"Yes."*
> *"What is your opinion?"*
> *"When she was at the State hospital she was not insane."*
> *"How was her health?"*
> *"She was in excellent physical condition."*

Recalling that reference had been made (in the hospital report) to Mrs. Burleson as "a psychopathic personality," the solicitor asked the meaning of this term.

> *"It is a congenital or inherited—more or less—condition," Doctor Horger said.*
> *"It is not insanity?"*
> *"No."*

During cross-examination by Sapp, Dr. Horger made explicit that the finding of "not insane" by the state hospital staff applied to the period while Mrs. Burleson was under observation there and was not intended as a report on her mental status prior to that time. He also noted that the report was not unanimous. Sapp pressed the point:

> *"You had a disagreement?"*
> *"Yes."*
> *"Some thought that she was sane, some insane?"*
> *"Some thought that she was psychotic; some thought that she was sane."*
> *"The majority opinion governed the report?"*
> *"Correct."*

When Mr. Spigner questioned him, Dr. Horger indicated that unanimous opinions were "very seldom" occurrences among the staff.

Dr. Fred Williams, hospital superintendent, testified briefly the next day, as did Dr. J.E. Freed. Drs. Horger, Freed and Williams all testified that in their opinion, Mrs. Burleson was pretending to be insane or "putting on a show" during her observation period at state hospital. Both Dr. Williams and Dr. Horger explicitly rejected paranoia as the cause of Mrs. Burleson's behavior, in direct conflict with the testimony of the two psychiatrists called as witnesses by the defense. Dr. Williams put it this way:

> *The true paranoiac feels absolutely justified in an act...and would not try to cover up his act. He would brag about it and say that he would do it again. It was the conclusion of the majority of our staff that Mrs. Burleson tried to conceal the facts, and to make us think that she was mentally wrong. It was our conclusion that she was not insane.*
>
> *I believe the patient knew what she was doing at the time. I would have to know the condition of the patient at the time to say whether she knew whether it was right or wrong.*

Her attorney, Claud Sapp, made a decision not to put her on the witness stand, so that there is no trial testimony by the defendant, but Mrs. Burleson's responses during interviews at the state hospital were read into the court record. An excerpt from a session with Dr. Cory Ham that pertains to the actual shooting is provided here:

Q   Did you ever think of killing Colonel Burleson?
A   Oh, no, never. I must have thought if Mrs. Knowlton was gone, I could have my place with my husband.
Q   Did you go to the Jefferson hotel more than once?
A   No, I went to the hotel about 11 a.m., sat in the lobby for a while, ate lunch in the dining room, then went out and sat in the lobby again. While there Mrs. Knowlton entered through the front door, passed near me and entered the passageway from lobby to cafeteria. I followed her into the cafeteria, walked around and in front of her.
Q   Did you say anything to her?
A   No, I shot directly at her heart. I heard a scream. I think it was her.
Q   What did you do then?
A   Well, I don't know. Don't know what I did with the gun. Must have put it in my pocket.
Q   Did anyone take hold of you?
A   I don't know. There was a lot of confusion around me. I do remember someone taking hold of me and putting me in a car, a very nice car. Doctor Ham, I don't see how I could have done this. I am a very nice sort of person, am I not?
Q   Is there anything else you wish to say?
A   I just want to say that I don't see how I could have done what I did if I had been in my right mind. Regardless of what provocation or justification I might have had, I must have been beyond my mental and physical control to have done what I have. I have told the truth. Do you believe I have?

In a different interview, she was asked by another examiner, "Why did you shoot her?" She replied, "Because she had taken my husband and broken up my home." In still another part of the hospital report, Mrs. Burleson was asked if she had "any plans for killing Mrs. Knowlton before you left Galveston?" She answered, "Only that I thought if I could eliminate Mrs. Knowlton as he had eliminated me by divorce, then we could be united."

In line with her examination by Dr. Ham, a section of the hospital report noted that Mrs. Burleson had taken "great pains" to tell the hospital staff about insanity in the family. This information, she clearly thought, would bolster her claim that she had not been in her right mind when she shot Isabel Reece Burleson. In another part of the report, however, she was asked, "Do you wish to be declared sane or insane?" She responded, "I'd rather have my sanity and be burned at sunrise, for I feel I am sane."

Had these responses been given on the witness stand, the jury would have seen both the inconsistencies in her testimony and, in the responses to Dr. Ham, the conflict with other eyewitness accounts and the autopsy. Sapp could not have known how these discrepancies would affect the jury and therefore kept his client off the witness stand.

CLOSING ARGUMENTS

At 11:39 a.m. on May 28, Spigner announced that the state had no more witnesses.[336] Judge Bellinger gave each side two hours for closing arguments, and Clint T. Graydon went first, speaking before the lunch recess. Claud Sapp was the sole closer for the defense, and Fletcher Spigner spoke last.

Assistant prosecutor Graydon paid tribute to the second Mrs. Burleson, the victim of the crime, noting that her son was present at the trial and that "his presence gives the lie to the fact that she was anything but what she should have been." *The State*'s reporter covering the trial noted that Colonel Burleson was "visibly moved" by this reference and "dried tears from his eyes." Graydon also attacked Mrs. Burleson's claim that "her home had been broken up," pointing out that she "had cavorted away from her husband." When he implied that she had abandoned Colonel Burleson at a crucial point in their marriage (in 1935) by departing Boston for Texas, Mrs. Burleson cried out, "Why I was deserted!"

(This outburst was ignored.)

Graydon's primary focus, however, was on premeditation. He called for the death penalty, "if the defendant is not insane" and proceeded to tell why he thought that she was not. What she had done was "made plans to sneak up on an innocent woman" and kill her, and those plans were made a long time before the day of the crime. She went to Honolulu, Graydon said, for the purpose of killing both Mrs. Burleson and Colonel Burleson but "lost her nerve."

> *Insanity has been the only defense offered.... The only difference is that she is more dangerous if she is insane than if she is sane. She is a murderess or a maniac and I believe she is sane.*
>
> *What she told about the Honolulu trip was at the bottom of all this.... She said that she went there to kill them and would plead insanity.*

Having failed in Honolulu, she came from Galveston to Columbia to implement "a scheme that was planned as magnificently as any war." Attorney Graydon concluded his remarks by saying, "If you put the law to her [the defendant], Columbia and South Carolina will be a better place in which to live."

Mr. Sapp, lead attorney for Mrs. Burleson, spoke next. He contended that Mrs. Burleson was insane, that Colonel Burleson's infidelity had driven her insane and driven her from her home with the colonel and, finally, that her conviction would violate an unwritten law in South Carolina that killing was justified when one's home was invaded. The excerpts that follow illustrate how he expressed these themes:

> *"Nothing I say will be to offend the sensibilities of anybody," the attorney continued, expressing sympathy for the woman who was killed and her family.*
>
> *"I contend that infidelity caused the defendant to become crazy, to lose mental and physical control and do the thing she did do.*
>
> *"If these infidelities were not true, Colonel Burleson, who sat here, was the only man who could dispute it. Why did he not take the witness stand and say they were not true?"*

Sapp then placed the blame for the marriage's breakup squarely on Colonel Burleson:

> *"May Walker Burleson was born at Galveston, into one of the finest families in Texas," Mr. Sapp said. "She ranked with anybody in the United States in society. She was as clean, high type, honorable girl as could grace the home of any man."*
>
> *"She married Lieutenant Burleson after his graduation from West Point. As long as she had youth, she was his wife, but when gray streaked her hair, he wanted somebody else who would give him wealth because he had spent all his wife had and there was a mortgage on her land."*
>
> *She was a fine, public-spirited, civic-minded woman, the attorney said, adding that she was chairman of the Democratic club in San Antonio and went to the Democratic national convention. "She was a woman of background, education, and charm, acquired in the courts of Europe and the best society in America."*
>
> *"I charge that Colonel Burleson brought wreck and ruin on himself," Mr. Sapp declared emphatically. "This man let this woman down without*

a dime. Under the laws of Texas, there is no alimony granted in the divorce, but under the laws of decency and honor in South Carolina, a man who lives with a woman doesn't kick her out after 27 years without providing at least the bare necessities of life for her."

In closing, Sapp appealed to the testimony regarding insanity and reaffirmed his belief that the "unwritten law" concerning home invasion in South Carolina applied in this case. After reviewing the testimony and citing his contention that the preponderance of evidence proved that Mrs. Burleson was insane, Sapp claimed that in all his experience he had never seen a sadder case.

"Since I tried my first murder case in 1911," he said in conclusion, "I have never seen a South Carolina jury harm a hair on the head of a man who had killed because his home had been invaded. If there is an unwritten law for men, why not for women? If circumstances had been reversed, the defendant would not have to plead insanity. I want you to find the kind of verdict you would want a jury down in Galveston, Texas to find, if your mother or your wife were on trial and her life and her liberty were at stake."

Solicitor Spigner spoke last, and his message to the jury was that Mrs. Burleson was not an insane person but an assassin.

"If you declare her not guilty," Solicitor Spigner addressed the jury in a solemn tone at the opening of his address, "It won't be six months in Richland County before another man or woman will kill because of a divorce."

"If you turn her out, there are men and women marked, and this jury would shoulder the responsibility.

This woman needs no more favors from you because of her means and influence than anybody would have. It is just another case."

When Solicitor Spigner referred to one Texas witness' testimony that Mrs. Burleson had said she could get away with killing by "pleading insanity," Mrs. Means of San Antonio, who had testified for the defense, arose in the audience and shouted, "She did not say that!"

Solicitor Spigner turned, half smiled and said, "Sister, it is too late now."

Sheriff T. Alex Heise escorted Mrs. Means out of the courtroom on orders of the presiding judge.

"If insanity is an acceptable defense in this case," the Solicitor said, as he continued, "I think we should dig up the bones of some of the people we have electrocuted and apologize to them."

He added that the second Mrs. Burleson was "harmless and defenseless" as she sat at the dining table when she was slain and that the defendant committed the act of an assassin.

THE VERDICT

In his charge to the jurors, Judge Bellinger reminded them that a person on trial was considered innocent until it was proved that he or she was guilty and that the burden of proof of guilt rested on the state. The burden of proof of insanity, however, belonged to the defense. Five possible verdicts were listed by the judge, along with the associated sentences:

Guilty of Murder (penalty: electrocution)

Guilty of Murder, with recommendation to the mercy of the court (penalty: life imprisonment)

Manslaughter (penalty: two to thirty years) with the jury privileged to recommend mercy, which would be considered by the court in sentence

Not Guilty because of insanity at the time the crime was committed (transfer of the prisoner to the State Hospital for the Insane for confinement until release under process of law)

Not Guilty[337]

The case was placed in the hands of the jury at 5:48 p.m. Over 250 spectators were present when the jury returned at 9:15 p.m. The verdict was "guilty of manslaughter with a recommendation of mercy." Mrs. Burleson, dressed in black, with her usual corsage of violets, heard the verdict without a show of emotion. Judge Bellinger delayed passing sentence, pending a decision by defense attorney Claud Sapp to file a motion for a new trial. A significant burden of uncertainty was removed, however, for Sam W. Cannon, state electrician and executioner for South Carolina, whose responsibility it was to throw the switch for all electrocutions at the state penitentiary. He would not have to electrocute his third cousin.[338]

The Sentence

After the verdict on Tuesday night, May 28, Sapp had made a motion for a new trial, but on Thursday morning he withdrew the motion, telling the judge, "The defense desires to withdraw the motion for a new trial and is ready for the defendant to be sentenced." Then Mrs. Burleson stood before the judge, who asked her attorney if he had anything to say. Sapp responded:

"I don't know of anything I can say," replied the defense attorney. "It's a most pitiful case. I have no quarrel with the jury's verdict.…I hope you can see your way clear to give her the minimum sentence…two years. She is 52 years old, and certainly any sentence in the penitentiary six months or longer will be the same to her."[339]

Judge Bellinger commended the defense for the way in which its lawyers had proceeded, but said that "the facts were against you." The judge noted that passing judgment on anyone was "a difficult burden," but indicated that the defendant had taken the life of another human being. "The laws of this state shall be respected by those of the higher walks of life the same as is expected by those of a more humble station." Bellinger called the crime an assassination and remarked that had the jury not recommended mercy he would have imposed the maximum sentence of thirty years.

May Walker Burleson was sentenced to twelve years in the state penitentiary. She spent the next three days in the Richland County jail, where she had been lodged since April 15, and was transferred to the South Carolina State Penitentiary for Women on Monday, June 3, 1940.[340]

INCARCERATION
AND RELATED PROBLEMS

A Rocky Beginning

Mrs. Burleson's arrival at the women's prison of the South Carolina State Penitentiary did not go smoothly. She began a hunger strike when she was returned to the Richland County jail after having been sentenced on Thursday, May 30. An official at the jail quoted her as saying, "I would have taken a just sentence. It was too much."[341]

On the following Monday morning, June 3, Colonel John M. Glenn, superintendent of the state penitentiary; Dr. M. Whitfield Cheatham, penitentiary physician; and three sheriff's deputies came to escort her to an automobile to transfer her to the institution where she was to serve her sentence. In their presence, she abruptly popped in her mouth and swallowed three tablets that she said contained strychnine. She was driven rapidly to Columbia Hospital, where her stomach was pumped, with six men holding her down during the process. No trace of strychnine or of any other poisonous substance was found.

After it was clear that she had not been poisoned, she was taken to the main penitentiary for fingerprinting and photographing, steps that were part of the identification recording process for prisoners. Finally, at 3:00 p.m. she was transferred to the women's prison—a delay of over three hours having been triggered by the pill-swallowing incident.

Dr. Cheatham, who had been in attendance during the whole affair, reported Monday evening that Mrs. Burleson had been placed in the hospital at the women's prison and was being watched over by attendants there. He indicated that she was "nervous but not ill."[342]

According to other witnesses, Mrs. Burleson acted "disagreeably" all Monday afternoon and was indignant that she had received a prison sentence.

When questioned by Dr. Cheatham, Mrs. Burleson said that she had hidden the tablets in three places at the county jail while she was confined there. The remaining pills were located and tested, but no report of their containing strychnine was issued. Mrs. Burleson said that the pills had been in her possession since the war.[343]

By late afternoon of June 3, 1940, May Walker Burleson was officially—and physically—an inmate at the women's prison within the state penitentiary of South Carolina. Her transition to there had been difficult, and she needed to come to terms with the fact that she was going to be in prison for years and to begin the process of integrating herself emotionally into the prison routine that was now her lot. In addition to making that adjustment, she was faced with a major financial issue that had been exacerbated by the trial.

FISCAL DIFFICULTIES

As a result of inheritance, May Burleson owned property worth perhaps $100,000 or more, but she had very little by way of liquid assets. Her problem consisted of several fiscal obligations that needed to be met, to wit: (1) a mortgage of $10,000 on her property held by the Hutchins Sealy Bank in Galveston and a joint note with her brother of $2,500 also held by that bank; (2) a fee of $4,000 due to Claud N. Sapp of Columbia, lead defense counsel at her trial; (3) a fee and reimbursement for expenses due to Bleeker Morse of Galveston, who assisted Mr. Sapp; (4) other trial costs, including expenses to witnesses and fees for the two psychiatrists from Maryland who testified for the defense. Deciding on and executing the actions to be taken would require the advice and help of legal counsel and, given Mrs. Burleson's circumstances, that of a family member or friend.

All these obligations needed to be settled as promptly as possible. The bank was insisting that it be paid forthwith, bills had been received from her lawyers and bills from the two psychiatrists who had testified for the defense at the trial were long overdue. The generic issue was conversion of property to cash. Efforts to sell some of May's property in order to clear these debts began promptly, but her unreasonable actions and unrealistic perceptions, including her refusal to pay her two lawyers, her brother's indecisive behavior and the bank's mounting pressure for closure turned those efforts into a saga that almost wrecked May's estate.

The bank soon began to move forward with foreclosure proceedings that would enable the bank's officers to sell enough of May's property to recover the funds that May owed the bank. Judge Wilson advised Richard Walker that under that process, the bids would be low and that a better procedure would be for a guardian to be appointed for May by the court on the grounds that May was of "unsound mind," the only permissible grounds for a guardian under Texas law. The guardian would have authority to sell property and could do so at fair prices. Sufficient property could be sold to meet all outstanding obligations, any surplus funds would go into May's bank account and the bulk of May's property would remain in her possession.[344] At first, Richard accepted his uncle's advice and promised to endorse a petition to the court by his uncle to have a guardian appointed. Judge Wilson moved forward with alacrity, but Richard changed his mind and declined to authorize the petition.

Two factors motivated Richard's reversal: (1) May's opposition, which was expected, and the chief reason for seeking a guardian, but Richard indicated that he was deterred by May's threat to "do away with herself" should a guardian be appointed; (2) the "unsound mind" grounds would reinforce the negative publicity already experienced by his family because of May's trial and conviction—and the possibility that those grounds could be linked to Richard's earlier mental problems, which would harm his business and be ruinous for his daughter Carol.[345] Judge Wilson was furious and notified Richard in a blistering communication that he would have nothing further to do with May's business affairs.[346]

Richard was able to convince May to let some property be sold, but she continued to block any systematic plan to sell and repay.[347] The bank went ahead with foreclosure proceedings.

The impact of Richard's vacillation and May's obstruction can be seen in the process to which her attorneys had to resort to secure compensation and in the correspondence excerpts concerning the fees submitted by the psychiatrists who testified at her trial.

THE ATTORNEYS

There was widespread wonder among lawyers as well as the general public at the leniency of the sentence received by May Burleson. Judge Herbert Wilson, May's uncle and an outstanding attorney, felt that her attorneys had done a superb job in saving his niece from a much harsher sentence, which easily could have been the death penalty.

In spite of her obvious guilt and escape from the severe sentence generally associated with such a crime, however, May Burleson wanted—and expected—if not acquittal, then at most a minimum prison sentence or a short stay in a hospital to cure her "temporary insanity."

Further, she wanted at least a short-term release from prison to allow her to straighten out her financial and other affairs, without the complication of having to do so within the confines of a state penitentiary. These expectations were not met, and May therefore felt her lawyers had not done the job for which they were retained. Hence, she refused to pay the fees they submitted. She also proceeded to sever her relations first with Mr. Sapp and then with Mr. Morse, to the dismay of Judge Wilson, who felt not only that the attorneys should be paid but also that Mr. Sapp, in particular, would be valuable when it came time to seek parole for May. The attorneys waited while the negotiations went on between the bank and Richard, during which Mrs. Burleson continued to ignore the bills for legal services that they submitted. After two and a half years of fruitless efforts to collect their fees, the lawyers availed themselves of the legal process. Mr. Morse struck first, filing suit in the Tenth District Court in Galveston to have Mrs. Burleson pay him for his services associated with the trial.[348] A jury of twelve men for the case was selected on Friday, January 8, 1943. In reporting on the beginning of the case, the *Galveston Tribune* stated that this was the first instance in "many years" in which an attorney had sued his client for fees.[349] On Tuesday, January 19, the jury found in favor of the plaintiff, and Mr. Morse was awarded the $8,255 fee he had requested.[350] Mrs. Burleson appealed, but the court of civil appeals affirmed the district court decision in May and refused a rehearing requested by Mrs. Burleson's lawyers in June.[351]

The lead counsel for Mrs. Burleson, Claud N. Sapp, filed his suit for $4,000 against his former client in the Richland County Court of Common Pleas on April 12, 1943. The presiding judge appointed Mrs. Alice Robinson Johnson, a Columbia attorney, to serve as guardian *ad litem* for Mrs. Burleson during the lawsuit.[352] Mr. Sapp was represented by F. Ehrlich Thompson of

Columbia. The case was scheduled to go to trial when the fall term of court opened on September 27, but a settlement was reached on September 7, 1943. The terms of the settlement were not reported.[353]

THE WITNESSES

The two psychiatrists whose testimony at the trial supported the insanity defense claim by Mrs. Burleson's lawyers—Dr. Esther Richards, affiliated with Johns Hopkins Hospital in Baltimore, and Dr. William W. Elgin, from Pratt Hospital in Towson, Maryland—were also victims of Mrs. Burleson's intransigence with regard to paying her trial expenses and Richard's decision not to seek appointment of a guardian. Some correspondence between March 1941 and November 1942 shows the frustration of these two physicians with their inability to locate anyone, including members of Mrs. Burleson's family, willing to assume responsibility for compensating them for their professional services in support of the insanity defense, even though two family members had urged the psychiatrists to testify.

Dr. Richards wrote to Richard Walker on March 26, 1941:

> *It will presently be a year since I went to South Carolina on the tragic errand of your sister's trial. Since that time I have written to Mr. Morse several times, asking what has happened to your sister, where she is, and what her mental state is. I have also asked him about the financial status connected with paying me for my professional services last May. He paid for my trip with the exception of $7. I charged $300 for testifying, which you will agree is a very reasonable fee. Mr. Morse wrote after the trial that he felt that the Baltimore testimony saved your sister from the electric chair. Mr. Morse told me at the time that I was in South Carolina that he could not pay me for several months. Almost a year has elapsed, and I have heard nothing from him. It seems to me that I am at least entitled to the courtesy of a response. I am writing to ask your advice as to what I should do in this matter. Who has charge of your sister's affairs?[354]*

This letter, written over a year after the trial, was the first in a lengthy exchange of correspondence involving Dr. Richards, Richard Walker, Bleeker Morse and Albert Delange (an attorney retained briefly by Mrs. Burleson).

In the course of this correspondence, Richard advised Dr. Richards of May's concerns that she be transferred to the Texas Penitentiary, that she be given temporary release to put her business and personal affairs in order and that her trial was unfair. He also told Dr. Richards that he believed that testimony given by her and Dr. Elgin had saved his sister from "severe punishment."

Dr. Richards responded succinctly and bluntly:

> *I wish so much that an effort could be made to place her in a state hospital in Texas. There is of course no question about the fairness of her trial and the diagnosis of her paranoiac state. For her own sake and the sake of all the rest of us, I hope that she will die in institution before she is ever released.*

Her mental condition, in other words, was justification for not imposing the death penalty, but it also should prevent her from ever again being released into society. These letters back and forth over paying the two Baltimore physicians lasted another nineteen months but produced no tangible results. Finally, in late October 1942, an exasperated Dr. Richards put her position bluntly to Richard Walker. She first reminded Richard that it was at his "earnest insistence and that of Judge Wilson" that Dr. Elgin and she had traveled to Columbia to testify—and that their testimony had saved his sister from the electric chair. (The "he" in the first sentence of the excerpt below refers to Judge Wilson).

> *In plain words it would seem to me that you or he, or some other member of the family, would feel morally responsible for this debt, advancing the money for the payment of the doctors' bills, and drawing up papers which later on would establish your legal claim to a refunding of the money. I realize of course that you are under no legal obligation to take this step, but if I were in the position of Mrs. Burleson's family, I certainly could not feel comfortable in my conscience to know that two physicians had saved my sister's life and remained unrecompensed for over two years.[355]*

On November 10, Dr. William W. Elgin wrote to Richard to endorse "whole-heartedly" the sentiments expressed in the letter from Dr. Richards.[356]

Removal of Debts

During May's time in prison, enough of her property was sold to pay her creditors. The Hutchins-Sealy Bank used the mortgage on Mrs. Burleson's property to enforce payment of her debt by sale of pieces of her property, and her attorneys used lawsuits to collect. Any surplus cash from the property sales made to clear her debts went into Mrs. Burleson's bank account.

Pre-trial estimates of the value of May's property put the worth at approximately $100,000. Beginning in late 1941, blocks of May's property were put up for sale to cover May's debts, which totaled about $25,000. The priority for these sales, which were forced by creditors, was not to protect the value of May's estate but to raise sufficient funds to pay off the debts (all of which were now long overdue) promptly. A formal evaluation of her property was not done when these sales were finished, but a detailed inventory at the time of May's death assigned a value of $43,000. The property listed included the old Walker residence, valued at $40,000, four other small acreage properties and several "minerals only in and under" listings. The list was much shorter than one that had been prepared soon after the estate of Clara Walker (May's mother) was settled, reflecting the property sales for debt-clearance and for some of May's expenses during her post-prison years.[357]

The author could not find explicit documentation that Drs. Richards and Elgin were paid, but he assumes that either Mr. Morse fulfilled that relatively small obligation with funds from his settlement or that Richard was able to have the fees to the psychiatrists paid from May's funds.

Prison Life

May Burleson was polite and respectful to guards and other prison staff, and she became and remained a model prisoner. Upon request, she would draw sketches of inmates or staff members. Although excused from hard labor, she "occupied herself in a garment mill" and was busy with needlework, sending pieces of her knitting to friends. Mrs. Burleson also directed a Christmas pageant that was put on annually during her tenure and organized a dramatic club.[358]

Her Newberry, South Carolina relatives visited her, but no official records of those or other visits could be located.[359] Another visitor was Gertrude

Thurmond, a sister of Governor Strom Thurmond, who, according to Mrs. Burleson, became a close friend and was sympathetic with Mrs. Burleson's plight. This contact with Miss Thurmond dovetailed with Mrs. Burleson's interest in states' rights, an interest that intensified during the 1948 presidential campaign, especially with the entrance into the race of Governor Thurmond as a state's rights candidate. From her prison cell, she subscribed to many newspapers and magazines, from which she clipped articles about the Thurmond campaign to paste in a scrapbook.[360]

The files of her correspondence in family records ended in 1941, and although regular correspondence would have been expected, it is not known what communication she had thereafter, if any, with Richard or Uncle Herbert while she remained incarcerated.

In August 1944, the South Carolina Probation and Parole Board agreed to consider a petition for Mrs. Burleson's early release that had been submitted by relatives who lived in Newberry.[361] That petition was turned down, but four years later, after she had served two-thirds of her sentence (eight years), the board acted favorably on her application.

She had seen earlier advertisements for clothes placed in the *New York Times* by the B. Altman Company and proceeded to order a complete wardrobe for her life after prison.[362] Thus, she was prepared to be well dressed when her release became effective.

Release from Prison

On Saturday, October 23, 1948, May Walker Burleson boarded a Delta Airlines flight at Capitol Airport that departed Columbia at noon for Houston, where she took ground transportation to her home in Galveston. As she did when she arrived in Columbia over eight years earlier, she had a number of pieces of luggage. These she checked after purchasing her plane ticket but carried magazines, candy and a large purse on board the aircraft.

She had been scheduled for release the next week, but prison officials wanted to avoid public fanfare with a lot of press coverage and released her early. Nevertheless, a reporter for *The State* newspaper was present and dutifully reported on Mrs. Burleson's departure outfit:

> *Dressed in a dull black dress and coat with black stockings and brown shoes to match, Mrs. Burleson's only bit of bright attire for her first day of*

freedom was a green jade set comprising necklace, earrings, bracelet, and ring, all mounted in white gold.

Markedly lacking in her dress was a large picture hat similar to those she wore at the trial following the slaying of her ex-husband's wife.

As she did at every session of her sensational trial eight years ago, she wore a corsage of violets, her favorite flower. Lacking, however, was the prayer book she always took with her into the court room.

Her long "new look" dress and coat and small hat gave her a distinct "grandmotherish" look that was far from her courtroom appearances eight years ago.[363]

Her support of presidential candidate J. Strom Thurmond of South Carolina was proclaimed by a big button pinned to her dress.

She refused to answer the question, but "threw back her head and laughed heartily" when asked if she planned to visit her former husband. Appearing "almost hysterically happy," Mrs. Burleson smoked one cigarette after another during her brief time at the airport. She was accompanied by Mr. and Mrs. Hugh K. Boyd of Newberry.[364] Before leaving the terminal to board, she waved and shouted good-bye to a reporter "whom, she said she hated to disappoint."[365]

8

AFTERMATH

RICHARD COKE BURLESON

Colonel Richard Coke Burleson was a field artillery officer with combat experience in World War I, and later, when he was graduated in 1923 with honors from general staff training school, he hoped—and truly expected—that if the United States ever was compelled to ready itself for war again, he would be appointed a brigade commander with rank of brigadier general. Overall, his performance record was excellent, and his competence as an officer was never an issue.

His stubbornness and abrasive behavior in some of his assignments, and especially his conflicts in his first marriage, accentuated by his wife's tendency to bring his military superiors into those conflicts, had hampered his career, however. By the late summer of 1935, he had been promoted to the rank of colonel, but his personnel file contained damaging records of reprimands, accounts of difficulties in his marriage and even long letters of complaint about his behavior from his wife. The publicity stemming from marital conflict subsided after the bitter divorce proceedings ended in October 1937, but a blistering "Unsatisfactory" rating on his performance while he was an artillery regiment commander in Hawaii in February 1939 stained his record. The rating derived from a conflict over an order issued by a superior during a field exercise and over Burleson's failure to file certain reports on time. From reading the report and Colonel Burleson's appeal, it was clear that the real issue was Colonel Burleson's attitude and manner toward the officers above him. The officer who prepared the report, a brigadier general, gave the following estimate of Colonel Burleson: "An officer of high technical ability. He lacks judgement [*sic*]. He is prejudiced and self-opinionated. He lacks proper respect for his superiors."[366]

The shooting in Columbia in 1940 and the subsequent trial revived and brought more (this time very sensational) negative publicity about his personal life to the attention of the army and the public in general, and the death of his second wife was a devastating personal loss. His performance evaluation, however, covering the period of October 12, 1939, through May 28, 1940, rated him "Superior" (the highest ranking on the form) and included a comment by the rating officer that Colonel Burleson "possesses great fortitude under serious personal suffering."[367] During the ensuing year, though, Colonel Burleson found it necessary for reasons of health to take several leaves of absence, ranging in length from one month to just over four months.[368]

One of Colonel Burleson's assignments during 1941 was to the Second Army as antitank officer. In that capacity, he helped implement two significant changes in weaponry. First, the 75 mm cannons that were the backbone of U S. field artillery units in World War I were replaced by 105 mm howitzers. Second, the army antitank arsenal was greatly enhanced by the addition of the 75 mm gun, which could destroy heavy tanks, against which the current 37 mm weapons were ineffective. Colonel Burleson became the public spokesman for this enhancement, with articles appearing in newspapers across the country during October 1941. An excerpt from a typical article follows:

> *"The 75s are capable of throwing out 20 shells per minute, and they will stop the biggest of tanks," Colonel Burleson declared, "Moreover, they are easy to move."*
>
> *Some of them are being mounted on half-tracks—armored scout cars which have tractor treads on the rear wheels.*
>
> *"When these half-tracks carry the 75s, they are known as tank killers,"* *Burleson asserted. "The idea is for these vehicles, which are faster than tanks, is to hunt them down and destroy them."*[369]

Colonel Burleson's place in the sun was brief, however, and on June 30, 1942, early in the war, he retired. In response to a request for "a brief general estimate of the officer," the lieutenant general who filled out the form for Colonel Burleson's final performance evaluation wrote: "An officer of broad experience and professionally able but who had passed the period of great usefulness before retirement by reason of an unfortunate frame of mind."[370]

As the war was ending, he was appointed to the Allied Commission on Reparations that met in Moscow in June and July 1945. This commission discussed the issue of Germany making reparations for damages inflicted on Allied countries during the war.[371] Colonel Burleson's personal life took a turn for the better when about seven months after his second wife was killed he married Ella Pendergast Roberts, a woman with whom he had been involved in the late 1920s before he reunited with his first wife, May Walker, in San Antonio.[372] A letter that Ella had written Colonel Burleson during that period was read at the divorce trial.[373] Richard and Ella Burleson soon took up residence in San Antonio and became active in the social life there.[374]

When May Walker Burleson was released from prison, however, Richard Burleson and his third wife decided immediately that they did not want to remain in Texas. They told Mr. and Mrs. Jack Burleson Miller that they were selling their San Antonio home and that the Millers could have whatever furniture from the home that they wanted.[375] It took some time for them to leave Texas and then the United States, but they sailed for Europe in July 1949.[376] Their home was in Paris, but they traveled in Southern Europe during the winter months.

When they came back to the United States, they did not return to Texas but took up permanent residence in Baltimore, Maryland. Colonel Burleson died on March 2, 1960. Ella Burleson died on May 28 of the same year.[377]

MAY WALKER BURLESON

Life After Prison

After her release from prison on Saturday, October 23, 1948, Mrs. Burleson flew from Columbia to Houston, arriving there about three o'clock that afternoon. After a brief visit there with friends, she spent Sunday in Galveston and arrived in San Antonio on Monday—ready to resume an active role in Texas politics. Reporter Kemper Diehl from the *San Antonio Light*, who interviewed her, had this to say about her self-image:

> *No stranger would know the well-dressed, stately woman, with the air of a grand dame, has just been released from the model prison farm at*

Columbia, S.C. Mrs. Jennie May Walker Burleson has served her term and is back home in her home state. Her head is high, her eyes are bright, and she is already knee-deep in activity.[378]

Mrs. Burleson talked passionately in a rambling interview about (1) her trial (she should not have been convicted, there being "bribery on both sides"); (2) a book that she was writing that would make some people "wish that they were dead" when exposed by the book and resultant motion picture; and (3) the things that she had done to help other women prisoners while she was confined in Columbia—but focused primarily on (4) the importance of states' rights, her main interest, and on the role that she expected to play in supporting Thurmond and Wright. She had experienced a bitter disappointment on Tuesday (her second day in San Antonio), when she went to attend a luncheon of the Alamo City Women's Democratic Club, hoping to speak on the topic of states' rights. She was stunned, however to

> *find that my club—that I had organized and worked to perpetuate—had declared openly for the candidacy of Truman and Barkley.*
>
> *I was disgusted. I was infuriated. I walked out. I was so disappointed that my club had betrayed its principles of democracy and stood by Truman and the infamous FEPC. I feel as if my child has betrayed me.*[379]

Nonetheless, Mrs. Burleson indicated that she was eagerly looking forward to meeting Governor Thurmond when he came to Texas and felt that she could "get some votes in the bag" for him. She had high hopes for his winning if the election got thrown into the House of Representatives.[380]

Once Truman had won the election, Mrs. Burleson's brief burst of activity and publicity ended, and she soon returned to her home in Galveston, where she found that her status, social and otherwise, had undergone a dégringolade. She had been found guilty of manslaughter and was seen generally as someone to be avoided, instead of someone to be welcomed, and was not part of a social circle. She had contact with her brother and old family friends, but her family relationships were strained rather than warm. One of her grandnieces recalls that when she was given candy by Aunt Maisie, her mother would take it away after Aunt Maisie had gone. Her grandnieces also recall that their Aunt Maisie sometimes left her home at 1202 Tremont in bathing attire with parasol and pipe in hand to walk to the beach, where she strolled alone smoking the long pipe.[381]

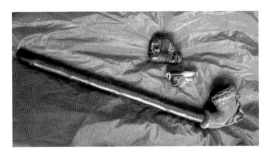

Above: Ornate pipe smoked by May Walker Burleson while strolling in bathing attire to and on Galveston Beach during her post-prison years. *Walker Family Collection.*

Right: Picture of May Walker Burleson in San Antonio in late October 1948, a few days after her release from prison. San Antonio Light, *October 27, 1948.*

Mrs. Burleson did try to participate in church and civic affairs, however. The rector of Grace Episcopal Church welcomed her, and at a luncheon meeting on January 25, 1951, of the St. Mary's Chapter of Associated Women of the church, she was appointed to the visiting committee.[382]

In civic affairs, she was more aggressive. When the city board of commissioners passed a resolution to change the name of Tremont Street, on which the Walker family home that she now owned was located, to Cohen Avenue, in honor of a beloved Galveston physician, she was a leader in a movement to protest the change. She appeared with the Tremont Street Committee at a board meeting in support of a protest petition already submitted by her group. The protest group had proposed that a memorial to Dr. Cohen be erected instead, and Mrs. Burleson was the group spokesperson at the meeting, pledging that the Tremont Street committee would "spearhead a campaign to obtain funds for a memorial to Dr. Cohen." The board rescinded its prior action in changing the street name, but asked for a fund campaign progress report in July of the next year.[383]

May Burleson died on August 30, 1957. Her obituary in the Galveston paper was brief, providing only the bare facts of her family connections.

Mrs. May Burleson

Private funeral services were held Saturday for Mrs. May Walker Burleson at J. Levy and Bro. funeral home. She died Friday in John Sealy Hospital.

Mrs. Burleson was the daughter of the late John C. and Clara Wilson Walker, pioneer Galvestonians. She was born October 22, 1888 in Galveston and resided at 1202 Tremont Street at the old family residence.

Survivors include one brother, Richard C. Walker of Galveston, and one niece, Mrs. Donald Cameron of El Paso.

Mrs. E.F. Dixon officiated at the funeral services, and burial was in Glenwood Cemetery in Houston.[384]

MAY WALKER BURLESON

A Reflection

Overview

May Walker Burleson valued her beauty and her social position, and she advanced the latter skillfully after her marriage, but she was also an ambitious woman who exhibited talent, competence, interpersonal skills, leadership and intelligence as she threw herself into the woman suffrage movement, civic and political activities and the study and practice of archaeology. Her character and behavior, however, were flawed. She wanted her marriage to succeed, but she seemed unwilling to work at building a strong marriage until it was too late. From the beginning, her absences, some brief, others long, from her husband signaled that being together was not a priority, at least when compared to spending time with her mother, working in the suffrage movement in New York, touring Europe alone after World War I while her husband returned home and going on archaeological expeditions. She refused to accompany Richard on assignments where the living quarters or social environment did not suit her.

Her immersion in activities outside the home suggested a strong need for independence, and when Richard sought a divorce, especially given his apparently habitual infidelity, one might have thought that she would welcome the opportunity to be shed of him. In her eyes, however, part of her identity was being the wife of an army officer, and she could not accept an end to the marriage. A clear illustration of her feelings was revealed just after the fall of 1934, during which she had experienced considerable success with her archaeological lectures (and likely could have found employment in the archaeology profession). She abandoned that pursuit to mount a desperate effort to contest a divorce suit brought by her husband. She articulated repeatedly her view that unfair loss of financial support had come with her divorce, but with the right attitude, May Burleson could have made it on her own financially. The fundamental issue was not fiscal support but her view of her identity, namely that her rightful place was that of Mrs. Richard Burleson.

May Walker Burleson could not accept defeat or be denied what she wanted, a character flaw that proved to be her undoing after the divorce. This was illustrated by the treatment received by her lawyers in both the divorce case and in the Columbia trial and by her astounding persistence in filing appeals long after the divorce case was truly over—a persistence that seemed to reflect mental imbalance.

Impact of Mental Health Issues

After the 1935 incident in Boston, May and Richard Burleson never lived together again. May Burleson began spending periods of time in hospitals, beginning with Walter Reed Hospital in Washington, D.C., in early 1935 for urgent care of a nervous breakdown. She spent from May through August 1935 in the psychiatric section of the John Sealy Hospital in Galveston, her admission there being triggered by worry over the impending divorce suit by her husband. The spring 1936 divorce trial ended with a verdict favorable to her, but that verdict almost immediately was set aside and replaced by a ruling that granted Colonel Burleson a new trial. She was overwhelmed that she would have to endure another trial and soon became a patient in the Fort Sam Houston Hospital. Based upon this, Mrs. Burleson's petition, filed by her attorney, to have the divorce trial deferred from the fall 1936 term of court until the spring 1937 term was granted. In October 1938, a year after a court denied her petition to have her spring 1937 divorce from Colonel Burleson overturned, she spent twenty-five days in John Sealy Hospital. In November, she was escorted by a nurse to Baltimore, where she was committed by Dr. Emily Richards to Enoch Pratt Hospital in Towson, Maryland. She remained there until January 1939 and, after her discharge, returned to Texas. After another brief stay in John Sealy Hospital, she remained hospital-free from March 1939 until March 1940, when, following her arrest, she was committed to the Waverly Sanitarium in Columbia, South Carolina. Her last documented hospitalization related to mental problems was in the South Carolina State Hospital for the Insane in Columbia, South Carolina, but this commitment was ordered by a judge solely for the purpose of a diagnosis. That diagnosis later was introduced as evidence at her trial.

With the exception of the last one, these hospitalizations all were triggered by a need to treat mental health episodes directly related to events during a lengthy divorce trial or by the result of that trial. The exact treatments that she received during her times in hospital could not be determined, but the treatment of mental illness in the 1930s was primitive and reflected a lack of knowledge of the causes of the condition.[385] Psychotherapy was in its early stages, and drug therapy did not yet exist.[386] Hydrotherapy was still in vogue, and while this treatment did have a calming effect on many patients, it could involve keeping a patient (restrained and) covered with warm water in a tub with only the head uncovered for hours. This procedure sometimes was repeated for days thereafter.[387] The details of Mrs. Burleson's various treatments could not be located, but the antipathy that she developed to baths most likely was a reaction to having undergone hydrotherapy. A treatment that she was fortunate to escape was the lobotomy, a surgical procedure in which part of the brain was removed. This procedure grew in popularity throughout the 1930s and often had tragic results. She also did not experience electroshock therapy, which began to be used in the late 1930s.

Her hospital stays seem to have calmed her down and helped blunt the anger and disappointment that she felt both as developments in the divorce trial unfolded and at the end when the divorce was upheld. The treatments that she received, however, neither "cured" her mental problems nor had any long-lasting benefit. In early March 1940, the strong re-emergence of her feelings about the divorce ended in a mental imbalance that resulted in her committing murder.

EPILOGUE

LAST WILL AND TESTAMENT OF
MAY WALKER BURLESON

When Jennie May Walker Burleson drew up and signed her last will and
testament in Galveston on October 15, 1951, her brother, Richard, her
closest living relative, was not named as a beneficiary, probably because
of her anger over property disputes following their mother's death and
the facts that Richard never once appeared in Columbia to support her
during the long pretrial and trial period and then pressured her during her
incarceration to sell property to settle obligations, such as attorney fees,
that she did not recognize.

The provisions of her will reflected the thoughts by which she was driven:
(1) the bitter breakup of her marriage that had defined her life since her
husband began divorce proceedings in 1935 and (2) the prominence of the
Walker family name.

The first thought—really an obsession—was reflected in a stipulation
near the end of her will:

> *I will and direct that the box of clothes (in the attic) given to my former
> husband Richard C. Burleson, U.S. Army, Retired, by his mistress Nellie
> Kemp von Ee and worn by him when he was married to me and the army
> trunk locker and black leather case containing love letters written to him by*

his mistress Nellie Kemp von Ee and love letters written to her by him, and love letters written to him by Ella Burleson his present wife when he was married to me, and used as evidence of his adultery in my suit for divorce against him, be sent to the Chief of Staff, U.S. Army Washington and examined by the officers of said office, with a copy of this instruction from this will.[388]

The referenced clothes were given to her husband in 1927, and the letters were written during the period between 1927 and 1931. Colonel Burleson had retired from the U.S. Army in 1942, so May Walker Burleson could not have hoped for these items to result in any action by the army high command. What she was seeking was post-mortem vindication that her requests to the chief of staff made during the divorce suit brought against her by her husband—to force Colonel Burleson to drop those proceedings—were valid and acknowledgement that those requests should have been acted on by the chief of staff.

May's second thought was reflected in a major bequest intended for the benefit of the cultural life of Galveston and that would enshrine the Walker family name for generations to come, but the conditions, fiscal and social, that she stipulated made it unlikely that this gift to the city would be accepted. The bequest was worded as follows:[389]

I will and direct that title to my property the building at 1202 Tremont Street, city of Galveston, garage and grounds named in my deed and furnishings designated in this will to remain in the building shall vest in the city of Galveston, Texas, for use and benefit of cultural groups of white citizens of Galveston named in this will. Viz.- The Galveston Art League, and other Art associations, Literary and musical groups, and cultural clubs and organizations composed of white citizens.

The building shall be used for meetings, exhibitions and social purposes by said named white groups. The building shall at no time be used by any political organization or individual for political purposes nor shall it be used by any fraternal organization, except members and alumnae of Pi Beta Phi national college sorority. It shall not be used by any group, cultural or otherwise, of negroes or any negro individual.

The name of her bequest and how that name was to be displayed was stipulated in Mrs. Burleson's will, namely that a bronze tablet be prepared and placed to the right of the front door affixed to the outside wall of the building stating in appropriate letters:

This building
The Walker Memorial Arts and Cultural Center
Was given to the City of Galveston
By
Jenny May Walker Burleson
in memory of her parents
John Caffery Walker
And
Clara Wilson Walker
and her brothers
John Caffery Walker, Jr.
Herbert Wilson Walker

It was noted in the will that space had to be left to add the name of her brother, Richard Clark Walker, at his death. The will also stated the following expectation:

As the Tremont St. property is willed to the City of Galveston I expect it to be tax free and for the City to make and effect all repairs such as reconditioning the furnace for natural gas, payment of utilities, keeping the grounds and premises in good order, by City labor. I also expect the city to pay the salary of a female manager or hostess to reside in the building.

Although the property and furnishings were willed the city, which was expected to contribute funds to operate the facility, the will directed that the Walker Center be administered by an independent governing board that was to be self-perpetuating, with the six original members named in the will. Cooperation between the board and the city was essential, but the will directed that executive authority for the Walker Center was to be exercised by the governing board. May Burleson's will provided for that board to receive funds from several sources, to wit: cash left in her account after her funeral expenses and any claims against her estate were paid, proceeds from the sale of the items of her personal property that were identified in the will and income from the properties for which she owned the mineral rights. The lands and mineral rights were willed to the City of Galveston, but one-half of any income from oil, gas or other minerals was willed directly to the Walker Center and the other half to Grace Episcopal Church in Galveston. These funds were not to be used for the salary of the hostess/manager or for building maintenance or operating expenses such as lights and heat, which were to be furnished by the city.

PUBLICITY ABOUT THE WILL

Within two weeks after May Burleson's death on August 30, both Galveston newspapers informed their readers about her will. On September 12, the day after the will was filed for probate, the *Galveston Tribune* ran a story that summarized the key points in the will that would affect the city (bequest of the Walker home for a cultural center, financial obligations that Galveston would need to assume, governing board for the cultural center, the wording of a bronze plaque and the stipulation that only white cultural groups could use the center).[390] A few days later, a picture of the Walker house on Tremont Street was published, "Home Given to the City," and accompanied by a caption that stated that the city attorney was studying the provisions of the will and that "if accepted" the home was to be used by white cultural groups.[391] On October 13, an article titled "Civic Clubs Eye Old Walker Home" noted that the city attorney and others were examining the "fiscal viability of accepting the bequest," but that the "Galveston Art League and other cultural and music groups" were at work to determine "ways and means" for the bequest to be accepted.[392] These groups needed a meeting place, and the historic ambiance and the location of the old Walker home apparently attracted their interest.

CHALLENGES, OBSTACLES AND RESOLUTION

After the will was admitted to probate on October 1, 1957, May's brother and her sole heir challenged the probate of her purported will in county court by suing First Hutchins–Sealy National Bank of Galveston, which had been named executor by his sister. The basis for Richard's suit was his contention that when she drew up the instrument, May "was not of sound mind nor in any respect capable of making a valid will."[393]

On June 25, 1958, given the developing tangle created by concerns of the Galveston city commissioners about accepting the bequest and by the Richard Walker challenge, the bank asked the court for a "declaratory judgment." Specifically, the *Galveston Daily News* reported that the bank "recites that 'serious questions and controversy' have arisen over the properties belonging to Mrs. Burleson and listed in her will and whether certain of the bequests listed in the will are valid. A court order construing the will and a declaration of the rights of the various parties is sought in the suit."[394]

Complete resolution of this matter would not be announced publicly until eighteen more months had passed, but in January 1959, barely six months later, Richard conveyed a one-sixteenth interest in the royalty from "oil, gas, etc." produced from all the land owned by grantor as the heir of Jennie May Walker Burleson, to Grace Episcopal Church in Galveston. Richard clearly had inherited all the mineral rights that had been assigned in May's will to be divided equally between Grace Church and the City of Galveston. Instead of the half share specified by May, he granted the church the sixteenth share. Public notice of this action was given in the newspaper under "Court Proceedings."[395] Richard received a letter of thanks from the rector of Grace Church, telling Richard that May had spoken about remembering the church in this way.[396] One could infer from this action that Richard's suit contesting his sister's will had succeeded, but the full story had yet to emerge. Richard Walker died in March 1959, so that the issue became one involving his estate.

Finally, on December 18, 1959, some nine months after Richard's death, articles appeared in Galveston newspapers that clarified how the matter was resolved. The key facts were reported as follows:[397]

1. The city of Galveston had decided earlier "not to accept the gift of the Walker house because it would involve spending tax money, and the cost of maintenance would be prohibitive."

2. The will of Mrs. Burleson, which was written largely in long hand, was declared "unenforceable" by the probate court since it was not a valid will.

3. Related to the second point, it was noted that under a property agreement made some years earlier between May and Richard, Richard would convey his interest in the Walker home to her, but that upon her death, the Walker house would pass back to him. The probate court and the attorney general had concurred that this agreement must be upheld, and the will was in violation of that agreement. Thus, even had the

will been otherwise valid, Richard or his estate would have been given possession of the house.

Simply put, Richard Walker, the sole heir at law of his sister, May Walker Burleson, had inherited all her property and possessions, including the Walker house.

In the settlement of the Richard Walker estate, it was decided that the sum of $7,535 would be contributed to the City of Galveston as a memorial to the Walker family. This was done in the form of a trust agreement, which stipulated that

> *the money should be used for furnishing and maintaining a room in a permanent type masonry building belonging to the city as a meeting or study center for cultural or charitable groups of the city, under regulations established by the board in 10 years. However, if at any time within the said 10 years the city does not elect to use the money for the purpose stipulated, the city may place the money in the hands of the board of trustees of the Rosenberg Library for a similar purpose.*[398]

The Galveston Board of Commissioners accepted the contribution and the stipulations thereto.

This bequest to the city and the assignment of "oil and gas" rights to Grace Episcopal Church apparently were Richard's way of honoring, to the extent that he deemed feasible, his sister's wishes as expressed in her 1951 will.

It is interesting that in no public reports of the deliberations of the Galveston Board of Commissioners was there explicit mention of the "white only" restriction placed on the proposed memorial center by the purported will of May Walker Burleson, because by the late 1950s, it should have been clear to the city officials that the days of government-owned facilities being open only to white citizens were numbered. Declining the gift of the house based on the cost of maintaining the house as a cultural center may have saved the board from confronting that issue. The bequest of money to the city from Richard's estate to establish a room for cultural groups to meet did not have such a stipulation attached.

The Walker family home that stood at 1202 Tremont Street, Galveston, Texas. This home was demolished in 1964. *Walker Family Collection.*

Bachelor home of Judge John Caffery Walker. This home was included on a tour of historic houses in Galveston held in 1977. *Walker Family Collection.*

FATE OF THE WALKER HOME

The old Walker home at 1202 Tremont Street did become Richard Walker's property after the probate court declared his sister's 1951 will to be invalid, and that real estate passed to his wife Caroline upon his death. In September 1964, shortly after the area was rezoned for business, Carol Cameron, daughter of Richard and Caroline and executrix for her mother's will, sold the property.[399] The last published picture of the home showed it in partial demolishment, with the following crude hand-lettered sign in front:[400]

DEMOLITION

DANGER

KEEP OUT

A Pilgrim Cleaners' establishment soon opened on the site.[401]

NOTES

Preface

1. Turner and Wilson, *Houston's Silent Garden*, 215–35.
2. Ibid., 236–37; Donna Cameron, personal communication with author.

Prologue

3. Cartwright, "Big Blow," 76–81, 114–19.
4. The disposal of bodies after the storm was indeed a horrific problem; for a general treatment, see Larson, *Isaac's Storm*, 239–42. For a discussion of the storm's impact on Galveston, the recovery efforts and the impact of subsequent storms, see McComb, *Galveston: A History*, 121–49.
5. Burleson, "'I Lived to Tell It,'" WFP.

Chapter 1

6. *Galveston (TX) Daily News*, September 6, 1908, 12.
7. Cullum, *Biographical Register*, Supplement 6B, 1,227.
8. *San Antonio (TX) Light*, May 4, 1936, 6-A.
9. *Galveston (TX) Daily News*, September 10, 1908, 10.

10. Marriage Record, State of Texas, County of Galveston, certifying the marriage of Captain Richard Coke Burleson and Miss Jennie May Walker on December 9, 1908.

11. *Galveston (TX) Daily News*, December 10, 1908, 12.

12. Captain Burleson's official military record shows him to be posted to the Watervliet Arsenal in New York from July 1, 1908, to April 4, 1909, but he was detailed to Cuba for January and February 1909, an assignment documented by newspaper accounts and family correspondence.

13. Maisie Burleson to Mrs. J.C. Walker, postcard from Watervliet, dated March 17, 1909, WFP.

14. *Galveston (TX) Daily News*, August 14, 1910, 6.

15. *Eau Claire (WI) Leader*, February 10, 1914, 5.

16. The founder and director of Chase Normal School, William Merritt Chase, 1849–1916, was an American painter known not only for his painting but also for his contributions to art education. His normal school became the Parsons School of Design.

17. *Eau Claire (WI) Leader*, February 10, 1914, 5. This quotation appeared in a syndicated column titled "Women Worthwhile," written by Selene Armstrong Harmon.

18. In late May 1908, a story was circulated about William Howard Taft, secretary of war in the Theodore Roosevelt administration. The story was that Taft, who had taken with him on an official visit to Panama an African American employed as a messenger by the War Department, asked the messenger to dine with him in the dining car of a train while the train was traversing North Carolina. This would have violated the segregation laws of the state. The story was denied by the secretary's staff, but it received widespread publicity. It seems likely that this incident triggered Mrs. Burleson's comment. See the *San Antonio (TX) Light*, May 20, 1908, 4.

19. Postcards written by May Walker Burleson, signed "M" for "Maisie," WFP.

20. *Galveston (TX) Daily News*, September 19, 1911, 12.

21. Ibid., January 3, 1912, 8.

22. Cullum, *Biographical Register*, Supplement 6B, 1,227.

23. Walton, *Woman's Crusade*, 53–68.

24. *Washington (D.C.) Post*, January 3, 4, 6,7, 8 and 9, 1913.

25. President Taft's position on the issue was reported in an article headed, "Taft to Protect Parade of Woman Suffragists," *Washington (D.C.) Post*, January 7, 1913, 1.

26. The three societies or organizations were the Woman's Suffrage Union of New York, the Woman's Suffrage Society of Connecticut and a group being assembled by Rosalie Jones, who was leading a band of hikers from New York that was expected to be joined by delegations from Virginia and Maryland. These and all other participants in the procession were to be under the general direction of the National American Woman's Suffrage Association, which had appointed Alice Paul to organize the event. *Washington (D.C.) Times*, January 10, 1913, 1.

27. *Washington (D.C.) Times*, January 10, 1913, 1.

28. See, for example, *Fort Wayne (IN) News*, January 21, 1913, 1.

29. Stovall, *Seeing Suffrage*, 24.

30. Inez Milholland, one of the most highly visible leaders of the woman suffrage movement, died just over three years later in November 1916. An account of her participation in the Washington procession is given in Lumsden, *Inez*, 81–91.

31. Brown, ed., *Official Program*, 5, 7, 9, 11, 13, 15.

32. Walton, *Woman's Crusade*, 68–71.

33. Brown, *Official Program*.

34. "General Orders No. 15," March 1, 1913, issued by Richard H. Sylvester, major and superintendent, Police Department, District of Columbia.

35. Brown, ed., *Official Program*, 15, 17; *New York American*, March 4, 1913, 3.

36. *Washington (D.C.) Post*, March 4, 1913, 1, 3.

37. *New York Times*, March 4, 1913, 1.

38. *Suffrage Parade Hearings*, 3.

39. The page number(s) in *Suffrage Parade Hearings* on which each of the following excerpts from the testimony of Mrs. Burleson may be found is given in parentheses following the excerpt.

40. *New York American*, March 4, 1913, 3. This review of the allegory was written by Genevieve Clark, daughter of Speaker of the House James Beauchamp Clark of Missouri.

41. *Washington (D.C.) Post*, March 4, 1913, 1.

42. *Galveston (TX) Daily News*, March 25, 1913, 5.

43. *Eau Claire (WI) Leader*, February 10, 1914, 5. Mrs. Burleson's decision to attend college was widely reported.

44. *Washington (D.C.) Post*, January 12, 1914, 2.

45. Ibid., August 2, 1914, 10.

46. Ibid., August 4, 1914, 10.

47. Ibid., July 30, 1914, 1.

48. Ibid., November 15, 1915, 19.

49. *Galveston (TX) Daily News*, March 17, 1915, 7; April 24, 1915, 5.

50. *Washington (D.C.) Post*, December 16, 1915, 11; *Galveston (TX) Daily News*, March 26, 1916, 7.

51. *Washington (D.C.) Post*, November 2, 1913, 29.

52. Ibid., January 1, 1916, 9.

53. Ibid., November 28, 1915, 12.

54. Ibid., December 4, 1915, 7. Woodrow Wilson and Edith Galt were married two weeks later.

55. Richard Burleson's assignment at Fort Myer was interrupted by two and a half months of detail to the School of Fire for Field Artillery, Fort Sill, Oklahoma, in the early part of 1914, *Biographical Register*, Supplement 6B, 1,227.

56. Ibid.

57. *San Antonio (TX) Light*, November 29, 1916, 8.

58. Ibid., October 28, 1917, 7.

59. *San Saba (TX) News*, December 27, 1917, 8.

60. Machado, *Centaur of the North*, 147–54.

61. Hurst, *Pancho Villa*, 99.

62. *San Saba (TX) News*, August 3, 1916, 6.

63. Cullum, *Biographical Register*, Supplement 6B, 1,227.

64. The Pershing Expedition was not successful in either capturing or killing Pancho Villa. See Hurst, *Pancho Villa*, 153–54.

65. Tuchman, *Zimmerman Telegram*, 149.

66. Ibid., 7.

67. Woolley and Peters, "Proclamation 1364—Declaring That a State of War Exists Between the United States and Germany," http://www.presidency.ucsb.edu/ws/?pid=598. See Tuchman, *Zimmerman Telegram*, 198–200, for a brief discussion of President Wilson's decision to seek a declaration of war.

68. Cullum, *Biographical Register*, Supplement 6B, 1,227.

69. Ibid., 1,228.

70. *Pennsylvania in the World War*, vol. 2.

71. *Short History and Illustrated Roster of the 107th Field Artillery.* Overall statistics are on pages 1–5. The remainder of the sixty pages describe the six batteries and other units.

72. *Pennsylvania in the World War*, vol. 2, 640.

73. Cullum, *Biographical Register*, Supplement 6B, 1,228.

74. Ibid.

75. A graphic description of this incident may be found in Garber, *Service with Battery C*, 81–82. Thirty enlisted men and three officers from the 107th were killed in action in World War I.

76. In *Pennsylvania in the World War*, this incident is simply reported. In *Service with Battery C*, author David Garber describes the removal as a blow to the men of Battery C and notes that Captain Whittaker later was exonerated by a trial.

77. *Pennsylvania in the World War*, vol. 2, 649.

78. Cullum, *Biographical Register*, Supplement 6B, 1,228.

79. Ibid., Supplement 7, 711.

80. Ibid., 710.

81. *Galveston (TX) Daily News*, February 19, 1919, 5.

82. Ibid., May 20, 1919, 7.

83. Postcards written in 1919–20 by May Walker Burleson, WFP.

84. *Galveston (TX) Daily News* November 1, 1919, 7.

85. Apparently a reference to a song written after the fall of Manila to American forces during the Spanish-American War. See chapter 1 in Vic Hurley, *Jungle Patrol: The Story of the Philippine Constabulary, 1901–1936* (Salem, OR: Cerebus Books, 2011).

86. Postcards written in 1920 by May Walker Burleson, WFP.

87. *San Saba (TX) News*, March 11, 1920, 1.

88. Cullum, *Biographical Register*, Supplement 7, 710.

89. Ibid.

90. *Galveston (TX) Daily News*, September 21, 1922, 5; January 5, 1923, 5; March 21, 1923, 7.

91. Burleson, "Aeroplane," 349.

92. Ibid.

93. Ibid., 358.

94. *San Saba (TX) News*, October 28, 1926, 1. This news item referred to Colonel Burleson, although his rank at that time was major.

95. Military Service Records of Burleson, Richard Coke, National Archives, National Personnel Records Center.

96. G.P Summrall to Board of Directors, Texas A.&M., June 5, 1925, MRRCB.

97. "Charles Pelot Summerall," Arlington National Cemetery, accessed April 13, 2013, http://www.arlingtoncemetery.net/summer.htm.

98. Cullum, *Biographical Register*, Supplement 7, 711.

99. Ibid.

100. Cullum, *Biographical Register*, Supplement 8, 178.
101. John W. Davis was defeated in the November 1924 presidential election by Calvin Coolidge, the Republican nominee.
102. *North Adams (MA) Transcript*, July 11, 1924, 6.
103. *Washington (D.C.) Post*, March 8, 1925, 10.
104. *Emporia (KS) Daily Gazette*, November 30, 1925, 4.
105. Cullum, *Biographical Register*, Supplement 7, 711.
106. Secretary of State Cordell Hull, a member of the U.S. House of Representatives from Tennessee in 1928, is best known for his service under FDR from 1933 to November 1944. He was awarded the Nobel Peace Prize in 1945 for his role in the establishment of the United Nations.
107. *San Antonio (TX) Express*, October 14, 1930, 8.
108. Ibid., October 25, 1930, 8; March 18, 1931, 6.
109. *Social Register of Washington, 1931* 45, no. 2, Social Register Association, 1930, WFP.
110. *San Antonio (TX) Light*, September 18, 1932, 20.
111. Ibid., April 17, 1933, 3.
112. Ibid., February 11, 1932, 3.
113. Ibid., April 10, 1932, 4.
114. Ibid., July 19, 1932, 2.
115. Ibid., August 28, 1932, 18.
116. Ibid., August 14, 1932, 3.
117. Ibid., August 17, 1932, 4.
118. Whitman, "As a Strong Bird."
119. *San Antonio (TX) Light*, April 19, 1933, 5B.
120. Ibid., February 28, 1932, 9.
121. Ibid., January 18, 1932, 4A.
122. Ibid., April 7, 1933, 3A.
123. Ibid., April 11, 1933, 4B.
124. Ibid., February 11, 1934, 3.
125. May Walker Burleson to Mira Hall of Pittsfield, Massachusetts, September 28, 1934, WFP.
126. *Foster's Daily Democrat* (Dover, NH), October 9, 1934, 5.
127. Ibid.
128. *Galveston (TX) Daily News*, October 15, 1934, 10.
129. In 1973, sixteen years after May's death, her niece, Mrs. Donald Cameron, who was the daughter of May's brother, Richard, donated her aunt's artifacts to the Rice University art collection. The curator of that collection provided Mrs. Cameron in 1978 with a list that

included his identification of each artifact, together with his "educated guess" for the period of the excavated object. J.F. Scott, curator, Rice University Art Collection, to Mrs. Donald Cameron, May 26, 1978, with an attachment listing all artifacts donated to Rice University by Mrs. Cameron, WFP.

130. *Galveston (TX) Daily News*, December 26, 1934, 3. A copy of the program for the attorney general's conference on crime was found in Mrs. Burleson's papers, WFP.

Chapter 2

131. Cullum, *Biographical Register*, Supplement 7, 711.

132. Order issued by cablegram, at direction of the secretary of war, August 9, 1927, MRRCB.

133. William W. Harts, brigadier general and military attaché, U.S. Embassy, Paris, France, to assistant chief of staff, War Department, Washington, D.C., March 2, 1928, MRRCB.

134. Ibid.

135. Ibid.

136. Ibid.

137. Ibid.

138. Cullum, *Biographical Register*, Supplement 7, 711.

139. May Walker Burleson to General Malin Craig, chief of staff, U.S. Army, November 25, 1935, MRRCB.

140. May Walker Burleson to the adjutant general, October 16, 1929, MRRCB.

141. Charles Lyman, the adjutant general, to May Walker Burleson, October 24, 1929, MRRCB.

142. May Walker Burleson to General Malin Craig, November 25, 1935.

143. Ibid.

144. "Reassignment of Colonel Burleson," a document prepared by the adjutant general for the chief of staff, March 23, 1933, MRRCB.

145. Senator Morris Sheppard to George H. Dorn, secretary of war, March 10 1933, MRRCB.

146. George H. Dorn, secretary of war, to Senator Morris Sheppard, March 20, 1933, MRRCB.

147. Senator Tom Connally to George H. Dorn, secretary of war, March 23, 1933, MRRCB.

148. The response in the letter from George H. Dorn, secretary of war, to Senator Tom Connally, March 30 1933, is typical, MRRCB.
149. Brigadier General Andrew Moses to Mrs. Richard Burleson, March 23, 1933, MRRCB.
150. Efficiency Report for April 3–June 30, 1933, MRRCB.
151. Incident report, Patrolman Daniel Byrnes to Boston police captain Thomas Towle, submitted February 26, 1935, MRRCB.
152. "Report of Investigation of Complaint that Lt. Colonel R.C. Burleson Had Threatened to Kill His Wife, etc.," submitted by Lt. Colonel L.B. Moody to Major General Fox Conner, April 16, 1935. References to records of interviews attached to this report will be hereafter "Moody Report," interview with ___, MRRCB.
153. "Moody Report," interview with Colonel Albert W. Foreman, February 23, 1935, MRRCB.
154. Ibid.
155. "Moody Report," interview with Colonel Brady G. Ruttencutter, Retired, March 1, 1935, MRRCB.
156. F.H. Nash, attorney at law, to Mrs. R.C. Burleson, February 25, 1935, MRRCB.
157. Statement signed by May Walker Burleson in presence of two witnesses in her room at the Fort Banks Hospital on March 4, 1935, MRRCB.
158. Interview with Colonel Ruttencutter.
159. Interview with Colonel Albert W. Foreman.
160. "Report of Investigation of Complaint."
161. Letter of Administrative Admonition to Lieutenant Colonel R.C. Burleson, from Major General Fox Conner, through chief of staff, Ninety-Fourth Division, May 14, 1935, MRRCB.
162. Ibid.
163. Colonel Burleson's appeal, which included a list of supporting letters, dated June 29, 1935, together with copies of the twenty-nine supporting letters, are included in the MRRCB.
164. Memorandum by Order of the Secretary of War, sent by the Acting Adjutant General to Lieutenant Colonel Richard C. Burleson, F.A., August 8, 1935, MRRCB.

Chapter 3

165. The discussion of the courtroom proceedings during the trial, including the testimony and the remarks by the lawyers, are based on the summaries provided in the *San Antonio Light* on April 25 and 30, and May 1–3, 5–6 and 10, 1936. Court actions, including the jury verdict and rulings of the trial judge, are documented by the summary court records that were preserved.

166. *San Saba (TX) News*, September 5, 1935, 7.

167. This trial lasted only one day, and the only official action taken was to continue the trial to the spring 1936 term. A transcript of testimony was not retained by the court; the description of the trial proceedings reflected accounts given in the *San Antonio (TX) Light*, November 20, 1935, 1; *San Antonio (TX) Express*, November 21, 1935, 5.

168. *San Antonio (TX) Light*, November 20, 1935, 1.

169. See "Separate Ways" earlier.

170. Two versions of the reason for a continuance were given in the press. The *San Saba News* and the *San Antonio Express* reported that after the reading of the love letters from other women, the plaintiff's attorney made the request. The *San Antonio Light* reported that the request came from the defense to permit attorney J. Franklin Spears to continue work in Austin as chair of a body investigating the state police. Surviving court records could not resolve the matter, but the *San Antonio Express* reported that the defense resisted the continuance. Mrs. Burleson made clear a few days later in a letter to General Craig that she was greatly disappointed when the continuance was granted. *San Saba (TX) News*, November 21, 1935, 1; *San Antonio (TX) Express*, November 21, 1935, 5; *San Antonio (TX) Light*, February 28, 1932, 9. May Walker Burleson to General Malin Craig, Chief of Staff, U.S. Army, November 25, 1935, MRRCB.

171. May Walker Burleson to General Malin Craig, chief of staff, U.S. Army, November 25, 1935, MRRCB. General Malin Craig served as chief of staff from October 2, 1935, until August 31, 1939. His predecessor was General Douglas MacArthur, and he was succeeded by General George C. Marshall.

172. See "Troubled Waters Beneath a Calm Surface" earlier.

173. May Walker Burleson to General Malin Craig, chief of staff, U.S. Army, November 25, 1935, MRRCB.

174. Ibid.

175. Ibid., November 26, 1935.

176. Ibid., January 9, 1936.
177. General Malin Craig, chief of staff, U.S. Army, to May Walker Burleson, January 14, 1936, MRRCB.
178. May Walker Burleson to General Malin Craig, chief of staff, U.S. Army, January 23, 1936, MRRCB.
179. Major General E.T. Conley to Mrs. Richard C. Burleson, January 28, 1936, MRRCB.
180. *San Antonio (TX) Light*, May 1, 1936, 4A.
181. Ibid., April 25, 1936, 2.
182. Ibid., April 25, 1936, 1.
183. See "Divorce Suit Announced" earlier.
184. See "Testimony Reconciliation" as follows.
185. *San Antonio (TX) Light*, April 25, 1936, 2.
186. Ibid., May 3, 1936, 1.
187. Ibid.
188. In an article in the *Galveston Daily News* on December 26, 1934, Mrs. Burleson's trip is stated to be of six weeks' duration. She stipulated four weeks in the course of testimony at the 1936 trial.
189. *Galveston (TX) Daily News*, December 26, 1934, 3.
190. *San Antonio (TX) Light*, April 25, 1936, 2.
191. See "The 1935 Incident and Its Immediate Consequences" for details concerning this incident.
192. *San Antonio (TX) Light*, May 1, 1936, 1.
193. Ibid., May 3, 1936, 1.
194. The police report for this incident was presented under "The 1935 Incident in Boston and Its Immediate Consequences" earlier. The accounts given by Colonel Burleson and his wife both differed in the details of the actual incident from the police report, but these differences were not significant in regard to impact of the incident.
195. *San Antonio (TX) Light*, April 25, 1936, 1.
196. Ibid.
197. See "Troubled Waters Beneath a Calm Surface."
198. *San Antonio (TX) Light*, April 30, 1936, 1.
199. Ibid.
200. Ibid.
201. Ibid.
202. Ibid.
203. *San Antonio (TX) Light*, May 1, 1936, 4A.
204. See "Troubled Waters Beneath a Calm Surface."

205. *San Antonio (TX) Light*, May 2, 1936, 1.

206. Ibid.

207. Ibid., May 2, 1936, 2.

208. The mental health problems of both Colonel and Mrs. Burleson are discussed under "Mental Heath Issues," pages 95–8.

209. *San Antonio (TX) Light*, May 2, 1936, 2.

210. Ibid., May 3, 1936, 1.

211. Ibid., May 5, 1936, 1.

212. Ibid., May 4, 1936, 6A.

213. Richard C. Burleson v. Jennie May Burleson, Cause No. 3007, District Court of San Saba County, Texas, Spring 1936 Term, May 6, 1936, Court Records, 212.

214. Ibid.

215. Ibid., 213.

216. *Galveston (TX) Daily News*, May 10, 1936, 1. The plaintiff attorney also charged that Carl Runge, one of the defense attorneys, had erred during final arguments by reading an extract from a divorce case to the jury.

217. Ibid.

218. Richard C. Burleson v. Jennie May Burleson, Cause No. 3007, District Court of San Saba County, Texas, Petition filed by Mrs. Burleson for income support during pendency of trial, filed August 1936.

219. Ibid.

220. *Burleson*, Ruling in Chambers at Mason, Texas, August 14, 1936.

221. May Walker Burleson to General Fox Conner, February 22, 1935, MRRCB.

222. Colonel G.M. Ekwurzel to Colonel Roger Brooke, February 21, 1935, MRRCB.

223. Colonel Roger Brooke to Colonel G.M. Ekwurzel, February 23, 1935, MRRCB.

224. Colonel Roger Brooke to Colonel G.M. Ekwurzel, telegram, copy undated, but sent on or about March 19, 1935, MRRCB.

225. Colonel Ekwurzel's response was not located in Colonel Burleson's personnel file, but in March 1935 there was no indication of pending action by the U.S. Army.

226. Colonel Roger Brooke to Colonel G.M. Ekwurzel, March 23, 1935,

227. "Psychiatrist Testifies in Divorce," *San Antonio (TX) Light*, May 5, 1936, 1.

228. May Walker Burleson to General Malin Craig, chief of staff, U.S. Army, November 25, 1935, MRRCB.

229. Petition dated November 4, 1936, filed with Court Records for *Burleson*, Cause No. 3007, District Court of San Saba, Texas, Fall Term, 1936.

230. Ibid.

231. Ibid.

232. Ibid.

233. *San Antonio (TX) Light*, April 15, 1937, 26.

234. May Walker Burleson to Secretary of War Harry Woodring, February 23, 1937, MRRCB.

235. Cullum, *Biographical Register*, Supplement 8, 178.

236. Ibid.

237. Secretary of War Harry Woodring to Attorney General Homer Cummings, February 19, 1937, MRRCB.

238. Attorney General Homer Cummings to Secretary of War Harry Woodring, March 4, 1937, MRRCB.

239. May Walker Burleson to Secretary of War Harry Woodring, February 23, 1937, MRRCB.

240. Ibid.

241. May Walker Burleson to President Roosevelt, February 23, 1937, MRRCB. In the fall of 1934, Mrs. Burleson received and accepted an invitation to a musicale at the White House.

242. *Burleson*, Spring 1937 Term, April 22, 1937, Court Records.

243. *San Antonio (TX) Light*, April 23, 1937, 3A.

244. *Burleson*, Spring 1937 Term, April 22, 1937, Court Records.

245. Petition filed by Jennie May Burleson, September 27, 1937, with District Court of San Saba, Texas, for a bill of review at the October 1937 Term of Court of Suit No. 3007, 1–12.

246. Ibid., 11.

247. Mrs. Burleson was filing a petition for a bill of review and would be the plaintiff when that cause moved forward in court. In the divorce suit, however, she was the defendant. In this section of her petition, both she and her husband are referred to as "plaintiff," and the reader needs to be aware that there are two cases at issue.

248. Petition filed by Jennie May Burleson, September 27, 1937, with District Court of San Saba, Texas, for a bill of review at the October 1937 Term of Court of Suit No. 3007, 2.

249. Ibid., 5.

250. Ibid., 9.

251. Although Texas law at the time did not provide for alimony, Colonel Burleson had not maintained his promised monthly payments to Mrs.

Burleson during the divorce trial period, and the settlement conferred on Mrs. Burleson did not compensate her for the full amount that the colonel was in arrears.

252. Petition filed by Jennie May Burleson, September 27, 1937, with District Court of San Saba, Texas, for a bill of review at the October 1937 Term of Court of Suit No. 3007, 10.

253. Jennie May Burleson v. Richard C. Burleson, Cause No. 3118, District Court of San Saba County, Texas, Fall 1937 Term, October 19, 1937, Court Records.

254. Burleson v. Burleson, No. 8792, Court of Civil Appeals, Court of Civil Appeals of Austin, Texas.

255. Jennie May Burleson v. Richard C. Burleson, Petition for Damages, District Court, San Saba County, Texas, filed October 19, 1937, Court Records.

256. *San Saba (TX) News*, October 26, 1939, 1.

Chapter 4

257. *Galveston (TX) Daily News*, October 22, 1937, 4.

258. *San Antonio (TX) Light*, May 16, 1938, 3B.

259. *Burleson*, Cause No. 3007, District Court of San Saba County, Texas, Spring 1937 Term, April 22, 1937, Court Records. Texas divorce law required a one-year waiting period before a party to a divorce could marry again.

260. W. Herbert Wilson to Richard C. Walker, May 18, 1936, WFP.

261. Richard C. Walker to W. Herbert Wilson, May 25, 1936, WFP.

262. W. Herbert Wilson to Richard C. Walker, November 14, 1938, WFP. The author could not confirm that Richard actually visited his uncle as requested.

263. Bill for stay at John Sealy Hospital, Galveston, Texas, for care of Mrs. Burleson during period October 6 to October 31, 1938, WFP.

264. The details of May Burleson's trip to Baltimore and her treatment in hospital at Towson, including her account of her Honolulu visit, subsequently were the subjects of testimony at her trial in Columbia and will be covered when the trial is discussed.

265. May Walker Burleson to Richard C. Walker, April 23, 1939, WFP.

266. Ibid., May 9, 1939, WFP.

267. Richard and his family moved from Galveston to the Los Angeles area in 1939.

268. May Walker Burleson to Richard C. Walker, May 23, 1939, WFP.

269. Richard C. Walker to William Herbert Wilson, July 19, 1939, WFP.

270. Bleeker Morse and Marion Levy were attorneys retained by May.

271. May Walker Burleson to Richard C. Walker, July 27, 1939, WFP.

272. Richard C. Walker to May Walker Burleson, July 29, 1939, WFP.

273. Ibid., August 9, 1939, WFP.

274. May Walker Burleson to Richard C. Walker, November 6, 1939, WFP.

275. Ibid., January 4, 1940, WFP.

276. Richard C. Walker to May Walker Burleson, January 10, 1940, WFP.

277. The Houston property that May and Richard inherited from their mother came through the Wilson side of the family and later became part of what is now known as the Tanglewood property, which comprises some of the most desirable (and expensive) residential property in Houston. Donna Cameron, personal communication.

278. Ibid.

279. May Walker Burleson to Richard C. Walker, February 13, 1940, WFP.

280. Ibid.

281. Ibid., February 23, 1940, WFP.

282. Ibid., February 28, 1940, WFP.

Chapter 5

283. These letters and the postcard are discussed in chapter 4, "Impact of the Divorce."

284. *The State* (Columbia, SC), May 24, 1940, 7.

285. Ibid.

286. Ibid., March 9, 1940, 5.

287. Ibid., March 11, 1940, 8.

288. Ibid., March 9, 1940, 5.

289. Cullum, *Biographical Register*, Supplement 8, 178.

290. *The State* (Columbia, SC), May 12, 1963, 1. The Jefferson remained a Columbia landmark until 1968, when it was demolished.

291. Telephone and email communications with Debbie Bloom and Margaret Dunlap at the Walker Local and Family History Center, Richland Library, Columbia, South Carolina.

292. *The State* (Columbia, SC), May 23, 1940, 9.

293. Ibid.

294. The State v. May Walker Burleson, Court of General Sessions, County of Richland, State of South Carolina, *Inquest and Indictment Records*. Author's note: A photocopy of part of this documentation was made at the Richland County Court House in the late 1990s. Unfortunately, the Burleson file is no longer available at the courthouse.

295. *The State* (Columbia, SC), May 23, 1940, 9.

296. Ibid., March 10, 1940, 11.

297. Ibid., January 20, 1940, 3.

298. Ibid., March 12, 1940, 7.

299. "Black-Clad Slayer Carefully Avoids References to Shooting," *The State* (Columbia, SC), March 9, 1940, 1.

300. Ibid.

301. *The State* (Columbia, SC), March 10, 1940, 1, 11.

302. Ibid., March 11, 1940, 1, 8.

303. Robert Archer Cooper, a lawyer, served as governor of South Carolina from 1919 to 1922, as a member of the Farm Loan Board from 1922 to 1927 and as U.S. district judge for Puerto Rico from 1934 to 1947. "South Carolina Governors: Robert Archer Cooper," SCIWAY, accessed September 2, 2015, http://www.sciway.net/hist/governors/cooper.html.

304. *The State* (Columbia, SC), March 11, 1940, 8.

305. Ibid., 1, 7.

306. Ibid., March 12, 1940, 1, 7; March 13, 1940, 1, 11.

307. Ibid., March 12, 1940, 1.

308. Ibid., March 13, 1940, 1.

309. Ibid.

310. Ibid., 1, 11.

311. Ibid.

312. Ibid., March 15, 1940, 1, 4.

313. Mr. Andrews's testimony was introduced earlier under "The Shooting."

314. State v. May Walker Burleson, Court of General Sessions, Richland County, SC, Inquest Records (this file is no longer available at the courthouse).

315. *The State* (Columbia, SC), March 16, 1940, 11.

316. Ibid., 1, 13.

317. Ibid.

318. Ibid., April 16, 1940, 1.

319. Ibid.

320. Indictment for Murder with Concealed Weapon Clause (South Carolina State Form S-9), indicting May Walker Burleson for murder of Isabel

Reece Burleson on the eighth day of March 1940. Form dated the third Monday of April 1940 and signed by A.F. Spigner, Solicitor (form copied from Burleson file at Richland County Court House, but the Burleson file no longer available there).

Chapter 6

321. *The State* (Columbia, SC), May 23, 1940, 1, 9.
322. The testimony of witnesses and the physical evidence at the trial are presented as reported in *The State* (Columbia, SC), May 23, 1940, 1, 9.
323. The events described in testimony by these witnesses were described under "The Shooting" and "The Arrest" earlier.
324 The testimony of witnesses and the physical evidence at the trial are presented as reported in *The State* (Columbia, SC), May 24, 1940, 1, 11
325. *The State* (Columbia, SC), May 24, 1940, 1.
326. The affidavits secured by Mr. Low included three by physicians who had examined Mrs. Burleson and no doubt would have been brought before the jury had Judge Bellinger admitted the divorce case records as evidence in the murder trial.
327. *The State* (Columbia, SC), May 24, 1940, 1.
328. Ibid.
329. Ibid., 7.
330. The testimony of witnesses at the trial as presented was excerpted from *The State* (Columbia, SC), May 25, 1940, 1,7.
331. See also testimony by Judge Wilson. Richard Walker's granddaughter Donna Cameron recalls being told that her grandfather met Caroline Sadtler when she was a nurse in the psych ward at Johns Hopkins Hospital. A certificate of marriage dated March 4, 1922, for Richard Walker and Caroline Miriam Sadtler, issued in Elkton, Maryland, was located by Ms. Cameron in the Walker family papers. From these facts and Dr. Richard's testimony, it may be inferred that Richard Walker sought treatment for psychological problems at John Hopkins before 1922 and that he returned for treatment again in 1931. There is no official record or indication of any need for treatment thereafter. Richard, however, was anxious that his episodes of mental difficulties not become widely known and hence avoided testifying about May's mental health—testimony that most likely would have generated questions about his mental health history. Such testimony in open court, he feared, would be harmful to his daughter,

and that harm would be compounded if it also were revealed that his grandfather Richard S. Walker had been treated for mental illness at a clinic in Cincinnati.

332. *The State* (Columbia, SC), May 25, 1940, 7. The words that appeared in the article were: to "kill time," but it is clear from the context that this was a misprint and that the wording should have been to "kill them."

333. The account of this session of the trial is based on the report in *The State* (Columbia, SC), May 26, 1940, 1, 3.

334. The excerpts below, both from testimony and from the South Carolina State Hospital report were taken from *The State* (Columbia, SC), May 28, 1940, 1, 11; May 29, 1940, 1, 7.

335. Unfortunately, this report was not preserved in court records; the summary statements and direct quotations from the report included in this chapter were taken from an article in *The State* of May 28, 1940, 1, 11, that gave an account of the trial proceedings on May 27.

336. A detailed report of the closing arguments was given in *The State* (Columbia, SC), May 29, 1940, 7. (1) The account of those arguments presented below is based upon that report and (2) The direct quotations enclosed in quotation marks were extracted from that report.

337. *The State* (Columbia, SC), May 29, 1940, 1, 7.

338. Ibid., May 31, 1940, 1.

339. Ibid.

340. Ibid.

Chapter 7

341. Ibid., June 4, 1940, 1.

342. Ibid., 1, 3.

343. Ibid., June 6, 1940, 13.

344. W. Herbert Wilson to Richard C. Walker, September 19, 1941, WFP.

345. Richard C. Walker to W. Herbert Wilson, May 16, 1941, WFP.

346. Night Letter, W. Herbert Wilson to Richard C. Walker, May 19, 1941, WFP.

347. Richard C. Walker to W. Herbert Wilson, July 10, 1941, WFP.

348. Ironically, May's father, John C. Walker, served as judge of the Texas Tenth District for a brief period in 1909.

349. *Galveston (TX) Tribune*, January 8, 1943, 16.

350. Ibid., January 19, 1943, 12.

351. Ibid., May 27, 1943, 12; June 17, 1943, 13.

352. *Columbia (SC) Record*, April 12, 1943, 1.

353. *The State* (Columbia, SC), September 8, 1943, 6.

354. Esther L. Richards, MD, to Richard C. Walker, March 26, 1941, WFP.

355. Ibid., October 29, 1942, WFP.

356. William W. Elgin, MD, to Richard C. Walker, November 10, 1942, WFP.

357. Revised Inventory and Appraisement of the Estate of Jennie May Walker Burleson, October 29, 1958, WFP.

358. *San Antonio (TX) Light*, October 27, 1948, C-1, C-7.

359. Both the South Carolina Department of Corrections and the South Carolina Department of Archives and History responded in the negative when asked if records of visitors with Mrs. Burleson were available.

360. *San Antonio (TX) Light*, October 27, 1948, C-7.

361. *Columbia (SC) Record*, August 8, 1944, 1.

362. *San Antonio (TX) Light*, October 27, 1948, C-7.

363. *The State* (Columbia, SC), October 24, 1948, 1.

364. The Boyds were distant relatives through the Wilson side of the family.

365. *The State* (Columbia, SC), October 24, 1948, 1.

Chapter 8

366. U.S. Army Efficiency Report, July 1, 1938–February 27, 1939, MRRCB.

367. U.S. Army Efficient Report, October 12, 1939–June 30, 1942, MRRCB.

368. U.S. Army Efficiency Files, June 1940–April 1941, and notations on reports during that period, MRRCB.

369. *Manitowoc (WI) Herald-Times*, October 14, 1941, 1.

370. U.S. Army Efficiency Report, August 14, 1941–June 30, 1942, MRRCB.

371. *San Antonio (TX) Light*, May 27, 1945, 4-A.

372. May's brother, Richard, noted in April 1941 that he had received from a relative in Baltimore in October 1940 a copy of a newspaper clipping that reported the issuance of a marriage license for Richard Burleson and Ella Roberts.

373. See the discussion of the spring 1936 trial in chapter 3, "Protracted Divorce Proceedings."

374. *San Antonio (TX) Express*, November 23, 1941, 10; *San Antonio (TX) Light*, June 10, 1947, 3B.

375. Betty Jo Miller (Mrs. Jack Burleson Miller), communication with author, February 2015. Jack Burleson Miller's mother was Armour Leigh

Burleson (Miller), and her father was Russell Burleson, brother of Richard Coke Burleson.

376. *San Antonio (TX) Light,* July 10, 1949, 37.

377. *Washington (D.C.) Post,* March 5, 1960, B2; May 31, 1960, B2.

378. *San Antonio (TX) Light,* October 27, 1948, C-1.

379. Ibid., C-7.

380. Ibid.

381. Donna Cameron, communication with author, May 2015.

382. *Galveston (TX) Daily News,* January 26, 1951, 17.

383. Ibid., July 3, 1953, 1.

384. Ibid., September 1, 1957, 20.

385. Consultation with Daniel Greenfield, MD, psychiatrist, in Millburn, New Jersey.

386. Prosono, "History of Forensic Psychiatry," and Buchanan, "Mental Illness in the 1930s," https://prezi.com/fcbq6xa4cdzi/mental-illness-in-the-1930s, provide an overview of the treatment options available and the approach to mental illness in the 1930s.

387. Forbush, *Sheppard and Enoch Pratt Hospital,* 44, 89, 90, 101, 129, 146.

Epilogue

388. Last Will and Testament of Jennie May Walker Burleson, October 15, 1951, WFP.

389. Ibid. Several excerpts follow, all of which are from Mrs. Burleson's Last Will and Testament.

390. *Galveston (TX) Tribune,* September 12, 1957, 7.

391. *Galveston (TX) Daily News,* September 15, 1957, 17.

392. Ibid., October 13, 1957, 29.

393. A Galveston newspaper clipping from either the *Daily News* or the *Tribune* that was retained in a family scrapbook located by Donna Cameron documents the filing of this suit. The clipping is undated, but it is certain that this challenge was filed soon after Mrs. Burleson's will was accepted for consideration by the probate court.

394. *Galveston (TX) Daily News,* June 26, 1958, 1.

395. Ibid., January 15, 1959, 2. A copy of the court record of this action is in the WFP.

396. The Reverend Lionel T. DeForest, rector, Grace Episcopal Church, to Richard C. Walker, January 14, 1959, WFP.

397. *Galveston (TX) Daily News*, December 18, 1959, 10.
398. Ibid.
399. Earnest money contract, executed May 21, 1964, WFP.
400. *Galveston (TX) Tribune*, September 4, 1964, 1.
401. Donna Cameron, communication with author, May 2015.

BIBLIOGRAPHY

SPECIAL SOURCE COLLECTIONS

Walker Family Papers

This collection was assembled by Donna Cameron, grandniece of May Walker Burleson. Letters and other papers that were in Mrs. Burleson's possession at the time of her death in 1957 form the core of the collection, but it also contains correspondence files left by other deceased family members, including letters to and from Mrs. Burleson's brother and her maternal uncle Herbert Wilson. The collection includes newspaper clippings, correspondence and other items from family scrapbooks. Documents from this collection, exclusive of correspondence, are listed in the general bibliography, followed by the WFP designation.

Military Service Records of Richard Coke Burleson

This extensive file was secured from the National Personnel Records Center, Military Personnel Records, St. Louis, Missouri. It includes assignment papers and other documentation for Richard Burleson's military posting from the time he was graduated from the United States Military Academy until he retired. Included are the official efficiency reports concerning his performance that were required to be filed at intervals throughout his career and the official correspondence involving his performance of duty. This file includes letters and other material placed there by Colonel Burleson, and Mrs. Burleson's lengthy correspondence with military officers, ranging from his immediate superiors to the army chief of staff and even President Roosevelt, is contained in these records. Documents from this file, exclusive of correspondence, are included in the general bibliography followed by the (MRRCB) designation. These records are the source of all letters to or from military personnel.

NEWSPAPERS

Newspaper stories were used to supplement the documentation throughout the book, but at three places in the story, newspapers served as the principal source.

THE YEARS 1930–33 FOR RICHARD AND MAY BURLESON

These were socially active years for the Burlesons as a married couple and years in which Mrs. Burleson was intensely involved in civic and political affairs as well as archaeological research. The *San Antonio Light* (San Antonio, Texas) and the *Galveston Daily News* (Galveston, Texas) furnished the documentation of these activities.

DIVORCE TRIAL PROCEEDINGS FOR RICHARD COKE BURLESON V. JENNIE MAY BURLESON IN SAN SABA, TEXAS, 1935–37

Although court records of the various pleas, petitions, verdicts and court rulings were maintained, the record of testimony and other courtroom proceedings was incomplete, and articles in the *San Antonio Light* (San Antonio, Texas) were used to document the daily court proceedings.

TRIAL OF MAY WALKER BURLESON FOR MURDER IN COLUMBIA, SOUTH CAROLINA, IN MAY 1940

Official court records for the indictment and the inquest were located, but in that the official trial transcript was not retained by the court, the series of daily articles in *The State* (Columbia, South Carolina) was relied upon for the testimony of witnesses and other proceedings at the trial.

OFFICIAL COURT RECORDS

COURT OF CIVIL APPEALS, STATE OF TEXAS

Burleson v. Burleson No. 8792, Court of Civil Appeals of Austin, Texas.

DISTRICT COURT OF SAN SABA COUNTY, TEXAS

Jennie May Burleson v. Richard C. Burleson, Cause No. 3118, Fall 1937 Term.

Richard C. Burleson v. Jennie May Burleson, Cause No. 3007, Spring 1936 Term, August and October 1936, Spring 1937 Term, Fall 1937 Term.

COURT OF GENERAL SESSIONS, COUNTY OF RICHLAND, THE STATE OF SOUTH CAROLINA

NOTE: The records listed below were photocopied in the late 1990s at the Richland County Court House, but the Burleson case file is no longer available in court records there.

INDICTMENT FOR MURDER WITH CONCEALED WEAPON CLAUSE (South Carolina State Form S-9), indicting May Walker Burleson for murder of Isabel Reece Burleson on the eighth day of March 1940. The State v. May Walker Burleson, Court of General Sessions, County of Richland, The State of South Carolina, *Inquest and Indictment Records.*

UNITED STATES DISTRICT COURT OF EASTERN NORTH CAROLINA

May Walker Burleson v. R.C. Burleson, March 23 and 24, 1937. Entry in General Minutes Book, National Archives at Atlanta.

ARTICLES, BOOKS, DOCUMENTS AND LETTERS

Brown, Mrs. Herbert, ed. *Official Program of the Woman Suffrage Procession: Washington, D.C., March 3, 1913*. Washington, D.C.: Press of the Sudwarth Company, 1913.

Burleson, Jennie May Walker. Last Will and Testament. October 15, 1951 (WFP).

———. "I Lived to Tell It" A Child's Experience in the Great Galveston Storm of 1900." (WFP, undated).

Burleson, Richard C. "THE AEROPLANE: A Means of Transport with Special Reference to Its Adaptation to the Conduct of War." *Field Artillery Journal* 15, no.4 (1925): 349–58.

Cartwright, Gary. "The Big Blow." *Texas Monthly* (August 1990): 76–81; 114–19.

Cullum, George W. *Biographical Register of the Officers and Graduates of the United States Military Academy at West Point, New York. From Its Establishment in 1802 to 1890*. Boston: Houghton-Mifflin, 1891.

———. Supplement. Vol. 5, *1900–1910*. Edited by Lt. Charles Braden. Saginaw, MI: Seemann and Peters, 1910.

———. Supplement. Vol. 6B, *1910–1920*. Edited by Col. Wirt Robinson. Saginaw, MI: Seemann and Peters, 1920.

———. Supplement. Vol. 7, *1920–1930*. Edited by C. Donaldson. Chicago: Lakeside Press, 1931.

———. Supplement. Vol. 8, *1930–1940*. Edited by E.E. Farman. Chicago: Lakeside Press, 1940.

———. Supplement. Vol. 9, *1940–1950*. Edited by Charles N. Branthan. N.p., 1955.

Earnest Money Contract, Executed May 21, 1964, in Anticipation of Sale of Walker Family Home. Signed by F.W. Harris, Agent for Carol Cameron, Seller, and Ormand G. Farine, Buyer (WFP).

Forbush, Bliss. *The Sheppard and Enoch Pratt Hospital, 1853–1970: A History*. Philadelphia: J.P. Lippincott, 1971.

Garber, David S. *Service with Battery "C," 107th Field Artillery, 28th Division, A.E.F.* Philadelphia: Nines and Sons, 1919.

"General Orders No. 15." March 1, 1913, Issued by Richard H. Sylvester, Major and Superintendent, Police Department, District of Columbia.

Hurst, James W. *Pancho Villa and Black Jack Pershing: The Punitive Expedition in Mexico*. Westport, CT: Praeger, 2008.

John Sealy Hospital, Galveston, Texas. Bill for Stay of May Walker Burleson from October 6 to October 30, 1938.

Larson, Erik. *Isaac's Storm: A Man, a Time, and the Deadliest Hurricane in History*. New York: Crown Publishers, 1999.

Lumsden, Linda J. *Inez: The Life and Time of Inez Milholland*. Bloomington: Indiana University Press, 2004.

Machado, Manuel A., Jr. *Centaur of the North: Francisco Villa, the Mexican Revolution, and Northern Mexico*. Austin, TX: Eakin Press, 1988.

Marriage Record, State of Texas, County of Galveston, Certifying the marriage of Captain Richard Coke Burleson and Miss Jennie May Walker on December 9, 1908.

McComb, David G. *Galveston: A History*. Austin: University of Texas Press, 1986.

Moody, Lt. Col. L.B. "Report of Investigation of Complaint that Lt. Colonel R.C. Burleson Had Threatened to Kill His Wife, etc." Submitted to Major General Fox Conner on April 16, 1935 (MRRCB).

Pennsylvania in the World War: An Illustrated History of the Twenty-Eighth Division. Vol. 2. Pittsburgh, PA: States Publication Society, 1921.

Prosono, Marvin. "History of Forensic Psychiatry." in *Principles and Practice of Forensic Psychiatry*, edited by Richard Rosner, MD, 14–30. London: Arnold, 1998.

"Reassignment of Colonel Burleson." Prepared by the Adjutant General for the Chief of Staff, March 23, 1933 (MRRCB).

Revised Inventory and Appraisement of the Estate of Jennie May Walker Burleson. First Hutchins–Sealy National Bank of Galveston, Prepared October 29, 1958 (WFP).

A Short History and Illustrated Roster of the 107th Field Artillery, U.S.N.G. Philadelphia: Edward Stern and Company, 1918.

Stovall, James Glen. *Seeing Suffrage: The Washington Suffrage Parade of 1913: Its Pictures and Its Effect on the American Political Landscape*. Knoxville: University of Tennessee Press, 2013.

Suffrage Parade: Hearings Before a Subcommittee of the Committee on the District of Columbia, United States Senate under, S. RES. 499, *March 6–17, 1913*. Washington, D.C.: Government Printing Office, 1913.

Tuchman, Barbara W. *The Guns of August*. New York: MacMillan, 1962.

———. *The Zimmerman Telegram*. New York: MacMillan, 1958.

Turner, Suzanne, and Joanne Seale Wilson. *Houston's Silent Garden: Glenwood Cemetery, 1871–2009*. College Station: Texas A&M University Press, 2010.

U.S. Army Efficiency Report for Richard Coke Burleson, Lt. Col., FA, (94th Div.), For Period April 3–June 30, 1933, MRRCB

———. Col., 13th FA, For Period July 1, 1938–February 27, 1939, Filed February 28, 1939, MRRCB.

———. Col., FA, Inserts Noting Medical Leaves During Period June 1940–April 1941, MRRCB.

———. Col., FA, 6th Division, For Period October 12, 1939–June 30, 1942, Filed July 9, 1942, MRRCB.

———. Col., FA, Hq. 2nd Army, For Period August 14, 1941–June 30, 1942, Filed July 9, 1942, MRRCB.

U.S. Army Special Efficiency Report for Regular Officers on Richard Coke Burleson, Lt. Col., FA, For Period June 11, 1918–September 7, 1918, MRRCB.

Walton, Mary. *A Woman's Crusade: Alice Paul and the Battle for the Ballot.* New York: Palgrave Macmillan, 2010.

Whitman, Walt. "As a Strong Bird on Pinions Free." *New York Herald,* June 26, 1872, 3.

WEBSITES

Buchanan, Miranda. "Mental Illness in the 1930s." Prezi. Accessed November 12, 2016. https://prezi.com/fcbq6xa4cdzi/mental-illness-in-the-1930s.

Patterson, Michael Robert. "Charles Pelot Summerall: General, United States Army." Arlington National Cemetery. Accessed July 19, 2015. http://www.arlingtoncemetery.net/summer.htm.

"South Carolina Governors: Robert Archer Cooper, 1919–1922." South Carolina Information Highway. Accessed September 7, 2015. http://www.sciway.net/hist/governors/cooper.html.

Woolley, John, and Gerhard Peters. "Proclamation 1364—Declaring That a State of War Exists between the United States and Germany." The American Presidency Project. Accessed July 18, 2015. http://www.presidency.ucsb.edu/ws/?pid=598.

ABOUT THE AUTHOR

T. Felder Dorn was graduated from Duke University in 1954 with a BS in chemistry and was awarded a PhD in that discipline in 1958 by the University of Washington. He was a member of the chemistry faculty at the University of the South in Sewanee, Tennessee, from 1958 to 1969 and then served four years on the program staff of the College Board in New York. From 1973 until 1991, he held administrative positions at Kean University in Union, New Jersey, serving as associate dean, dean and vice president for academic affairs. His last ten years at Kean were spent as professor of chemistry. He retired in 2001. Felder Dorn and his wife, Sara Ruth, have resided in Millburn, New Jersey, since 1973. They have three children and three grandchildren. Dorn has previously published four books: *Challenges on the Emmaus Road: Episcopal Bishops Confront Slavery, Civil War, and Emancipation* (University of South Carolina Press, 2013), *Death of a Policeman; Birth of a Baby: A Crime and Its Aftermath* (Xlibris, 2012), *The Guns of Meeting Street: A Southern Tragedy* (University of South Carolina Press, 2001) and *The Tompkins School, 1925–1953: A Community Institution* (Attic Press, 1994).

Visit us at
www.historypress.net